THE LEGAL CODE

OF ÆLFRED THE GREAT

EDITED

WITH AN INTRODUCTION

BY

MILTON HAIGHT TURK, Ph. D.

WHITE PROFESSOR OF ENGLISH IN HOBART COLLEGE

HALLE.

MAX NIEMEYER

1893

PREFACE.

The preparation of a separate edition of Ælfred's Legal Code is due to the conviction that the nature of this work rendered desirable its consideration from a literary point of view. Philologically also its existence in one very old manuscript gives it among Anglo-Saxon Law-Books a peculiar value. But its chief claim to special consideration rests upon its author's great significance in Anglo-Saxon Literature. King Ælfred's literary tastes and occupations strongly colour this work; indeed in the Introduction the lawgiver is plainly supplanted by the man of letters, who, even in the actual laws, often presses close to the view. To prepare this monument for a place among Ælfred's literary works is the object of the present edition.

The last edition from the Mss. (Thorpe's, 1840) gave E rather inaccurately. We print from our own copies E, B, and the fragments Ot and Bu. The parts of the Vulgate used by Æ. in his introduction are given parallel to Ms. E. Besides the Bibliography and description and examination of the Manuscripts, with a discussion of the sources of Lambarde's text, an attempt is made to elucidate the literary characteristics of the work, to define the position of the laws called Ine's in it, and, as well as may be, to ascertain the probable date of its publication.

Although our citations are, with few exceptions, independent, yet the Bibliography owes a considerable debt to Professor Wülker's "Grundriss zur Geschichte der Angelsächsischen Litteratur", as must every work of this kind in the department of Anglo-Saxon. Furthermore, the consideration of the order of Æ.'s works in the "Grundriss", Schmidt's excellent treatise on the Beda, and the paper "Zu den Gesetzen der Angel-sachsen", by Dr. F. Liebermann, have all been of much use. For personal favours in connection with this work the editor is further indebted to Prof. Wülker and to Dr. Liebermann. The Rev. Samuel S. Lewis., M. A., F. S. A., Fellow and Librarian of Corpus Christi College, Cambridge, has laid him under obligations by many kind acts, including securing for his use from the Rev. F. J. A. Hort., D. D., LL. D., Professor in Cambridge, opinions on important points in Ælfred's use of Biblical sources. To these gentlemen and to the Rev. T. K. Cheyne, D. D., Canon of Rochester Cathedral, for placing the Textus Roffensis at his disposal, the editor wishes in this place to return hearty thanks.

Leipsic, July 1889.

Contents.

Part Second — Text.

General Note.

The selection and arrangement of texts and variant readings are explained on pp. 24—5. In the Anglo-Saxon texts the use of italics indicates the completing of the ordinary abbreviations, or an insertion from some other text, the only kind of emendation that the ed. has permitted himself. In the Vulgate text italics designate words not translated.

In the variant readings every accented word is included, though the basic text may have an accent as well. On the other hand, the want of an accent found in the basic text does not constitute a variant reading. Furthermore, in making up the lists of variants no regard has been paid to such unmeaning differences as those between þ and ð, an abbreviated and a complete word, or a large and a small letter. A number of words together in the variants indicates generally a deviation in their order, rarely a word added or substituted. 'Vac' indicates a word wanting, a hyphen often designates an erasure within or at the end of a word, 'above' or 'ab'. points to an insertion above the line.

PART FIRST.

INTRODUCTION.

I. BIBLIOGRAPHY.

A. Manuscripts of Ælfred's Code.

925—50. **E.** Ms. of Corpus Christi College, Cambridge, No. 173. P. 65—104, Code complete.

1000—25. **Ot.** Ms. of British Museum Cottoniana Otho B XI. Three burned leaves, reset as 49, 50 and 52—3. First leaf of Code, XXXVI (40) to XXXIX (43), and last leaf.

1025—50. **Bu.** Ms. of British Museum Burney 277. A double leaf: XLIV (Ine Introd.) to LXVII (Ine 23).

1075—1100. **G.** Ms. of British Museum Cottoniana Nero A I. Fol. 45a—48a and 51a—57b, Code to Introd. 49,5.

1100—25. **H.** Ms. of Rochester Cathedral called Textus Roffensis. Fol. 9a—31b, Code complete.

1125—50. **B.** Ms. of Corpus Christi College, Cambridge, No. 383. P. 13—42, Code incomplete, beginning to IV (3) and XXXVII (41) to XXXIX (43) being wanting. — Also p. 6, the shorter and p. 83—4, the longer, text of Peace between Æ. and Guthrum, Appendix C.

B. Editions of the Code.

1568. LAMBARDE. *APXAIONOMIA*, sive de priscis anglorum legibus libri, sermone Anglico, vetustate antiquissimo, aliquot abhinc seculis conscripti, atque nunc demum, magno iurisperitorum & amantium antiquitatis omnium commodo, è tenebris in lucem vocati. Gulielmo Lambardo interprete. Londini, ex officina Joannis Daij. An. 1568. (4 to).

Fol. 0b—44a Code with a free Latin translation by Lamb. (0 b Ines æ, Leges Inæ Regis; 18b Præfatio in leges Aluredi regis; 26b Ælfredes æ, Leges Aluredi Regis.) Text from unknown sources. Cf. p. 17 and p. 23. — Fol. 44b—46a gives longer text of Peace betw. Æ and Guth., slightly different from B.

1644. WHELOCK. (2nd edition of Lambarde.) *Aρχαιονομία*, etc., as above. Gulielmo Lambardo interprete. Sexcentis in locis a libro ipsius castigata, quo pro exemplari utimur; cum multis aliis additionibus. Accessere in hac nostra ultima editione leges Henrici primi, nunc primum

1*

4

editæ, ex manuscripto in fisco regis habito: Una cum Glossario earum antiquo ex manuscripto codice olim S. Augustini Doroboriensis. Canta-brigiæ: ex officina Rogeri Daniel, celeberrimæ Academiæ typographi. MDCXLIIII. Prostant Londini apud Cornelium Bee, sub Insignibus rega-libus in vico vulgo vocato Little Britain. (Folio.)

P. 1—35 Code with transl. (1 Ines æ etc.; 15 Præfatio etc.; 22 Ælf. æ.) Translation only revised. — Ælf.-Guth. follows Code.

1721. WILKINS. Leges Anglo-Saxonicæ Ecclesiasticæ & Civiles. Accedunt Leges Edvardi Latinæ, Guilielmi Conquestoris Gallo-Normannicæ, et Henrici I. Latinæ. Subjungitur Domini Henr. Spelmanni Codex Legum Veterum Statutorum Regni Angliæ, quæ ab ingressu Gui-lielmi I. usque ad 'annum nonum Henr. III. edita sunt. Toti Operi præ-mittitur Dissertatio Epistolaris admodum Reverendi Domini Guilielmi Nicolsoni Episcopi Derrensis De Jure Feudali Veterum Saxonum. — Cum Codd. MSS. contulit, Notas, Versionem & Glossarium adjecit David Wilkins, S. T. P. Canonicus Cantuariensis, Reverendissimo in Christo Patri ac Domino Domino Guilielmo Divina Providentia Archiepiscopo Cantuariensi, &c. &c. a Sacris Domesticis & Biblioth. Londini, Typis Guil. Bowyer, impensis Rob. Gosling ad Portam Medii Templi Bibliopolæ. MDCCXXI. (Folio.)

P. 14—46 Code. (P. 14 Leges Inæ; p. 28 Leges Ælfredi.) Text on inside, transl. on outside columns, with variant readings and copious historico-legal notes below. Text is substantially Lamb. Mss. E and H are used in variants and occas. in text. — P. 47 Foedus Ælfredi & Guthrumi Regum. L.'s text with Lat. transl. and foot-notes.

Proposals concerning this edition appeared some time before. Hickes as Præfatio shows, desired it made, and Wm. Elstob worked upon it. Wilkins began his work in 1716. He reprints Lamb.'s and Whelock's prefaces and their foot-notes.

1832. SCHMID. Die Gesetze der Angelsachsen. In der Ur-sprache mit Uebersetzung und Erläuterungen herausgegeben von Dr. Rein-hold Schmid, Professor der Rechte zu Jena. Erster Theil, den Text nebst Uebersetzung enthaltend. Leipzig, F. A. Brockhaus, 1832.

P. 14—57 Code (P. 14 Ine's Gesetze; P. 32 Ælfred's Gesetze), text and German translation parallel. The Introd. is here divided into chap-ters, substantially as now, but termed: Mosaische Gesetze. The Text is Wilkins's. — A second part was not published; Thorpe brought so much new material that a second edition of the whole was made, which super-seded this and is always meant by the citation 'Schmid'.

1840. THORPE. Ancient Laws and Institutes of England; comprising Laws enacted under the Anglo-Saxon Kings from Æthelbirht to Cnut, with an English Translation of the Saxon; The Laws called Edward the Confessor's; The Laws of William the Conqueror, and those ascribed to Henry the First; also Monumenta Ecclesiastica Anglicana, from the seventh to the tenth century; and the Ancient Latin Version of the Anglo-Saxon Laws. with a compendious Glossary, &c. Printed by command of His late Majesty King William IV under the direction of the Commissioners on the Public Records of the Kingdom. MDCCCXL. (Volume the First; containing the Secular Laws.)

P. 44—151 Code in proper Ms. order und Engl. Transl. on opposite pages. Text (not very accurate) of E with variants from B, G, and H. — Ælf.-Guth. is given p. 152—7 accdg. to B (both texts) with transl. To Vol. I is prefixed a list of Mss. where the designations are assigned that have been retained and augmented since. The Introd. is short.

This edition was begun by R. Price and our Code was of the part already in press at his death. Th. retains Price's work upon it.

1858. SCHMID. Die Gesetze der Angelsachsen. In der Ursprache mit Uebersetzung, Erläuterungen und einem antiquarischen Glossar herausgegeben von Dr. Reinhold Schmid, Professor der Rechte zu Bern. Zweite, völlig umgearbeitete und vermehrte Auflage. Leipzig: F. A. Brockhaus. 1858.

P. 20—105 Code, text on left, German and ancient Latin transl. on right hand pages. (Latin of Introd. 1-48 wanting. P. 20 Ine's Gesetze; p. 58 Ælfred's Gesetze, Einleitung; p. 68 Ælfred's Gesetze.) Text and variants are Thorpe's, but old misplacement of Ine's Laws retained from Schmid I, and many of B.'s chapter headings are given. — Ælf. Guth. P. 106—9 accdg. to Thorpe and Lamb. with transl. From Wanley's Catalogue, chiefly, Ed. has compiled the first detailed account of Mss. containing A.-S. Laws; he gives also a useful introduction and a learned Antiquarian Glossary.

This, the best edition of A.-S. Laws, is still very lacking, especially from a philological point of view. A new edition is therefore in preparation for the 'Savigny Stiftung'. From its editor has already appeared, as a valuable addition to Schmid's information concerning Mss.:

1884. F. LIEBERMANN. Zu den Gesetzen der Angelsachsen. Zeitschrift der Savigny Stiftung für Rechtsgeschichte. Fünfter Band. Germanistische Abtheilung. S. 198—226.

Here Bn is mentioned for the first time and the first two leaves of Ot. The relation of the Mss. is discussed and mistakes of Th.-Sch. corrected. For the ancient Latin Version much is done.

C. Extracts from the Code.

1566—7. A Testimonie of Antiquitie, shewing the auncient fayth in the Church of England touching the sacrament . . . ., aboue 600 yeares agoe . . . . Imprinted at London by John Day . . . .

The first A.-S. publication. At the end Decalogue according to Ms. E (10 wanting). Reprint: 1849 and 1875. Ƿodcunde Lar 7 þeowdom. Others under original title.

1610. M. FREHER. Decalogi, orationis, symboli Saxonica versio vetustissima. Anno MDCX. Place not given. Decal. reprinted from above.

1623. W. L'ISLE. A Saxon Treatise concerning the Old

and New Testament, ... a second edition of A Testimonie of Antiquitie, etc. .... London, printed by John Haviland ....

1639. H. SPELMANN. Concilia, decreta, leges, constitutiones, in
re ecclesiarum orbis Brittanici, ... opera et scrutinio Henrici Spelmann.
Primus tomus .... Londini .... (Folio).

P. 354—364 Præfatio, seu apparatus R. Alur. M. etc.; p. 364—375
Leges Eccles. Alur. M. R. Angl. etc.; p. 182—186 Leges Eccles. Inæ etc.
Lamb.'s text and transl.

1650. M. Z. BOXHORNII Rudimenta Religionis Christianæ Antiquissima Saxonum & Alemannorum linguâ scripta. Lugdunensis Bata-
vorum.

Entire introd. accdg. to Lamb., exc. Decalogue, accdg. to Freher and
the Testimonie.

1713. J. G. ECCARDI Monumenta Cathechetica Theotisca,
Hanoveræ. Decalogue reprinted from Freher.

1727. J. SCHILTERI .... Thesaurus Antiquitatum Teutonicarum,
Eccles., civil., literarium. Tomus Primus ... Ulmæ sumptibus Danielis
Bartholomæi.

Tomi Primi Pars Altera (third numbering). P. 76—7 Decal. Eccles.
Anglo-Saxonicæ sub Rege Aluredo; p. 89 Synod. Apost. Epistola ....
quæ in Concilio Hierosolymitano scripta .... Actor. XV. 23—29 ....
Text of Lamb.-Whelock, with many blunders.

1737. D. WILKINS. Concilia Magnæ Brittaniæ et Hiberniæ,
a Synodo Verolamiensi A.D.CCCCXLVI. ad Londinensem A.D.MDCCXVII.
.... a Davide Wilkins, ... collecta. Vol. I (446—765) Londini
sumptibus R. Gosling .... (Folio).

P. 186—191 Rex Saxon. Ælfred, Præfatio; p. 191—194 Leges eccles.
Ælf. M. regis Angl.; p. 58—59 Leges eccles. Inæ regis occid. Saxon.
Text substant. that of Wilkins's Leges. Mss. named are not used.

1798. J. OELRICHS. Angelsächsische Chrestomathie .....
Hamburg u. Bremen. P. 45 Die zehn Gebothe, ex Leg. A. Sax. Wilkins's
Text, with errors.

1838. H. LEO. Alt- u. Angels. Sprachproben. Halle. No. 8,
p. 39—51, König Ina's Gesetze (complete). Text of Schmid I.

1847. F. W. EBELING. Angels. Lesebuch. Leipzig. No. 2, Aus
den Gesetzen König Ine u. Ælfred.

1849. L. F. KLIPSTEIN. Analecta Anglo-Saxonica. New York,
Putnam. Vol. I, No. 24, From A.-S. Laws.

1850. L. ETTMÜLLER. Engla and Seaxna Scopas and Boceras.
Quedlinburg und Leipzig. No. 10, Aus den Gesetzen der Ags. P. 56 Ine,
p. 57 Ælfred. Text of Wilkins.

c. 1855. T. MÜLLER. Angels. Lesebuch (never publ. complete).
No. 10, p. 88—92, Gesetze König Ine's. No. 11, p. 92—6, Ges. König
Ælfred's.

1861. M. RIEGER. Alt- u. Angels. Lesebuch. Giessen. P. 159,
Aus Ælfreds Gesetzen; P. 161, Aus Ine's Ges. Text of Thorpe emended.

1870. F. MARCH. Introduction to Anglo-Saxon. New York. P. 43, Laws of Alfred.

1880. A. S. COOK. Extracts from the Anglo-Saxon Laws. New York, Holt. P. 2—4 Ine; p. 4—6 Ælfred. Text of Thorpe emended.

1880. K. KÖRNER. Einleitung in das Studium des Angelsächsischen. 2. Teil: Ags. Texte. Heilbronn. No. 14, p. 54—7, Einleitung zu Ælfred's Gesetzen. Text of Schmid emended.

1884. H. SWEET. Anglo-Saxon Reader. Fourth Edition (No Laws in previous editions). Oxford, Clar. Press. No. XI, p. 51—3, From the Laws (Ine's). Text of Ms. E.

1888. F. KLUGE. Angelsächsisches Lesebuch. Halle. No. VII, p. 33—5. Aus den Gesetzen (Ine's). Text reprinted from Sweet.

D. Translations of the Code.

c. 1113—20. Vetus Versio (Ve.), an ancient Latin translation comprising, with most other codes, that of Æ., which is given first (Ine being in all old Mss. at the end of the code). The rendering was made as the first part of the Law-Book of Henry I by a cleric no longer altogether master of the A.-S. tongue. He probably belonged to East Middle England.[1]) This Code in this Version is found in a number of Mss.[2])

c. 1150. Hk. Holkham Ms. f. 34—53. Code complete.

c. 1175. Dm. Ms. Brit. Mus. Cott. Domit. VIII. f. 107—109 b. Beginning of code.

c. 1190. R. Ms. Brit. Mus. Reg. 11. B 2. f. 118—136. Code.

c. 1190. M. Macro Ms. Beginning lost. f. 46—49. End of code.

c. 1250. T. Ms. Brit. Mus. Cott. Tib. A 27. f. 104 b seqq. Code.

c. 1290. K₂. Ms. Brit. Mus. Cott. Claud. D 2. made under Eduard 1. Makes use of f. 2—4 Ine, f. 5 seqq. Æ. from Intr. 49 on.

c. 1300—25. Co. Ms. C. C. C. C. No. 70. f. 2 Ine, f. 5 seqq. Æ. (wi. Intr.).

c. 1425. Br. Ms. C. C. C. C. No. 96; Br. Ti. Ms. Cott. Tib. E. XIII. Two Mss. of Bromton's Chronicle, written in the 14th century, which makes use of Ve. from Intr. 49 on, putting Ine first.

Ve. was published except Introd. 1—48 incl. by Thorpe[3]) from T compared with Br. Hk. and M., and by Schmid[4]), who adds variants from Bromton.

Of modern translations we have LAMBARDE[4]) a Latin paraphrase; WHELOCK[4]), Lamb. with corrections; WILKINS[4]), Latin, closer than Lamb., but with many blunders; SCHMID[4]), German, the best extant; THORPE[4]) a fair English translation; GILES in 'The Whole Works of King Alfred the Great. Jubilee Edition. London 1858.' Vol. III (bound with II), No. XXI, a bad English translation, not complete. The translator wishes to show by using a large number of non-existent words, how

[1]) cf. B., Liebermann, p. 199.   [2]) cf. same, p. 202—6.
[3]) cf. B., Vol. II, p. 447—472.   [4]) cf. B.

8

much Modern English resembles A.-S. He proves conclusively that it is very different. His translation is unintelligible to one not acquainted with Anglo-Saxon.

E. Writings concerning the Code.

1678. J. SPELMANN. Ælfredi Magni..... Vita. Oxonii (Folio). P. 62—67.

1831—2. F. PALGRAVE. The Rise and Progress of the English Commonwealth. Anglo-Saxon Period. . . London. Vol. I, p. 47—8.

1840. THORPE. (cf. B) Vol. I, p. X.

1851. R. PAULI. König Ælfred und seine Stelle in der Geschichte Englands. Berlin. P. 164—176. Translation by THORPE, R. Pauli's Life of Alfred the Great. London. (Bohn's Lib.) 1853. — An interesting and instructive account.

1858. SCHMID. (cf. B.) P. XXXV—XXXVII and p. XXXIX—XLI.

1877. B. TEN BRINK. Geschichte der Englischen Litteratur. Bd. I, P. 89—90. Translation by KENNEDY: Early English Literature. London (Bohn's Lib.). 1883. P. 71.

1885. R. WÜLKER. Grundriss zur Geschichte der Angelsächsischen Litteratur. III. § 454—459.

1887. G. KÖRTING. Grundriss zur Gesch. der Englischen Litteratur. I. § 59.

The language of Thorpe's ed. of Ms. E of the Code finds phonological treatment in:

1883. O. PRIESE. Die Sprache der Gesetze Aelfred's des Grossen und König Ine's. Strassburg. (Dissertation.)

F. Other Works of Importance.[1]

1722. F. WISE. Annales Rerum gestarum Ælfredi Magni, auctore ASSERIO Menevensi. Oxonii.

1840. T. D. HARDY. Guilielmi Malmesburniensis Gesta regum Anglorum. Engl. Hist. Soc.

1851. PAULI. (cf. E.) P. 212—240. Transl. also.

1859. J. BOSWORTH. King Alfred's A.-S. Version of Orosius. London. Introd. P. VIII.

1871—2. H. SWEET. King Alfred's West-Saxon Version of Gregory's Pastoral Care. London. E. E. T. S. Introduction; p. XXXIX—XLII. — A.-S. Text here. Latin in Migne, Patrologiae Latinae Tomus 77. P. 14—127.

1876. R. WÜLCKER. Ueber die Quellen Laʒamons in Paul u. Braune's Beiträgen zur Gesch. der Deutschen Spr. u. Litt. Bd. III. P. 527—532, on Ælfred's Beda. — A.-S. Text in J. SMITH. Historiæ Ecclesiasticæ Gentis Anglorum libri V . . . . auctore . . . Bæda. Cantabrigia·, 1722. P. 471—649. Latin also; better in A. HOLDER. Bædæ Hist. Eccl. gent. Angl. Freiburg u. Tübingen, 1882. or G. MOBERLY. Oxford, 1881.

---

[1] Useful in determining the date of the code.

1877. TEN BRINK. (cf. E.) P. 94—103. Translation. P. 74—81.

1885. A. LEICHT. Zur Angelsächsischen Bearbeitung des Boetius, in Anglia Bd. VII, p. 187—202. — A.-S. Text in S. FOX. King Alf. A.-S. Version of Boethius de Cons. Phil. London (Bohn), 1864. Latin: R. PEIPER. A. M. S. Boetii Philos. Consolationis Libri V. Lipsiæ, 1871.

1885. WÜLKER. (cf. E.) III. § 438 — 486, espec. § 439 — 452. The starting-point of III, Chapter II, on the date. Accepted by all following.

1886. H. SCHILLING. König Ælfred's Ags. Bearb. der Weltgeschichte des Orosius. Halle. — A.-S. Text in H. SWEET. King Alfred's Orosius. Part I. London: E. E. T. S. 1883. Latin also; complete in ZANGEMEISTER. P. Orosii Hist. adversum paganos libri VII. Vindobonæ, 1882.

1887. A. EBERT. Allgemeine Gesch. der Literatur des Mittelalters im Abendlande. 3. Band. Leipzig. P. 239—248.

1887. KÖRTING. (cf. E.) I. § 53—60.

1889. J. WICHMANN. König Aelfred's Angels. Uebertragung der Psalmen I—LI. Leipzig (Diss.), also Anglia Bd. XI, p. 39—96.

1889. A. SCHMIDT. Untersuchungen über König Ælfred's Bedaüber-setzung. Berlin (Diss.) cf. sub 1876.

II. THE MANUSCRIPTS.

A. History and Description of each Ms.

1. Ms. E.

This manuscript is to be found in the Library of Corpus Christi College, Cambridge, as No. 173 (according to the old enumeration S. 11). Thither it came through the gift of Archbishop Matthew Parker, who, in collecting from various sources Mss. relating to Saxon antiquities, took this one from the Cathedral Library of Christ Church, Canterbury, where it had been since the beginning of the eleventh century. It seems to have been brought thither from Winchester, where it was written and attached (but not immediately) to the well-known Parker Chronicle, with which it is now bound in one volume. — Shortly after Parker found it, it was used for the text of the Decalogue found in the Testimonie[1]), which Joscelin, Parker's secretary, is believed to have edited at the latter's instance in 1566—7. Lambarde in 1568 must then have known it; whether he used it at all is doubtful. About this time E was used to gloss and complete the fragment G, probably by Joscelin. Wilkins in 1721 gave occasional variants and textual emendations from it, which Sch. I in 1832 followed. Thorpe in 1840 printed it in full, whom Sch. II in 1858 followed.

The volume is a small folio; it is of very heavy parchment and well preserved. The Ms. of the Chronicle in the beginning of the volume, written by different hands at different times, is the best extant. Itself beginning a layer, our code,

---

[1]) cf. 1 C.

complete and unaccompanied by any other laws, occupies pages 65—104. It is written throughout in the same hand. The hand is very round and large, and equally fair and clear throughout. The text remains perfectly plain, except that in a few places it is rubbed somewhat dim, the parchment being so very hard and smooth that the ink did not take good hold, and a few pages are spotted as if splashed with water. There are, however, practically no doubtful readings whatever. Occasional holes in the parchment, a few pages of which are rough, with flaws, were avoided by the scribe. The scribe makes a wide margin, which he rarely oversteps, by means of scratched lines. In the same way he marks off the lines, twenty five on the page. He puts the numerals designating the chapters generally in the space left on the last line of the chapter preceding; if there be none, he either leaves a place at the end of the first line of the new chapter, or he puts the numeral in the middle of a line by itself. He never puts a numeral on the margin, nor at the left just before the beginning of a chapter, where we would naturally place it. The chapter headings occupy nearly five pages, the rest of the fifth and all the sixth page are then left blank. The text then begins with a number of capitals, of which the first, D, is merely marked out very large, probably to be made in red or illuminated, which was never done. Each chapter begins with a capital from $1^{1}/_{2}$ to 3 lines deep; some of these are quite ornate, but in black ink only. At the end of each chapter is a punctuation mark consisting of two dots with a comma just below them. Capitals smaller than those beginning the chapters, but not of uniform size, are used within the chapters to begin sentences and clauses. Here the capital G like the modern letter (only with square corners) is never used; the other, shaped like the small letter ($ʒ$) alone appears and being of all possible sizes is hardly to be distinguished in many cases from the small $ʒ$.[1]) The dot above the line is the only punctuation within the chapter. Such a dot appears also on each side the numerals and occasionally also between X and V.

---

[1]) On this account in printing we must be guided occas. by the sense.

Only once (*oððe æt ·his swister borenre* 42, 7) is anything of importance added above the line and then the customary comma-like mark designates the place of insertion. It is worth notice that the first three *y*'s (*scyle, borʒ bryce, cynʒes*) are in the old form, with points toward the left, in imitation, no doubt, of the Ælfredian original. Besides the common A.-S. *s*, the long *s* is also found throughout the Ms. There are a considerable number of accents.

On palaeographical grounds this Ms. is to be assigned to the second quarter of the tenth century.

2. Ms. Ot.

This manuscript is in the British Museum catalogued as Cottoniana Otho B XI. The volume is now a collection of 53 badly burned leaves, carefully reset in pages of thick paper and beautifully bound. The Ms. came to the Museum with the Cotton collection after it was partially destroyed in the great fire of 1731 at Ashburnham House. Originally[1]) the Ms. contained the Chronicle to 1001 copied from the Parker Chronicle, Ælfred's Beda, our Code, and part of the Laws of Æðelstan. The Code is in the same hand with the Chronicle and was therefore probably made at Winchester, possibly at Canterbury.[2]) — No use seems to have been made by editors of this Ms. of the code. Lieb.[3]) gives some variants from the first two of the three leaves.

The Ms. was an octavo volume of good parchment. All that now remains of our code, are the charred fragments of three leaves, reset, wrong side first, as f. 49, 50 and 52—3 (the last leaf is set in two pieces, whose relation to each other escaped apparently the restorer). Fol. 49 contains the chapter headings to LIII, fol. 50 the Laws XXXVI (40) *hundniʒontiʒ* to XXXIX (43) *weorþunʒe*, 52—3 contains CX (lne 66) to end. The handwriting is exceedingly regular and ornate; in shape it is more elongated than that of E. There are 27 lines on the page. Enough can easily be deciphered to show that

---

[1]) Cf. Wanley's Catal., p. 219.

[2]) Cf. above, under Ms. E.

[3]) Cf. I B, p. 219—21. Before Lieb. it was not known that fragments of our code remained in this Ms.

in respect of capitalization, the placing of numerals, etc., Ot
is entirely similar to E. Occasionally a letter stands above
another (*i* above *y* in *gyf*, to imitate the original) and sometimes a letter is inserted above a word with the use of the
comma, as in E. Ot seems to have had no accents.

This Ms. is assigned to the first quarter of the eleventh
century. This date is sufficiently established by its being
together and in the same hand with the copy of the Chronicle
to 1001.

3. Ms. Bu.

This manuscript is to be found in the British Museum,
catalogued as Burney 277.[1]) It is one of a large number of
miscellaneous fragments, mostly Latin, that have been attached
to blank leaves in a large folio volume. It is a double octavo
parchment leaf, which was used as a book cover and is punc-
tured with holes made in sewing. On one side of it a great
part of the text is obliterated. It was the inside double leaf
of its layer and gives therefore a continuous text, extending
from XLIV (Ine Introd.) *æfter* to LXVII (Ine 23) *mæges.* —
The hand here is not a fair one; the letters are elongated
similar to Ot. It follows the same rules as to placing nume-
.rals, etc., as the other Mss. There are 25 lines on the page.
No accents are to be seen in the fragment.

This Ms. is to be placed in the second quarter of the
eleventh century.

4. Ms. G.

This manuscript also is in the British Museum, in the Cottoniana Nero A I. It is said to have come from the Cathedral
Church of Worcester. It may be one of the Mss. collected at
the instance of Archbishop Parker; to Joscelin, Parker's secretary, are ascribed the glossing and completing of this Ms.
accdg. to E. It then passed, like many copies etc. by Nowell,
Lambarde and others, into the collection of Sir Robert Cotton.
— Thorpe 1840 printed variants from it, which Schmid II
1858 followed.

This is an unhandy volume, very small, not more than

---

[1]) It was not known until Liebermann, cf. I B, p. 203.

duodecimo, and very thick. It is of heavy parchment. Many
layers throughout the volume, which is a collection of laws,
are wanting. What remains, however, is in an excellent state
of preservation.[1]) Leaves 45 a—48 a contain the chapter headings
of our code. Immediately upon these on the same page, 48 a,
follows, '*Romzescot sꝑ azifen on scs. petrus mæssedæz* etc.', then,
still on the same page, '*Ælc man þe riht demeð* etc.', which
extends to fol. 50 b. On the blank part of this page is written
a Latin version of Ælf. Introd. 49, 9, presumably by Joscelin
according to Bromton[2]). Leaves 51 a—57 b contain the text of
the code to Introd. 49, 5 *ðæt*, within two words of the end of
the Apostolic Letter. — The hand of Headings and Introduction
is unquestionably the same with that of the pieces separating
them. It is round and not especially beautiful. The scribe
leaves almost no margin and gets 19 lines on the small page.
Capitals are sparingly used. The *D* of *Drihten* (the first word)
is here altogether wanting. A number of careless mistakes are
made, E. g. *Be þan ðe mannes zestalize* for *zeneat stalize* LXVI.
G has a large number of accents. The headings of this Ms.,
excepting I and XLIV (*Be ines domum*), are glossed in Latin,
by Joscelin according to Bromton, no doubt, who puts Ine's
Laws before the rest of the code and omits these two headings.
The text is glossed from Ms. E., some words being crossed because wanting in E., and then all the rest of the code is added
accdg. to E., except the chapter headings inserted over each
chapter, which are sometimes from G. All this is the work
of Joscelin. As no erasures were made, the Ms. is not injured,
and the additions may be simply disregarded.

This Ms. seems to belong to the last quarter of the eleventh
century.

5. Ms. H.

This manuscript is in the strong room of Rochester Cathedral,
where it has been for some seven centuries. It is commonly
called Textus Roffensis, also Chronicon Claustri Roffensis. It
was made in the reign of Henry I at the command of Bishop
Ernulf of Rochester, who died in 1124. That it was written,

---

[1]) Full contents Lieb. (I. B) p. 203.
[2]) Cf. I. D. Vetus Versio, last mentioned Mss.

however, in Canterbury rather than in Rochester concludes
Liebermann from the fact that the scribe, having copied down
Cnut's gift to Christ Church, Canterbury, then stops, leaving
the rest of fol. 58 blank. — Lambarde used this Ms. in 1576
in the 'Perambulation of Kent'[1]), p. 307—312, though evidently
not in the 'Archaionomia' 8 years before. Thos Hearne[2]) published
'Textus Roffensis, Oxonii, 1720' with the omission, however, of
all pieces that had already appeared in the two editions of the
Arch. (and were about to appear a third time in Wilkins's
Leges). Wilkins 1721 used H with E for variants and occasional emendations, Thorpe 1840 gave more variants from it.

The Ms. is a quarto on heavy parchment, a thick volume.
It alone contains the laws of Æðelbirht of Kent, as well as
the two codes ascribed to Hlothar and Eadric and to Wihtræd,
of Kent. Fol. 9 a to 31 b contain our code complete.[3]) It is
written in a very fair hand, but its neatness is marred by
many erasures and numberless instances of letters or even
words above the line, the customary comma being used as a
sign. Like the Ms., the corrections, apparently in the same
hand, are carelessly made and while they often bring the Ms.
into conformity with its original, must in many instances take
it farther from it. The Ms. is to be read as it stands, as the
corrections are old ones and, many erasures having taken
place, the original readings are undiscoverable. The margins
here are of considerable width and there are but 17 lines on
the page. The chapter headings are crowded into two columns
on the page. The numerals are in red here and throughout
the Ms., where as in other Mss. they are repeated at each
chapter. There is a greater profusion of capitals here than in
the before mentioned Mss. Occasionally the old y with the
points toward the left appears, copied presumably from the
original. H has very few accents.

This Ms. as already shown, belongs to the first quarter
of the twelfth century.

---

[1]) See Grundriss I § 9.
[2]) See Grundriss I § 37.
[3]) See Schmid, p. XXIII, for full contents.

6. Ms. B.

This manuscript is in the Library of Corpus Christi College, Cambridge, No. 383 (19, 2). It may have been used by Lambarde, but in later days its existence has been unknown until Thorpe. Liebermann has assigned it to Essex or that neighbourhood. — Th.-Sch. have variants from it.

This Ms. is a small octavo on parchment. In it our code originally stood complete p. 1—48 (in all probability), but before the pages were numbered the first layer was lost and the fourth, of 12 pages, was bound in its place; the sixth leaf of the second layer was also lost. What now remains stands therefore on 30 pp. numbered 13—42. These contain [1]) IV (3) *oðres bisceopes* to the end of XXXVI (40), and XXXIX (43) *dazas to eastron* to end of the code. On the page numbered 6 is found the shorter, and on pp. 83—4 the longer text of the Treaty of Peace, Appendix C, both in the same hand. — The handwriting of B is neat and clear, but very compressed in every way; the scribe, keeping fair margins, gets 26 lines on the page. The numerals are left to be made in red; so is the first letter of every chapter, the first two lines beginning back from the margin to give space for it.

The numerals were never made, but the capitals were supplied much later by a very indifferent penman, who made in red ink awkward round capitals that never take up the space left for them. The same hand inserted also in red in a very slovenly manner in the space left of the last line of a chapter and on the right hand margin a set of chapter headings, — this continues throughout the volume, which is a collection of legal documents — introducing on the margin many new ones, where B, like all other Mss., makes no new chapter and requires no such heading.

Still another and much later hand has been at work on B, supplying in black ink on the margins omissions noted in the Ms., using a sign consisting of a circle with a dash through it, and occasionally adding a letter, or 7. These additions are altogether foreign to B and easily distinguishable from it, and can only be taken into the text, if taken at all, in italics, like

[1]) Full contents Lieb. (I. B), p. 202.

a reading from another Ms. New accents are also recognisable and are to be rejected always. — As to the chapter headings just montioned, although they are cited as belonging to B, it must be borne in mind that the original set of headings that undoubtedly preceded B were like those of older Mss. and very different from these later additions.

This Ms., later additions aside, belongs probably to the second quarter of the twelfth century.

7. Lamb.

Lambarde's Archaionomia, 1568: To the information already given [1]) may be added the following from Lamb's preface:

Obtulit mihi superiori anno Laurentius Noelus diligentissimus inuestigator antiquitatis, mihique multa et iucunda consuetudine coniunctus, ac qui me (quicunque in hoc genere sim) effecit, priscas Anglorum legos, antiquissima Saxonum lingua et literis conscriptas, atque a me (quoniam ei tum erat trans mare eundum) ut latinas facerem ac peruulgarem vehementer flagitauit . . . . Jam vero ne quis domi nostræ has natas esse leges arbitretur, plane suscipio atque profiteor magna fide et religione ex vetustissimis (ut quæ ante quingentos annos, uti coniectura autumo, saxonicis depicta sunt literis) exemplaribus fuisse desumptas, quorum pleraque in Reuerend. in Christo patris, atque optime de Antiquitate meriti, D. Matthei Cantuariensis Archiepiscopi Bibliotheca, alia aliorum in librarijs visenda supersunt.

This is all the direct information at hand towards settling the interesting question as to the sources of Lamb's text, which Whelock, Wilkins and Schmid I practically reprinted. L. was born in Kent in 1536, admitted to the Society of Lincoln's Inn in 1556. He studied under L. Nowell and for professional purposes took up the study of Saxon customs and jurisprudence. The Arch. was the first fruit of both legal and Saxon studies.[2]) Considering the tremendous difficulties attendant upon the study of A.-S. at that time [3]), it is not likely that at his age L.'s knowledge of the language was very great, and we are led to suppose that his edition was prepared in the absence of his teacher Nowell.

---

[1]) Cf. I, B.
[2]) Cf. Bibliotheca Typographica Brittanica, Vol. I, p. 493—509.
[3]) Cf. Grundriss I, § 14, L'Isle's preface, over 50 years later.

As to the sources L. might have used, there is good ground for believing, independent of a comparison of his text, that he knew three of the four principal Mss. now in our possession. H Lamb. did not know at the time he edited the Arch. This is shown, according to Sch., by his comment on the text of Æðelbirht in that Ms., 'Harum autem exemplar haud scio an aliud usquam extet, ac propterea hunc librum magni facito quisquis es, qui eum nactus fueris. W. L. 1573 in gratiam antiquitatis'. Undoubtedly had Lamb. known of the existence of these Kentish Laws in 1568 he would have taken them up into his edition.[1] L.'s remark in the preface points to E and B, the Corpus Mss., as Parker's Library for the most part went thither. B contains a number of pieces otherwise known only in Lamb.; other indications as to it are wanting. It does not contain all the laws in Lamb., though it has most of them and may well have had all when complete. There are some documents in it, however, that are not found in Lamb., which might have been expected if he knew B. E Lamb. undoubtedly was acquainted with, for Joscelin had used it a year or two before for his text of the Decalogue in the 'Testimonie', the only A.-S. print that L. could use as a pattern and whose publisher he also patronized. Joscelin's having glossed the G fragment of our code (from E) makes it likely that L. knew G also. That Lamb. used more than one Ms. is clearly indicated by the words above, 'ex vetustissimis exemplaribus fuisse desumptas'.

Furthermore, Lambarde undoubtedly was acquainted with Bromton's Chronicle[2], containing the ancient Latin version excepting 1—48 of the Introd. Probably he knew the Ve. for this part also. Br. was used for glossing in G. There is still a Ms. of it and one of the complete Ve. in Corpus Christi College. There are also Mss. of both among the Cotton Mss. It is not possible to suppose he could have remained ignorant of the existence of this Latin version. That he should not mention it is natural, as it would take from him the chief credit of his editorship, viz: his translation. We do not believe, either,

---

[1] Cf. Lamb.'s remarks at end of his preface, reprinted by Wilkins.
[2] Cf. L, D and Lieb., I., B.

that L. could have made this translation from the A.-S. unaided,
and it is worth notice that he gives a paraphrase so loose
that it might as well have been made from the Latin as from
the Anglo-Saxon text. — In considering Lamb.'s readings we
shall treat this subject farther.

B. Relation of the Mss. one to another.

1. Readings of the Mss.

At the head of the Mss. just described stands E, both for
its age and because it gives altogether the most correct text
of the code, copied conscientiously at a time when Æ.'s Laws
were still of vital importance from an Ælfredian Ms. in his
capital city. Probably the scribe reproduced the original Ms.
as to paragraphs and externals altogether, but, striving simply
to copy syllable by syllable his original, he was not exempted
from clerical errors. Such appear occasionally: E. g. 1. Skipping *wisan budan* in 7 *eow hefigran wisan budan to healdanne*,
Int. 49, 3; probably as he wrote *an* of *hefigran* his eye rested on
an of *budan* and he proceeded from there. 2. Skipping one
line from *gelæstanne*, Ælf. 1, 2, to the same word in the line below.
Similar mistakes occur in Ælf. 30 and 39, 2. Other errors are
clerical ones of small account. The text was meant for a good
copy and it is such.

The value as a copy of each of the other Mss. is in proportion, in general, to its agreement with E and that again
seems about in proportion to the antiquity of each Ms. The
scribe of E in the second quarter of the tenth century had an
Ælfredian original which he respected; as time went on Æ.'s
laws lost their importance and in the later collective Mss., G
and especially H and B, the scribes grow careless and a
considerable personal element is introduced into the work
of each.

Nearest to E stands Ms. Ot. There are very few established variant readings in the fragments that are left.
These are:

Headings XXVII *monnes wif* (*wifmonnes* E G H); Ælf. 40 *monnes*
conjectured to be wanting because there seems to be no room for it on
the line (*monnes* E H B Lamb.); 42, 2 *cyrican þonne* is conjectured at

2*

ðonne cyrican E H because an *e* is found where *n* ought to stand. Lamb. has *cyricean* ðonne. The clause, *oððe æt his snister borenre*, 42, 7, found in text of Ot., is above the line in E, yet certainly old. Further Ine 70, 1 *wilisces*, as H B Lamb. st. E *wilisc*, and 76, 2 *ætfealle* as H B Lamb. st. E *æ fealle*, the former certainly correct.

There are many points of resemblance between the two Mss. Ot has in I *him mon* with E. against *man him* of G H, Ot keeps in 42, 7 *sweoster borenre* of E against *sw. æwum borenre* H Lamb., &c. As the Ms. of the Chronicle contained in the same vol. and written by the same hand as Ot, is a copy of the Chron. Text now found with E, one naturally considers the possibility that E and the Parker Chron. were then together, and that the copy of both texts was made shortly after 1001, to which date the Ot Chron. extends, probably in Winchester, possibly in Canterbury, where the entries in the Parker Chron. after 1001 were made. The evidence just collected is not sufficient to determine the question. The variations do not absolutely establish, it seems to us, the independence of Ot, still, considering how little of the Ms. remains, they must make its dependence very doubtful. Ot is, however, certainly closely allied to E, prob. copied from same Ms.

Bu also stands not very far from E. Its variants are:

Ine: 3, 2 vac. *his* before *hlafordes* (*his* E H B Lamb); 5 *ʒeærne* (*ʒeierne* E H B Lamb); 5, 1 vac. *he* bef. *cirican* (*he* E H B Lamb); 6 *habbe* (*aʒe* E H B Lamb); 6, 2 vac. *he* after *ʒebete* (*he* E H B Lamb); 6, 3 *mon* (*ðonne* E H B Lamb), *bure* (*ʒebure* E H B Lamb); 6, 5 *bið on ʒebeorscipe ʒeciden* (*on ʒebeorscipe hie ʒeciden* E Π B Lamb); 8 *hine* (*him* E H B Lamb); *mid XXX* (vac. *mid* E H B Lamb); 12 *monna liese* (*mon aliese* E H B Lamb); 13, 1 vac. *oð* before *VII* (*oð* E Π B Lamb); 13, 1 with 14 makes LVIII (with Π, against E B); 14 *he* (*se* E H B Lamb); 15, 2 with 16 makes LX (with Π, against E B); 16 *he* (*se* E H B Lamb); 20 *lesanne* (*aliesanne* E H B Lamb); 21 *ðeofðe* (*ðeof* E H B Lamb); 21, 1 vac. *ðonne* before *dirneð* (*ðonne* E H B Lamb).

It will be seen that these variations are, excepting perhaps the change in division of chapters, of very slight importance. Only two are shared by any other text and it is not difficult to attribute all directly to the scribe of Bu and to suppose for Bu an original very closely in agreement with E and its original. Bu itself is to be regarded, like Ot, as a younger representative of the group of which an Ælfredian Ms. is the source and E the oldest member.

G is younger and departs more from E:

Headings I *man him* H (*him mon* E Ot), LIII *man rihtes* (*he him ryhtes* E, *hine man ryhtes* H), LXXIX *he þæt mote aðe* (*he mote aðe* E, *he mott þæt mid aðe* H), CVI *ceace* H (*ceape* E). Introd. 11, 3 *habbe sylf* (*self hæbbe* E H Lamb), 11, 6 *æt ðas temples dura* (*to ðære dura þæs temples* E H Lamb), 12, 2 *hie faran freo* Lamb. (vac. *faran* E H), 13, 1 *hyne ymbe ne sierede* Lamb (*hine ne ymbsyrede* E, *him ne syrwde ymbe* H), 17, 1 *ʒyf ðonne he idæʒes sie dead* (*ʒif he ðonne sie idæʒes dead* E Lamb, *ʒif he þonne byþ idæʒes dead* H), 18 *ʒetæcan* Lamb (*ʒereccen* E H), 20, 1 *sylfe* (*ilce* E H Lamb), 21, 1 *twam daʒum oððe þrim ær* (*twam daʒum ær oððe ðrim* E H Lamb), *nyste ʒif he hit ðonne* inserted, the clause *se hlaford bið unscyldig* being taken to belong to this sentence, Lamb (vac., said clause belongs to preceding sentence E H), 21, 2 *sy he þæs ylcan domes wyrðe* (*ðæs ilcan domes sie he wyrðe* E H Lamb), 21, 3 *se oxa sie* Lamb. (vac. *sie* E, *sy se oxa* H), 28, 1 *ʒà ladiʒe* (*ʒeladiʒe* E H Lamb), 34 *sceaððan ʒe hie nahwer nê ne deriað* (*sceððað ʒe ne hie nawer deriað* E, *scyþþað 7 ne hy nawer deriað* H, *sceapæþ ʒe hi ne hi na hwær deriað* Lamb), 43 *swiðe rihte 7 swiðe emne* Lamb (*swiðe emne* E, *swiþe ryhtne dom* H), 49, 3 *hefigran wisan budan* H Lamb (vac. *wisan budan* E), *ùs ða eallum ʒelicode* (*us eallum ʒelicode ða* E Lamb, *us eallum ða ʒelicode þa* H), 49, 5 *þæt is* H (vac. *is* E Lamb). — Less important: Insertions: 15 *hym*, 23, 1 *he*, 25, 2 *he*, 28, 1 *ôn* H, 28, 2 *he* H, 41 *on* Lamb; Omissions: 15 *he* H, 15, 1 *his*, 21, 1 *inne*, 24 *wið*, 25 *na*, 28, 2 *hit*, 34 *þa*, 35 *swa* H Lamb, 40 *þæs*, 49, 2 *ðonne, to*; Substitutions: 12 *he* (*hio*), 19 *for* Lamb (*wið*), 31 *se* H Lamb (*he*), 33 *þà* (*no*), 36 *oððe* H (*and*), 47 *ðone* (*hine*), 49, 5 *is* (*wæs*); Slight Changes: VII *cyricena* (-*can*), XXXVIII *fæhðum* H (-*ðe*), LVI *þeofe* (-*fum*), CIII *cu* (*cuus*), CV *sceatum* H (-*te*), CXII *siðcundes* (*ʒes-*), 3, 1 *ðone* (*þam*), 3, 2 *sæ* H (*sæs*), 8 *ʒebete* (*bete*), 21, 3 *ðeowne* H Lamb (*ðeowmennen*), 22 *delfe* (*ad-*), 30 *ʒaldorcræft* Lamb (-*tiʒan*), 35 *ʒesylle* Lamb (*selle*), 49, 3 *rihton* (*ʒer-*); Mistakes: IV *burh* H (*borʒ*), CXVIII *þeofwealh* (*þeow-*), 49, 3 *wyrcað* (*wyscað*); Blunders: LXVI *ʒestaliʒe* (*ʒeneat st.*), CI *mannes tale* (*stale*), 10 *wyce* (*wyrc*), 29, 1 *witoman weotuman*, 32 *of* (*ofer*), 49, 5 *ðeow* (*ðe eow*).

Of all these variations only that in 21, 1 has any effect on the sense and it is easy to see how that might arise. The many agreements of Lamb with G probably indicate only the use of G by Lambarde. Only a few are supported by H. The variations are not sufficient to put G out of the class to which the beforementioned Mss. belong. The scribe of G had an original not much different, we should judge, from E. He was somewhat careless, writing rather fast, and introduced often words of his own, still oftener a new word-order.

The two remaining younger Mss., H and B, bear some

outward marks of having had a common original. H gives
as *CXXI* in the headings *Be blaserum 7 be mordslihtum* and
joins it, with this number, to the end of the code, leaving
then a space of two lines before proceeding to the next piece
in the collection. The chapter headings preceding B are lost
and it has no numbers, but this same piece follows immediately
the laws in B also. This would indicate that both H
and B were copied from a Ms. where this piece followed Æ.'s
code. As this could only be the result of chance, it could
hardly occur in many Mss., so that a common original for H
and B would be expected. There are, however, important
points of difference between these two Mss. H against EOtGB
puts XXIII (25) after the next three closely related chapters
as *XXVI.* This change is undoubtedly on account of the
related subject of the two chapters thus brought together.
Lamb. for the same reason brings up 26 and puts it after
XXIII (25); Thorpe-Schmid do the same by both XXVII and
XXVIII (26, 27, 28). This change is entirely in accord with
the spirit of the scribe of H towards the text, for we note
often deliberate changes in phraseology and word order,
whereas the sense of the whole is as a rule kept well in
mind. B's peculiarities are largely omissions through care-
lessness, less regard for the sense being shown. Such being
the case, this change in H, considerable as it is, may be, with
other lesser alterations[1]), laid to the account of the scribe of
H as well as to any predecessor. The change must have
been made deliberately by some scribe, the other is beyond
peradventure the original reading. B's principal differences
from H, being unsupported as a rule by any other Ms., may
be laid to the door of B's scribe. In this way a belief in a
common original for H and B is not impossible. At all events
these two Mss. stand somewhat apart from EOtBuG. Lists
of variants of these Mss. from E would be far too bulky to
be useful. The arrangement of the text furnishes every faci-
lity for making comparison. Important additions to our knowledge of the text are made by neither of these Mss. They

---

[1]) See under Bu two other changes in lne 13, 1 and 15, 2. Often H
supports E against B, often however they agree against E.

correct occas. clerical errors in E, but serve on the whole only
to show the excellence of that text.

The later chapter headings of B would require a separate
consideration if they deserved any at all. They vary greatly
from all other Mss. and are therefore given parallel to those
of E. They are not valuable, however, except to show how
far a late version may depart from the original form; they
are clearly the result of the arbitrary will of the scribe.

The text of Lambarde is, as already indicated[1]), in all
probability not from any one Ms. Lamb. and Vetus Versio have
in common, however, certain variations from all Mss. that
would at first sight indicate that he and the maker of Ve. had
related and peculiar Mss. before them. Lamb-Ve. give two
additions to the Decalogue, restoring parts in 3 (*ðu 7 ðin sunu 7*
ðine dohter 7 ðin ðeowe 7 ðine wylne 7 ðin weorcnyten 7 se
cuma þe biþ binnan ðinan durum Lamb) and 8 (*wiþ ðinum*
nehstan Lamb) according to the Vulgate. In Intr. 15 7 *hit*
onbestæled sie . . . . mæʒe is omitted and in Intr. 49, 2 *þæt him*
belampe substituted for *þæt him ne speow* to agree with the
Vulg. Lamb-Ve. concur also in omitting the last three sections
of XVI (18, 1; 18, 2; 18, 3), and Lamb with Bromton, the worst
source of Ve. readings, puts a clause that belongs at the end
of 18, 1 at the end of XI (10) against all Mss. The supposition
that these agreements of Lamb and Ve. spring from a common
A.-S. source is, nevertheless, to be definitely rejected. In the
Ve. the variations in the Introduction are simply the result of
adopting Vulgate readings instead of translating the A.-S., a
course which the translator adopts very often where Lamb.
does not agree with him. The omission in XVI is on account
of the subject-matter of the parts omitted and is also to be
ascribed to the translator. Lamb's additions and alteration
present an interesting question. Ælfredian they could not
possibly be. Æ. would not have translated *ancilla* by *wylne*, but
by *þeow mennen, þeowenne* or *mennen*, nor *jumentum* by *weorc-*
nyten, but by *neat* or *nyten*, nor *advena* by *cuma*, but by
utancumene or *elðeodiʒe*. *þæt him belampe*, short as it is, is an
unfortunate substitution for *þæt him ne speow*, as the conjunction

---

[1]) See p. 17.

is changed to a relative without any antecedent. It may be that these bits of Anglo-Saxon appeared as very late glosses on some A.-S. Ms. We are not however inclined to date them earlier than the third quarter of the 16th century. Joscelin's Dictionary [1]), or his collections for it, seems to us their most probable source. The same wish to agree with the Vulgate and Ve. did not cause L. to translate any difficult passages. In agreement with Bromton, however, he made undoubtedly the other changes mentioned. Many other changes in headings are undoubtedly arbitrary alterations of Lamb. accdg. to his view of the requirements of each case. These variations aside, Lamb. follows, where G remains, that Ms. and E pretty closely. In the other parts his readings are generally those of E, though in certain places, as IX—XIII his text shows a remarkable resemblance to B. He has a number of its late glosses and many chapter headings like those found only in the late collection on the margins of B. Perhaps L. used G as it now stands, with the glosses and giving all that was to be found in E except its chapter headings. Whether he used B or not, it can hardly be doubted that he possessed some lost collective Ms. too, which he used more, perhaps, in other parts of his collection, where so many Mss. as exist of our code were not at hand. But his chief variations are probably of unworthy origin, his text is composite, and were the supposed lost Ms. found we could not expect from it any addition to our knowledge of the text of this Code.

Conclusion as to the Text. Our investigation gives the following scheme of Mss., from which Lamb and Ve. must be omitted:

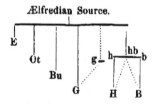

In printing we accordingly give E and B, as most widely separated, in full, parallel to each other. Ot, B and G are given

---

[1]) See Grundriss I § 8.

as variants from E. H is given variant from B, where B exists; otherwise it is printed in full or — where the space is occupied by the Vulgate Extracts — given variant from E. How much of the text really remains in the mutilated fragments Ot and Bu, and the consequent value of their variants, will be seen by reference to Appendices A and B, where they appear in full, page for page and line for line, with the parts wanting supplied in italics from E. Peculiar readings of Lamb-Ve. are noted in the variants, also readings of Lamb are adduced where they agree with one Ms. against the others in some remarkable variation.

2. Phonological Complexion of the Mss.

Our principal Ms., E, has already received the grammatical treatment it so well deserves from Priese.[1]) He gives it detailed consideration and in reply to Schmid's statement that it was Mercian, shows it to be a West-Saxon monument. Though written two centuries later, the Mss. H and B each deserve a similar detailed consideration. As each is but part of a large collection, such a treatment should include many other monuments besides ours, and even were this not the case, the work is beyond the limits of our space. Both show, as will be seen, many late forms, but B seems to be more uniform in this respect, whereas H retains in many places the forms of its original, which in others it supplants with more modern forms. For the fragments Ot Bu G we have attempted a classification of the phonological variants from E, which, in view of the existence of Priese's work, will sufficiently illustrate the phonological peculiarities of each. In the case of the latest and longest of these, G, it must, however, be admitted that the results are rather cumbrous. This fragment, moreover, like H and B, is a part of a collection; indeed only Bu stands utterly alone.

The language of Ot is in general that of E. Very few of the variations possess great significance.[2]) They are:

---

[1]) See I E. Unfortunately the untrustworthy character of Thorpe's text detracts at times from the value of Priese's work.

[2]) In parenthesis are forms that occur elsewhere in E.

26

a for *æ*, *maᵹum* 42,1 end, cf. Priese 6.
o for *a* (*o*), *londes* Ine 67, cf. Pr. 14.
e for *æ* (*e, a*), *ofsleᵹenum* X; *æ* for *e* (*æ*) *cwæðað* 42, 5.
eo for *i*, *sweoster* 42, 7, cf. Pr. 15.
io for *eo* (*io*), *hiora* XVII.
i for *y*, *twyhindum* XXIV.
y for *i*, *ᵹyf* 42, 1, 3, 4; Ine 67; *forᵹyfen* 42, 7; *forᵹyfene* 43.
ŷ for *î*, *stŷle* XXI.
y for *ie* (*i, y* I uml. of *eo*), *cyrlisces* XXXII. Pr. 18.
ŷ for *ie* (*ê* I uml. of *êa*), *tymp* Ine 75, *lyfað* 42, 6.
          ie, î (I-uml. *êo*), *ᵹestryndon* 41, *flys* Ine 69. Pr. 18.
Unaccented: *eo* for *e, o*, *bisceopes* 40, 41, *bisceopum* XV.
Doubled-Cons.: *ð*: *oððcra* XLIII, *l*: *forstollenne* Ine 75.
Also *borh* (*borᵹ*) IV, *cyninᵹes* (*cynᵹes*) VIII, *dumbra* (*dumbera*) XIV.

A similar examination of Bu's variants yields more of
interest. This Ms., in direct contradiction of G, shows the tendency to make *y* (umlaut of *u* as well as of *ea, eo*) give place
to *i* and very often to *e*. Still it displaces *i* with *y* a few
times. Perhaps we are to argue that *i* and *y* are not distinguished and the closed *e* and *i* had likewise become confused.
The tendency here shown is remarkably strong. The variations
are as follows (the numerals refer to Ine):

a for *æ*, *habbe* 5, 22, (also 6 for *aᵹe*) optative.
æ for *a* (*æ*), *wræce* 9. Priese 1, p. 7.
          e (*æ, a*), *ofslægenan* 21 end.
ê for *â* (*ê*), *þæm* 1; 2; 21, 1 twice.
e, i for *y* (I uml. of *u*), *ofspereð* 17, *scildig* 4, 11, *kining* 23, *kininᵹes* 6;
          15, 2; *unsinᵹian* 21, 1. Pr. 18.
          y, ie (*i*, I uml. of *ea* br. of *a*), *ofslehð* (E *ofstihð*) 16, *ᵹederneð* 17,
          dirneð 21, 1 (cf. below *nyhtum*).
          y, ie (*i*, I uml. of *eo* br. of *e*), *werce* 3, *forwerce* 5, 1, *sixtiᵹ* 19,
          cirlisc 18.
e, i, y for *y, e, i* (after palatal), *ᵹeld* (verb) 22, *anᵹeldes* 22, *anᵹelde*
          22. — *ᵹafolᵹildan* 6, 3. — *forᵹylde* 9.
i for *ie, y* (*i*), *ᵹeirne* 5, 1, *betiᵹen* 15, (cf. *betwyᵹen* 18).
ê for *ŷ* (I uml. of *û*) *ᵹecepan* 16, *remeð* 21, 1 (cf. *ᵹecypan* 21).
î for *ie* (*î, ŷ*, I uml. of *êo*), *hrime* 20.
y for *i* (*y, ie*, pal. uml. of *ea*, br. of *a*?), *nyhtum* 2, 8. Pr. 19.
ŷ for *î* (old), *swycne* 15, 2. Pr. 8.
eo for *ie* (I uml. of *eo*), *þeofðe* 7, 2, *weorðe* 8.
ie for *eo* (I uml. to *ie*), *wierðeð* 21, 1.
ie for *î*, *sien* 4.
o for *eo*, *forcund* 20; *eo* for *o*, *ᵹefeohtan* 6, 4.
eo for *io* (*eo*), *freoh* 3.

éo for *ìo (éo)*, *beon* 7, 2.
ŷo for *ìo (éo)*, *byon* 15, 1.

In Unaccented Syllables:

an for *um*, *middan* 6, 4.
œ for *e*, *eallœs* 7, 1. Gen. sing.
e for *a*, *mœӡes* (nom. pl.) 21, 1; 23, *hereteame* 15, *healden* 1, *sweriӡen* 19.
a for *e*, *ӡefeohtan* 6, 4.
o for *a*, *ӡefullod* (E *ӡefulwad*) 2, *buton* 2; 3, 2; 20.
    e, *biscope* 13.
um for *on*, *nyhtum* 8.
y for *e*, *ӡewitnysse* 3, 1; 7, 1 (cf. *ӡewitnesse* 13).

    Also *wed (dd)* 8, *bebycӡe (ӡӡ)* 11, *manna (n)* 22, *ӡehealdenne (n)* 1, *wereӡilde (werӡ)* 15, *huslӡenӡa (ӡea)* 19, *berӡan (ӡean)* 22, *wisie (ӡe)* 5, *sweriӡen (ian)* 19 and *ӡeӡildanum (ӡeӡildan)* 16.

Ms. G shows a great mass of variations. The principal characteristic of the Ms. is the introduction of *y* for a great number of sounds of every sort of origin. This is in contrast to Bu. G is fairly consistent in its introduction of new forms and exhibits, we take it, the West-Saxon conditions or tendencies at its time. Examples follow [1]):

a for *œ*, *habbe* 11, 3; 12, 4; *habben* LXXXII, *habbon* 23.
    œ (a), *stal* XC, *ofslaӡen* 21, 1; *ofslaӡenes* LXV, *ofslaӡenum* X.
    ea (br. of *a*), *ӡaldorcrœft* 30.
a, œ for *o* (before nasal), *man* (always), *land* (always), *handa*, *ӡefanӡenum* LVI, *ӡanӡe* CXIII, *ânfôn* 30, *anfenӡe* XII (cf. *onfenӡe* XVI), *andsœce* LXXXV, *naman* (always), *fram* (always), *ӡesamnodan* 49, 3; *ðan*, *mœniӡe* 49, 1; *þœnne* LXXX; 28, 3; *ðœne* (eum) 45, (still *moniӡfealdum* 49, 3).
œ for *e (œ)*, *œlðeodiӡ* always; for *a (œ)*, *stœfe* 16.
e, è for *œ*, *è hwet* 24, 1, *seӡe* 8, *restedœӡ* 3, *befestað* XVIII, *stele* 28, *slepe* 29.
e for *y*, *brece* LXXXIX; *è* for *ie* (I uml. of *éo*), *flese* CXIII.
i for *io* (U uml. of *i*), *wituma* 12, 4; for *u*, *awiht* 26.
i, y for *y, e, i, ie* (after pal) *anӡilde(e)* C, *werӡild* CXVI, *deofolӡyld* 49, 5; *ӡylde*, *ӡyf*, *aӡyfe* 12, 3; *ӡyft* LXXV.
i for *y* (I uml. of *u*), *bicӡe* LXXV, *ӡebicӡe* 11, 1, *bebicӡað* LV, *ðurhðìrliӡe* 11, 6; *drihten* 1.
    y (*ie*, pal uml. of *eo*, *ea*), *riht* LXXXII, *rihtes* LII, LIII, *unrihte* 9, *rihte* 21, 1, *rihton* 49, 3; *slihte* XVII, XXIV.

---

[1]) Arabic numerals refer to Introd. Examples without reference occur often. Forms in brackets occur in E or in W.-Sax. generally.

y for old *e*, Goth. *i*, *swyltan* 14, *lybbe* 17.

Teut. *i*, *byst*, *fryþe*, *fryðstowa* 13, 1, *ys*, *hys*, *hyt*, *hyne*, *hym*, *syððan*, *syndan*.

i (*y*) (borrowed words) *cyrice*, *eʒypta* 1, 1.

eo, *io* (O uml. of *i*), *clypiʒen* 48, *hyra* (cf. *hira*).

e, *brynʒe* 11, 6; *ʒecyrdon* 49, 1; *œwyrdlan*, *ʒewyrde*.

eo, *e*, *i*, *wyrcum* XLVII, *swylce* (cf. *swilce* 11, 2), *ʒehwylces* C, *ylcan*.

ie, (I uml. of *eo*), *hyre* 11, 4; 29.

e (I uml. of *a*), *sylle* 19, *ʒesylle* 21, 3; *wyrʒe* 15, 1.

ie (*i*, *y* I uml. of *ea*), *fyrd* XCV, *wylysces* LXXVI, *dyrnum* XCVI, *forhwyrfdon* (*e*) 49, 3.

ie, *i*, (*y* I uml. of *eo*), *cyrlisces*, *cyrliscre* XII; etc.

ŷ for *ê* (I uml. of *ô*), *ʒehyne* 35.

ie (I uml. of *êa*), *cypmanna* LXIX, *cypmannum*, *nytena* XXII, *un-alyfedes* XCIII.

ê (I uml. of *êa*), *alyfe* 12, 3; *nydes* 13, 1; *ʒymelcasnesse* XXXIII.

ie (I uml. of *êo*), *frynd* 28, *flyman* LXXIV, *ʒehyre* 34, 1; *ʒehyranne* 40, *ʒetrywe* 28, 3; *ðyfðe* LXXXI.

ie for *ê*, *nietene* 31, *niedþearf* 49, 5; cf. above.

u for *y* (I uml. of *u*), *ʒemune* 3.

y for *u* (uml. to *y*), *becyme* 42, *utancymenan* 47.

eo for *io* (*eo*), *seofoðan* 3, *seo*, *heo*, *feoh* 17, *freok* 11, 1; *freonne* 15.

ye for *ie* (*e*), *nyehstan* 13, 2; *eo* for *ie* (I uml. of *eo*) *ʒeornnesse* 13, 2.

In Unaccented Syllables:

a for *e*, *findan* 21, 1, *bebicʒan* 23, *fryðstowa* 13, 1, *leasunʒa* XXIX; etc.

o (*a*), *butan* (always), *ʒemettan* LXIV, *sendan* 49, 3; *ʒesamnodan* 49, 3; *syndan* 49, *ofworpad* 21, 3.

œ for *es* (*œ*), *nihtœ* CXVII; *y* for *i*, *wylysces* LXXVI, *scyldyʒ* 17.

c for *a*, *orceapunʒe* 11, 1; *utʒanʒen* 16, *healdenne* 49, 5; etc.

eo for *o*, *bisceopum* XV. Prob. *e* only indicates pronunc. 'sch.'

o for *a*, *ʒesamhiwon* LXXXII, for *e*, *habbon* 23.

u for *o*, *unbeweddude* 29, for *e*, *dearnunʒa* LXXI, 6.

ea for *a*, *sunea* 12, 3; *ʒewitnessea* 8; *a* for *ea*, *wyrcað* 3, 1; *bereccan* 15.

an for *um*, *minan* 13, 2.

e dropped, *wœpn* XVII, *dumbra* XIV, *niedhœmde* XXIII, XXVII.

Also *ʒeahsodon* (asc) 49, 3, *spœce* (*sprœce*) 41, *œðenum* (*hœð*) 49, 2; *tihlan* (*htl*) CXV, *werfœhte* (*hðe*) XCVIII, *ceaste* (*cease*) 18, *wiste* (*ss*) 23, 1; *sceatum* (*tt*) XLVIII, *bicʒe* (*ccʒ*) LXXV, etc.

The text of Lamb. offers little of interest phonologically: *e* is frequently dropped from the end of a word, as in Ms. B, after *ʒ*; in general however it shows nothing new as against the other Mss. Here again there are indications of a composite text. To a great extent the forms coincide with E, still there are many, especially in certain places, as IX seq., that greatly resemble B. In the part remaining of G variations from E are apt to coincide with G. Where Lamb resembles B, the variants from E are quite numerous, otherwise they are not great in number nor in importance. This being the case, none are adopted in the variant collections. Were their interest greater than it is, so old an edition would be but poor authority for phonological variants.

III. LITERARY OBSERVATIONS.

Chapter I.

THE COMPOSITION OF ÆLFRED'S CODE.

1. The purpose of this chapter is to examine Æ.'s code, to determine its sources, so far as possible in a purely literary consideration, and to explain its construction. We shall in so doing take occasion to compare translations and adaptations with their originals and to discuss any other literary questions of import. A word at the outset as to division of our monument. Former editions separate it into three parts: 1. Introduction [1]); 2. Laws of Ælfred; 3. Laws of Ine. The Mss. recognize none of these divisions. The best authority proceeds without paragraphing to the end of 48, makes a second paragraph of 49 to 49, 5, a third, which is numbered I, of 49, 6 to 49, 8, and a fourth, unnumbered, of 49, 9 and 10. This last is the Introduction Proper to the Laws in distinction from the Historical Introduction preceding it. With II begin the actual Laws and the division into numbered paragraphs, or chapters, continues without any further distinction to the end of the document. Our code has suffered in the past from a too zealous separation into parts, and we prefer as far as possible to regard it as a whole, though gathered from different sources. Yet, as for convenience of reference we retain the threefold division with its three sets of numbers, so merely for the purposes of our present consideration we may make the following division:

1. The Historical Introduction; To Introd. 49, 8.

---

[1]) Less aptly termed Ecclesiastical Laws and so referred to by Bosw.-Toller Dicty.

2. The Introduction Proper; 49, 9 and 10.

3. The Miscellaneous Laws; II(1)—XXXIX(43).

4. The Code concerning Bodily Injuries, XL(44)—XLIII(77).

5. The Laws called Ine's, XLIV (Ine Introd.) to End.[1])

The first part is partly translation — from the Mosaic Law and the Letter of the Apostles from Jerusalem — and partly original; it will require two sections for its consideration, the original parts being best considered first. Our remarks on 2. and 3. can be given in one section.

2. The Original Parts of the Historical Introduction: Its Construction; Comments.

Having completed his translation from the Mosaic Law, Æ. says (49): *Þis sindan ða domas þe se ælmihteza zod self sprecende wæs to moyse 7 him bebead to healdanne.* This is Æ.'s statement of his sufficient reason for putting these laws before his people, for, unlike all others, they were given by God himself and He ordered their fulfilment.[2]) Æ. proceeds, adapting incidentally Matt. V, 17,[3]) *7 siððan se âncenneda dryhtnes sunu ure zod þæt is hælend crist on middanzeard cwom, he cwæð ðæt he ne come no ðas bebodu to brecanne ne to forbeodanne, ac mid eallum zodum to ecanne,* pointing out that these Mosaic Laws are not abrogated by Christ under the new dispensation, for He desired but to augment them with all good (laws).[4]) Then comes the second important point, *7 mildheortnesse 7 eaðmodnesse he lærde:* this prepares the way for the rendering of the Apostolic letter and indicates at the same time the reason for giving it, viz: that, having introduced the harsh injunctions of the Mosaic Law ('an eye for an eye, a tooth for a tooth'), Æ. avoids a too literal interpretation of them and modifies very greatly their effect by adding to represent the dispensation of Christ the peculiarly mild and encouraging precepts of the Apostolic

---

[1]) Strictly speaking 5. should be subdivided into (1) Ine's Introd. XLIV, and (2) Ine's Laws.

[2]) *Self* shows this to be Æ.'s intent.

[3]) Nolite putare quoniam veni solvere legem, aut prophetas: non veni solvere, sed adimplere. Vulg.

[4]) Better than Schmid, 'mit allem Guten zu vermehren'.

Letter. The two extracts together present a fairly complete view of Biblical teaching in these particulars.

Immediately upon the Letter follows the paragraph (49, 6—8) numbered I and designated in the chapter headings as '*Be ðon þæt mon ne scyle oþrum deman buton swa he wille þæt him mon deme*'. Only the first three sentences of this paragraph, however, are at all in the form of an injunction. This injunction, while recalling to mind Matt. VII, 1, 2,[1]) is closely connected with the final clause of the Apostolic letter (*7 þæt ʒe willen þæt oðre men êow ne don, ne doð ʒe ðæt oþrum monnum*); it is in a manner deduced from it: *Ʒeðence he þæt he nanum men ne deme þæt he nolde ðæt he him demde, ʒif he ðone dôm ofer hine sohte*. It is as well the spirit of all law and justice, the underlying principle of all lawgiving: *Of ðissum anum dome mon mæʒ ʒeðencean*, says Ælfred, *þæt he æʒhwelcne on ryht ʒedemeð. Ne ðearf he nanra domboca oþerra.*

The author does not now pass, as he well might, at once to his own laws, or to the introduction to them; he wishes to construct, rather than imagine, the bridge that shall connect the Apostolic injunctions with his own ordinances, just as he had carefully joined the former to the Mosaic commandments. His next sentence joins on closely to the introductory sentences of the Letter. There we read: *ða æfter his ðrowunʒe ær þam þe his apostolas tofarene wæron ʒeond ealle eorðan to læranne, 7 þa ʒiet ða hie ætʒædere wæron, moneʒa hæðena ðeoda hie to ʒode ʒecerdon*. The part now reached begins: *Siððan ðæt þa ʒelamp þæt moneʒa ðeoda cristes ʒeleafan onfenʒon;* it continues: *þa wurdon moneʒa seonoðas ʒeond ealne middanʒeard ʒeʒaderode, 7 eac swa ʒeond anʒelcyn, siððan hie cristes ʒeleafan onfenʒon, haleʒra biscepa 7 êac oðerra ʒeðunʒenra witena*. Thus Æ. conducts the reader from the Apostles and their times to England and the middle ages. With a renewed reference to the compassion taught by Christ, he relates how these synods resolved that secular lords might accept a money fine for a first offense, except only in the case of betrayal of a lord[2]),

---

[1]) Nolite iudicare, ut non indicemini. In quo enim iudicio iudicaveritis, iudicabimini. Vulg.

[2]) We note here Æ.'s severity where the kingly power might be touched. Cf. Pauli (I, E) pp. 168 seqq.

against which he proceeds on scriptural grounds to deliver a severe denunciation, closing with an imitation, the sense being however quite new, of Matt. XXII, 37, 39.[1]) Relating then how fines for various offenses were fixed and recorded in the synod-books, he is ready to proceed to the Introduction Proper to his own Laws, which names these books as the first source of his compilation.

Good as are the grounds that Æ. alleges for introducing his Biblical extracts, and apt as the historical account is, that connects and follows them, an underlying reason is still, we think, left to be inferred. Only in the Preface to the Pastoral Care does Æ. express himself on this head. The same general purpose, however, undoubtedly inspires both undertakings. Æ. knew the ignorance of his advisers in the state to be more lamentable than that of his clergy. As he gave Gregory's great work to the latter for their instruction, so, on the occasion of formulating a code of laws, he opened to his statesmen and people in the tongue they could understand the ancient commandments of God through Moses and the recommendations of the Holy Apostles for the Christian conduct of life. We may note here at the outset that a very different idea of his Law-book occupied Æ.'s mind from that of a mere publication of a certain number of his ordinances for the use of his kingdom.

3. Comparison of Ælfred's Translations with the Vulgate: The Decalogue; The Rest of the Mosaic Law, with Lists of Omissions, Alterations, Augmentations; The Apostolic Letter; Summary.

There is, as might be expected, no original from which Æ.'s extracts from the Bible could have been taken as they stand. There are numerous changes and omissions due to Æ. himself. The Text of Exodus, however, that he altered for his purposes, was the Vulgate, not any Pre-Hieronymic text. This is shown not only by comparison with the existing Pre-Hieronymic fragments, but also by Ælfred's agreement with the Vulgate against the Septuagint (the original of all Pre-Hieronymic texts), wherever they interpret the Hebrew differently. The version of the

---

[1]) Diliges Dominum Deum tuum ex toto corde tuo .... Diliges proximum tuum, sicut teipsum. Vulg. Note that all the references point to studies in Matthew.

Epistle from Jerusalem is also undoubtedly taken from the Vulgate.[1]) That Æ. used a text altogether corresponding to the present Vulgate — the Clementine — is certainly not to be supposed, but his translation is far too free to allow of determining the peculiar readings of the Ms. before him, except in rare cases; we make our comparisons accordingly with the standard Vulgate text, which unquestionably answers well the purpose.

The Decalogue as given by Æ. must be omitted from any comparison of his adaptation with the original to determine its fidelity. In his chief deviation, viz: the omission of the entire Second and part of the Fourth and Tenth commandments, Æ. but conforms to the custom of the Church. Lambarde and other editors have pointed to the second Nicene council as the reason for the omission of the Second, though it is worth notice that Æ. adds as the tenth Chap. XX, v. 23, of similar purpose, but of much narrower scope.[2]) Just why he does this is hard to see. As to the commandments in the middle ages, we may quote from the Speaker's Commentary, ed. Cook, p. 337. "In those copies of the commandments which have been used in different branches of the church for the instruction of its members, the form has almost always been more or less abbreviated of a part or the whole of those which are most expanded in Exodus and Deuteronomy, namely the Second, Third, Fourth, Fifth, and Tenth." Just how much of Æ.'s paraphrase is original and how far he is following an older Latin paraphrase is an interesting question, but no evidence has been found upon it.[3]) In most cases Æ. merely omits parts, following otherwise the Vulgate text closely. He has, however, two renderings that are unknown to any Bible text:

(1) The change of *Dominus* (always transl. *Dryhten*) to *Crist* in "*Crist geworhte heofonas* etc.", the proper translation being retained just below in 7 *forðon dryhten hine gehalgode*. This can not, well authenticated as the reading is, be attributed to the mistake of a scribe. In all probability it is Æ.'s own

---

[1]) For the above information we are indebted to Dr. F. J. A. Hort.

[2]) That is, in Æ.'s view. To the Hebrew the two meant quite the same.

[3]) Dr. Hort kindly examined into this matter.

deliberate rendering. That such a rendering would be quite possible is shown, for example, by the A.-S. poem "Crist", where Christ, rising at the last day to deliver his judgment, describes how he created the world, going on later to relate his own birth and ministry upon earth.[1]) As the word *"Dominus"* is so often used in the New Testament for Christ, it is easy to see how confusion could creep in, and how in this case Æ. should translate the single word — there is no *"Deus"* with it here — by *Crist* instead of *Dryhten*.

(2) In the fifth commandment the last clause, *"quam Dominus Deus tuus dabit tibi"*, is put immediately after the first, changing the sense altogether, i. e. *Ara ðinum fœder 7 þinre medder, ða þe dryhten sealde*. This change is probably due to the ambiguity of *terra*. In Exodus it means "land" (limited portion of earth), but Æ. took it to mean the earth generally. This interpretation left no room for a reference of the following words to *"terram"* and so we may suppose that Æ. assumed them to refer to the first clause.[2]) The A.-S. relative would be the same, and the Latin relative, if not before him in some unrecognisable abbreviation, would not trouble Ælfred, especially as it agrees perfectly with the *"tuam"* at the end of the first clause. Æ. accordingly transposed the clauses to make the supposed reference clear.

The adaptation from the rest of the Mosaic Law may be subjected to a detailed examination to show Æ.'s relation to his original. It extends from Exodus XXI, v. 1 to XXIII, v. 13. The entire 36 verses of Chap. XXI are taken with deviations only in an occasional clause or expression. In XXII Æ. becomes more free, omitting part of 6 and of 7, changing 8, omitting 9, omitting part and changing the order of the clauses of 10 and 11, omitting 12—15, then altering a good deal in 16—29, omitting last part of 29 and all 30, but taking the last verse 31. In Chap. XXIII Æ. omits vv. 3 and 5, translating the rest to v. 9 very freely; omits then all to the last part of v. 13, with which he closes his adaptation from Exodus. From the subjoined lists of his deviations from his original, it

---

[1]) Cf. Grein, Bibl. d. Ags. Poesie, Vol. I (line 1380 seqq).
[2]) Dr. Hort offers this explanation.

will be seen that he handled his Biblical source with considerable
freedom, judiciously adapting rather than slavishly rendering
it. He seems almost invariably master of the sense and one
or two mistakes go rather to prove his independence. His work
throughout bears high testimony to his excellent judgment in
the use of his original. Following are the deviations:

Omissions: Clauses not necessary to the sense are often
omitted: XXI, 4, 6, 18—19 (with good discernment here, the
end of 19 being brought cleverly into more intelligible expression), 22, 30; XXII, 4, 5, 24. Other omissions affecting the sense
are to be noted: XXI, 9—10, *juxta morem filiarum faciet illi.
Quod si alteram ei acceperit*, 22 end, giving husband right
to fix penalty for injury to his wife; XXII, 8, Æ. carefully omits
applicabitur ad deos and also 9 where *deos* occurs again,
(cf. XXII, 20, *diis, to god geldum; diis, to ðinne dryhten.*) 12—15
entire, concerning goods committed to another's charge, 29—31
all omitted except first and last clauses. Such a commandment
as *primogenitum filiorum tuorum dabis mihi, viri sancti eritis mihi*
Æ. could hardly be expected to adopt. XXIII, 3, *Pauperis quoque non misereberis in iudicio* is rejected with evident reason.
Most interesting as showing at once Æ.'s practical purpose and
throwing light upon the spirit of his time is the omission of 5,
*Si videris asinum odientis te iacere sub onere, non pertransibis,
sed sublevabis cum eo.* We are reminded here of the difficulties
caused the Heliand poet not long before Æ.'s day by many
Christian conceptions and injunctions. At the end of 9 the
repeated reference to the bondage is omitted, also 10—12 conc.
tilling soil, keeping sabbath-day, etc. The choice of 13 to close
the extract is evidently for its repetition of the first commandment, with which Æ. opens.

Alterations: XXI, 2, *servum Hebraeum* to *cristenne þeow;*
8 is rearranged considerably, *populo autem alieno vendendi non
habebit potestatem* is transl. first, then that part of the verse
preceding it, *populo alieno* being a second time given; 20—21,
order of the given instances altered; 30, *quidquid fuerit postulatus* changed to *swa ðæt witan to ryhte finden;* XXII, 1, *quinque boves* to *twegen,* 3 end placed after v. 1 for the sake of
clearness, 7—8, for *furto ablata fuerint, si invenitur fur* Æ.
inserts *gif he hit self stæle,* for *si latet fur, gif he nyste hwa*

hit stæle. 10—11 is much altered: from *nullusque hoc viderit*
is taken opposite sense, *ʒif he ʒewitnesse hæbbe*, and thereto
is joined the end of 11 as *ne þearf he þæt ʒeldan;* then *nullusque hoc viderit* and the rest is given. 18, strange mistake of
putting *quam virgines accipere consueverunt*, belonging to the
preceding ordinance, but not translated with it, before *maleficos,*
thus gaining the utterly different meaning of *þa fæmnan þe
ʒewuniað onfón ʒealdorcræftiʒan . . . ne læt þu ða libban*, a
peculiar and very severe injunction. XXIII, 1, 2 is represented
by a strong polemic against evil and seditious speech, that is
hardly a translation, although it shows a clear idea of the
meaning of the text; cf. Æ.'s Law XXIX (32). 4, in *si occurreris
bovi inimici tui erranti, reduc ad eum, reduc* is changed to
ʒecyðe, an alteration of the same significance as the omission
of v. 5 (which see). 6 is freely and strongly translated, 9 also
is very free.

Augmentations: Mostly the addition, common in all Æ.'s
transl., of synonyms and explanatory phrases: XXI, 10, *þæt is se
weotuma aʒife he hire þone;* 13, *nedes ofsloʒe oððe unwillum oððe
unʒewealdes.* Of more significance is *sie he feores wyrðe 7 folc
ryhtre bote, ʒif he friðstowe ʒesece*, a thoroughly A.-S. addition
to the Latin *constituam tibi locum in quem fugere debeat.* 14,
per industriam, of ʒiernesse 7 ʒewealdes; 16, *convictus noxae, 7 hit
onbestæled sie þæt he hine bereccean ne mæʒe.* XXII, 3, *buton
he nied dæda wære*, is Æ.'s own. 18, *maleficos, ʒealdorcræftiʒan
7 scinlæcan 7 wiccan;* 26—27, *si clamaverit, ʒif ðu swa ne
dest, þonne cleopað* etc.; 29, as if to compensate for the omission
of *De bobus quoque* etc., *ʒonʒendes 7 weaxendes.* XXIII, 9, is
much expanded.

The version of the Epistle from Jerusalem, taken from
Acts XV, vv. 23—29, affords subject for a few comments. The
only differences worth notice between Æ. and the Vulgate are
that he omits the local address of the Epistle in v. 23, having
just made use of it, that he alters *tradiderunt animas suas* into
wilniað hiora sawla sellan in v. 26, and that he adds a clause
at the end. This final clause is very interesting. It does not
come, as Thorpe and Schmid suppose, from Matt. VII, 12. It
is a very ancient interpretation in the text of the Acts (vv. 20
and 29) found in Greek and several ancient versions, being

38

as old as the second century. Here it is doubtless a bit of an old Latin text adhering to a Vulgate Ms. Such old Latin survivals in Vulgate Mss. are very common.[1]

Summary: We find that Æ. used for his historical introduction: Exodus XX, 1—3, 7—10 (beginning), 11—16, 17 (shortened), and 23; XXI entire; XXII, 1—5, 6—8 (in part), 10—11 (in part), 16—29, and 31. XXIII, 1, 2, 4, 6—9, and end of 13; — Acts XV, 23—29, including an ancient reading in 29 not belonging to the standard Vulgate text. The use, already noted[2]), of Matt. V, 17, VII, 1, 2 and XXII, 37, 39, in the original part of the Introduction may here be recalled to mind.

4. The Sources of the Laws as given in the Introduction Proper. Divisions of the Laws. II—XXXIX: The Miscellaneous Laws.

As Ine's Introduction told of those that had most assisted him in the preparation of his laws, so Æ. wishes to mention the sources from which his collection had been compiled. This he does, without any break, in close connection with his historical recital. This he had closed with the following words: *hie ða on monezum senoðum monezra menniscra misdæda bote zeselton 7 on moneza senoð bêc hie writan, hwær anne dom, hwær oþerne.* These clauses belong, we think, to the sense of the opening sentence of the part now under consideration, where Æ. proceeds: *Ic ða ælfred cyninz þâs togædere zezaderode 7 awritan het, moneze þara þe ure forezenzan heoldon ða ðe me licodon* (here is an anacoluthon which Ve. corrects with *reservavi*) *7 maneze þara þe me ne licodon ic âwearp mid minra witena zeðeahte 7 on oðre wisan bebead to healdanne.* Æ. then goes on: *forðam ic ne dorste zeðristlæcan þara minra awuht fela on zewrit settan, forðam me næs uncuð hwæt þæs ðam lician wolde ðe æfter ûs wæren,* and then finally, *ac ða ðe ic zemetle anðer oððe on ines dæze mines mæzes oððe on offan mercna cyninzes oððe on æþelbryhtes þe ærest fulluhte onfenz on anzelcynne, þa ðe me ryhtosle ðuhton ic þa heron zezaderode 7 þa oðre forlêt.* We have divided these sentences into three parts, to show how Æ. indicates three, or rather five, sources of his laws, yet the whole seems

[1]) For this interesting information we are also indebted to Dr. Hort.
[2] See pp. 31, 32, 33.

to belong together and its references are indefinite and interconnected one with another. While we take *þás* to refer to ordinances recorded in the *senoð-béc,* yet the context indicates that in Æ.'s mind his laws as collected from them are foremost. The laws of synods were not altogether ecclesiastical and Æ.'s reference to the betrayal of a lord shows that he did not wish to be so understood. In fact Æ. seems to mean by them all the laws *þe ure forezenzan heoldon.* The laws of the three kings, though not the resolutions of ecclesiastical synods, were still both in their origin and content largely ecclesiastical and, in an indefinite way, Æ. includes them with the rest. All this must be borne in mind in noting, for convenience's sake, the following five sources: 1. Synodical Laws, 2. Æ.'s own Laws, 3. Laws of Ine, 4. Laws of Offa, 5. Laws of Æðelbirht. As to the use made of these sources, Æ.'s own statements lead us to expect that he adopted but few laws entirely his own [1]; most of his collection is therefore from the adoption or revision, as he indicates, of laws from the other sources. With a view to our future discussion of Ine's Laws, however, attention may here be drawn to the indefinite and inexact character of this whole paragraph, and the way in which the laws "of the days of Ine, Offa or Æðelbirht" are mentioned all together. As already shown, this mention of the laws of the three kings is to some extent a repetition of what is said at the beginning of the paragraph, a particularisation induced by and in contrast to the mention just made by Æ. of himself and his own laws. In like manner the clauses following this mention of the kings parallel those above after the first reference to the laws that Æ. had collected. No reference is made to a particular lawbook of any single king, and, evident as is their general intent, these concluding clauses, thus introduced, do not, we are convinced, furnish sufficient ground for the statement that Æ. must have revised or excerpted the code of each one of the kings and that the code of no one of the three could appear unrevised in Æ.'s compilation.

---

[1] It is quite likely that Æ. had in use some laws of his own before this code was compiled, whose earliest possible date is after many years of peace.

The division of the Laws has already been made at the outset in dividing the entire Code. It remains but to state its grounds. Ine's Laws are so called because Chap. XLIV, entitled *Be ines domum,* is evidently the formal introduction to the code of King Ine of Wessex. The placing of Æ.'s revision of Æðelbirht's code concerning bodily injuries, which XL—XLIII readily appears to be, in a separate section, is merely for purposes of treatment. Only in subject matter is it distinguished from the laws preceding it; formal distinction there is none. This leaves Chapters II (1)—XXXIX (43) to be considered together as "Miscellaneous Laws".

It is not our purpose in considering these laws to endeavour to search out a source for the single chapters. Such a treatment of them would be legal, rather than literary, in character. The object of our observations here can only be to verify by actual investigation the information as to the sources used already gathered from Æ.'s own words. A considerable use of Ine and Æb. is shown outside these miscellaneous laws. The examination of these yields rather indefinite results. The loss of Offa's code is of course serious hindrance. It is, however, pretty clear that Æ. could have adopted but few laws not suggested to him by an ecclesiastical or Biblical [1]) source or by some law of the three kings; there are apparently not many entirely original laws of Æ. Yet in most of these the suggestion is all that is borrowed, the law is really Ælfred's and to him unquestionably is to be ascribed the whole character of this part of his code. How important a part in it Offa's Laws play, must probably remain an unanswered question. That a number of them were used by Æ. here, there can be no doubt, but probably they underwent, as others did, a thorough revision. The supposition of Palgrave [2]) that Offa's Laws occupied in a second promulgation of Æ.'s code for Mercia the place in which Ine's Laws are found in what he calls "the statute for the West-Saxons", is to be positively rejected. There is no evidence of any sort for such an assumption, and the fact that

---

[1]) Compare 9 with Intr. 16; 23—4 with Intr. 21; 32 with Intr. 8 and 40—41. Is 13 possibly suggested by Deut. XIX, 5, quoted by Gregory in Past. Care and found in Æ.'s transl., Chap. XXI?

[2]) See I, E.

Ine's Laws occupy such a position as they do, affords, as will be shown [1]), no ground for alloting to Offa's Laws a like place in a supposititious publication of which neither in Ms., nor ancient translation, nor ancient tradition any trace whatever can be found.

5. XL—XLIII: Ælfred's Revision of Æðelbirht's Code concerning Bodily Injuries.

The second part of the laws is interesting by reason of the insight it gives into Æ.'s work as a reviser. Its source, or perhaps more accurately model — for the salient point, the penalty, is almost always altered by Æ. — is found in Chapters 32—72 of the Laws of Æðelbirht [2]) as preserved in the Textus Roffensis.[3]) Here we have a list of fines that follows in general the order of the parts of the body from head to foot. In some places, however, as 38, 56, 66, this order is broken; again provisions seem to be repeated, as 45, 49, while others that should occur are wanting. All these are meagre in expression, some doubtful in meaning. Æ.'s revision is in four chapters, but the fourth, under the convenient title, *Be monnes eagwunde 7 oðerra missenlicra lima*, includes a great number of provisions; the whole occupies 44—77 in the new numbering. 44—64 go in the most exact order from crown to toe. 44 adds to the penalties for an injury to the head in Æb. 36, 37; 45 is Æ.'s own, but cf. Æb. 33; 46 (ear) doubles fines of Æb. 40, 39; 47 (eye) revises Æb. 43, 44; 48 (nose) displaces Æb. 45, 48; 49 (tooth) revises Æb. 51; 50 (cheek) displaces Æb. 46, 47, 50. 51 (throat) is Æ.'s; so also 52 (tongue). 53 (shoulder) shows the same penalty as Æb. 38; for 54 and 55 (arm) cf. Æb. 53. In 56—60 Æ. fills out Æb. 54, 55 by alloting a provision to each finger and the nail thereof, a notable instance of his love of order. He now returns 61 to the trunk, cf. Æb. 61; then comes 62 (thigh) for Æb. 67, and 63 (shank) Æ.'s own provision; 64, cf. Æb. 70, 71, provides for each toe in exemplary detail. — This part is carried through with perfect regularity, as well as great

---

[1]) See below p. 46.
[2]) Publ. by Wilkins, p. 1, Thorpe, Vol. I, p. 1 and Schmid, p. 2.
[3]) See p. 14.

exactness and even fulness of expression, and constitutes, so far as it goes, a perfect code by itself. To this Æ. adds a number of miscellaneous regulations, most of which have no counterpart in Æb. For 65 cf. Æb. 64, for 68 Æb. 38, for 71 Æb. 69. Many of these are of a complex character, referring to different parts of the body at once, as 66, 1 and 71, some refer to no part in particular, as 74.

This brief sketch of Æ.'s work here can hardly fail to have brought to view its salient point, the strong sense of order and clear conscious purpose that actuate it. The form of Æb.'s provisions — a mere collection of curt notes — did not please Ælfred, the order in which they were arranged was not satisfactory to him: he did not, therefore, content himself with simply altering the size of the fines, but, in spite of the great labour involved, constructed in place of the old code a new one satisfactory to his sense of order and to his views of literary propriety.

6. XLIV—CXX: The Laws called Ine's: Their relation to the Code: Ms. Evidence; Views of Schmid; The Compendious Character of this Work; Right of Ine's Laws to be considered an Intrinsic Part of it; These Laws not revised by Ælfred, but interpolated by his Predecessors.

We have already in dividing the Laws drawn attention to the fact that as Chapter XLIV appeared the introduction to the Laws of Ine, and that the chapters following could accordingly be regarded as Ine's Laws. Not only has this natural assumption in the past been freely made, but indeed all editors, excepting Thorpe, have separated this part of the Code from the rest, placing it then on chronological grounds before the "Laws of Ælfred" as the "Laws of Ine". Authority for this proceeding there is none. Six A.-S. Mss. and all the old Mss. of the Ve.[1] agree in showing that Æ.'s code did not exist without this part of it, and of Ine's Laws, independent of Æ.'s code, there is no more trace than of Offa's. The evidence being thus all on one side, no argument should be necessary, in spite of the course taken by so many editors in contradiction to the

---

[1] Only Bromton and one or two other late adaptations of Ve. put Ine's Laws first for the same reason as the edd.

Mss. Yet Schmid, the last editor of the Laws, not content with placing "Ine's Laws" before Ælfred's, goes so far as to refer[1]) to "die Vermuthung, dass Aelfred seine Gesetze für Westsachsen in Verbindung mit Ine's Gesetzen publiciren liess"! As Ine's Laws were otherwise unknown to us, this "supposition" may be stated to be correct!

Though for such a remark as this a refutation merely on Ms. grounds be sufficient, Sch.'s expressions in concluding his consideration of the question as to Æ.'s relation to the laws of the three kings, open a new field of controversy and demand that we show the position of these laws in the Mss. to be not unnatural, but altogether right, proper, and to be expected. Sch. says[2]): "Wir müssen uns bescheiden .... eine einigermassen sichere Antwort auf diese Frage geben zu können, nur müssen wir darauf aufmerksam machen, dass die Annahme am nächsten liegt, Aelfred habe gar keine Publication der beibehaltenen ältern Gesetze für nothwendig erachtet, sondern nur in sein Gesetz aufgenommen, was er ändern oder neu hinzufügen wollte. Es blieb Sache der Richter, das neue Gesetz mit den ältern geschriebenen und ungeschriebenen Rechtsnormen, wie sie in jedem Lande in Gebrauch waren, zu vereinigen". However well this statement might apply to other A.-S. kings, it involves in this case a real misconception of the nature and aims of the work. Æ.'s code was meant to be a legal compend. We gather indications and proofs of this from the most diverse sources. The spirit displayed by Æ. in his whole political and literary activity leads us to expect such a work from him, when once he takes the rôle of lawgiver. The purposes that caused him to strive so mightily to put all in the state on a firm and lasting basis, the aims shown in the translation of so many great works to raise the standard of learning among his people, lead us to expect of him now a different course from merely altering or adding a certain number of laws, leaving all the rest, along with the question of its retention or rejection, to his incompetent judges. More than this, Æ.'s own words in the Intr. are opposed to Schm.'s view.

---

[1]) See (I, E) p. XXXVII.
[2]) See (I, E) p. XL.—XLI.

44

He says distinctly that he did take up into his code laws of
his predecessors that he wished to retain; he expresses most
clearly his preference for such laws before his own to make
up this code. Strongest, however, is the evidence gathered from
our consideration of the code itself. We see clearly from Æ.'s
omissions and changes in his rendering of Biblical injunctions
that, without putting them on a par with his own ordinances,
he still intended them to be studied and observed by his people.
This and his account of the work of the mediaeval synods,
shows how in his eyes his compilation extended over the whole
period from which any tradition of laws was preserved. And,
as always, he gathered from the past to make good for the
future, alive to the important question *hwæt þæs ðam lician
wolde þe æfter ûs wæren.*

There is surely no possible ground for doubting the compendious character of this work, nor can there be any question
as to the labour expended upon its compilation, evidenced by
the revision just examined. That in such a work these laws,
the standard law of the West-Saxon kingdom, should appear,
seems on the face of it self evident. And the necessity of it
becomes more clear from a comparison of them with the rest
of the code. They are found to contain a large number of
provisions, wanting otherwise in the code, yet absolutely necessary to it. In the first part we find ecclesiastical laws, laws
concerning the rights of lordship, of inheritance; Æ. goes so
far as to fix the responsibility for the misdeeds of a deaf mute;
he mentions various special cases of assault, certain special
cases of murder and two of theft [1]); but for the great mass of
cases of theft, harbouring thieves, receiving stolen goods, etc.,
he has no provisions whatever. The omission of these in such
a compend of law would be inexplicable. Their absence in
this part of the collection is wholly justified, however, by their
presence in great numbers among the laws that Æ. had re-
served for the last place in his code. Æ.'s laws against stealing
from a church are about the only possible additions to the
remarkable collection already in his hands on that subject.
Here thievery seems to be regarded from every imaginable

---

[1]) Viz: 6,16, but 9,2; 12; 22 bear more or less upon it.

point of view: robbery in general and forcible spoliation (10), a servant's theft (22), former theft of a new-made serf (48), theft with or without the wife's knowledge (7), theft of wood (44), of mast (49), of meat (17), of a man (53); then concerning a thief caught in the act (12), catching a thief (18, 37, 28), catching a thief and letting him go (36, 72, 73), harbouring a fugitive (30), concerning slaying a thief (16, 35), concerning stolen goods (47, 75, 35, 1, 46), not to mention a stranger taken for a thief (20) and the slaying of the same (21). To the subject of murder fewer chapters are devoted and Æ. accordingly introduces quite a number among the miscellaneous laws. There can be no question that Æ. collected his laws with regard to those already found in the code of Ine, to which he intended to give a place in his law-book. This is the reason that the newer part of his code rarely, if ever, comes in contact with this older part. Analogous is his course in omitting penalties for wounds from his miscellaneous laws, having resolved upon a revision of Æb.'s collection on that subject. As to the position given Ine's Laws, it may be that he regarded the rest of the laws as a compilation from sources older than Ine's time, or at least as old, whereas the code bearing Ine's name was the present standard law of the kingdom, and he therefore puts these after the Biblical extracts and lets Ine's Laws follow them. At all events, the position of the laws called Ine's as an intrinsic, inseparable, part of Ælfred's Code, attested to by all the Ms. tradition, is equally well established as consistent with the aims of the author and the character of his work.[1])

The relation of Æ. to this part of his code is, none the less, by no means so close as to the other parts of the compilation. There are substantial grounds for asserting that Æ. did not revise the laws of Ine. This is indicated by the retention of the original introduction, which points to the adoption of the code bodily; it is evidenced also by the retention in it of one or two provisions supplanted by similar ones in Æ.'s other laws (cf. Ine 45 with Æ. 40, and Ine 6, 2 with Æ. 15), it is put beyond peradventure by an examination of the entire code. We find in it not only utter disorder as to arrangement,

---

[1]) Cf. Pauli (I, E) p. 165, near the foot, apparently unknown to Sch.

46

but the same subject treated from the same point of view in many places (cf. the list just given concerning theft), sometimes, as 18 and 37, 16 and 35, in particular, the same provision appears twice in nearly the same words. Compare the condition found here with the results of our examination of Æ.'s revision of Æb., and the impossibility of believing in any Ælfredian revision of Ine must appear. Only the chapter headings are Æ.'s work.[1]) We have already [2]) done what we could to reconcile Intr. 49, 9 with this fact; we will only add here that the absence in so inexact a statement of a special clause saying that this standard law of the kingdom had been taken up bodily into the code, is less to be wondered at if we consider that such a statement would be purely formal and have no practical value, in as much as this code was well known to West-Saxons and its retention complete was patent to all. Nor has, in fact, the idea of a revision found friends at any time. Schmid[3]) considers it, because of Æ.'s statement in 49, 9, to follow from Palgrave's statement that Ine's Laws are annexed to the statute of Alfred.[4]) Palgrave did not mean it so, however, for he says, "The laws of Offa have not been preserved in their original form, and we cannot distinguish them in the capitulary of the King of Wessex. But the Laws of Ina are annexed etc.", which shows that he believed Ine's Laws to be preserved here in their original form.

Though right as to an Ælf. revision, Pal. is wrong in considering, or permitting the inference, that these laws appear in their original form. They are preserved to us by Æ. in the form in which, as the current law of the kingdom, he found them in his day. But we doubt if one half the code really existed in Ine's time. Ine having been the first great West-Saxon law-giver, the code naturally retained his name, but through so long a period it received many accretions. The very condition that argues most strongly against an orderly Ælfredian revision is proof positive of a careless interpolation and augmentation by Æ.'s predecessors. Take away all long chapters and all chapters repeated from or suggested by preceding

---

[1]) Cf. below p. 47.   [2]) Cf. p. 39.
[3]) P. XL.   [4]) See I, E.

chapters, and perhaps something like the original code would
be the result. It would, at all events, then gain a resemblance
in form to the collection of legal notes known as Æðelbirht's
Code, which undoubtedly bears the stamp of great antiquity.

7. Conclusion: Construction of the Code as a Whole; The Chapter Headings; Critical Comments.

The different parts of Æ.'s code that accdg. to our division
we have now considered in order, had, if we consider the Introduction as one part, each its separate origin. The order of
time in which the parts arose seems to be exactly the reverse
of their order in the Code. Ine's Laws lay ready before Ælfred, the revision of Æðelbirht was resolved upon and probably
made before the miscellaneous laws were collected, and, whether
the translations in the Introd. were made before the completion
of the code or not, they were destined unquestionably for it [1]),
and the entire Introd., including the original parts, in all probability was not written until the rest of the work was done.
Prefixed to the whole is the last of Æ.'s manifold labours in
connection with this undertaking — the chapter headings. This
set of headings is itself quite interesting. It belongs to the
literary, rather than to the legal, character of Æ.'s work. Æ.
found, we believe, no chapter headings in Ine. There are none
to this day in the old Kentish laws. In the Pastoral Care
and other Latin writings appear headings over the chapters
indicating the contents of each. These are placed all before
the text as a sort of synopsis or table of contents. Our headings
are quite similar in form to those in P. C. and are possibly
modelled directly after that translation. That they are not of
legal origin seems to be shown also by the fact that they are
not given to every law nor to laws alone. After the various
parts of his code were in place and connected together Æ.
wrote out this set of headings, covering loosely most of its
contents. It begins not at the first law nor at the beginning
of the code, but immediately after the translation; it includes
Ine's introduction as a chapter and it leaves many a law to
make one chapter with the law preceding it, without recognising

[1]) The Decalogue, as Wülker suggests, may well be an exception.

its subject in the heading. The set of titles thus made becomes here as in other works a sort of table of contents for the whole. According to it, not according to separate subjects or provisions, the division into chapters was then made.

The great value of this code for law and history has been sufficiently emphasized already by others and is not likely to be underestimated. From our own observations it is difficult to gather any homogeneous results, as each investigation lay in a different field. A word may be said however as to the literary significance of the work. One thousand years have elapsed since its composition; the ordinances of the Apostles were nearer to Æ. in time than are his laws to us. We must bear this in mind in forming an estimate of this undertaking. Let us think what it meant to form in that day such a conception of a code as his! The fidelity and prudence with which he carried out his plan are remarkable. In the selection and adaptation of extracts from the Bible, in the establishment of an historical connection between them and his laws, in the selection of the various laws to add to his conscientious revision of Ædelbirht and to the code already in his hands, Æ. displayed his for that time remarkable learning and his for all time admirable traits of mind, literary taste and judgment combined with political foresight. Yet to the largeness and worthiness of Æ.'s idea of a legal compend covering all human history the greatest recognition is due. The work itself is small, but it bears testimony to the greatness of its author.

Chapter II.
THE DATE OF THE CODE.

The question of the order in time of Ælfred's literary productions has had to be treated with practically no aid from direct testimony of any sort; to this fact, no doubt, is due the great difference of opinion on this point that has long subsisted. Pauli [1]) and Bosworth [1]) give the arrangement: Boethius, Beda,

---

[1]) See p. 8.

Orosius, Pastoral Care, referring to W^m of Malmesbury's [1]) remark that the text of Boet. was glossed or explained for Æ. by Asser. Ten Brink [2]), without mentioning his reasons, adopts the order: Oros., Beda, Boet., P. C. A new light was thrown upon this matter by the first detailed investigation of it, that of Wülker in the Grundriss.[2]) Here the place of P. C. at the head of the list is attested by expressions in Æ.'s preface, and that of Boet. at the end by his additions to the text. Wülker further draws attention to the varying relation of the rendering to the original, and points out that a free treatment of the matter at hand indicates increased literary experience. Thus Handbook, P. C., Beda and Oros. are put in the first period of peace, before 893, while Boet., with the Soliloquies and 'De videndo Deo', is assigned to the closing years of Æ.'s life, 897—901.

The arguments here offered and the conclusions reached have justly commended themselves to those that have since had occasion to deal with this question: Schilling [3]), Ebert, Körting, Wichmann [4]) and Schmidt have in turn accepted them. Schilling and Schmidt indeed have done more: their detailed examinations of the relation between the A.-S. and Latin texts of Oros. and Beda respectively have furnished strong confirmation of the order given, which now seems as well established as such a hypothesis can be. The character of each of the great translations is now definitely ascertained. In the P. C., which Æ. in the preface declares to have been written by him as he learned the meaning of the Latin from four clerical assistants, words are treated quite freely, but each clause is translated without any attempt at adaptation of the matter given. This agrees well with Æ.'s statements. Not yet master of the Latin, he could not give exact translations nor did he yet feel equal to altering or handling freely the work before him. Although, as Sweet [5]) says, P. C. is not a translation in our sense of the term, neither is it an adaptation; it is a careful 'rendering' of the sense of the Latin original. Beda, however, as Schmidt

---

[1]) See p. 8, Hardy, II, 122. [2]) See p. 9. [3]) For all these, see p. 9.

[4]) Wichmann adds to the list of Æ.'s works the doubtful 'Psalms', which, on internal evidence as well as on W^m of Malmesbury's testimony, he considers Æ.'s last production.

[5]) See p. 8.

Turk, Ælfred the Great.   4

shows [1]), is for the most part a remarkably literal translation. A large number of chapters, however, are omitted altogether, for which there is often some reason discernible [2]); there are also smaller omissions, alterations, condensations, but (a fact often remarked and lamented) only very slight attempts to add anything from the king's knowledge of the subject. The actual translation is generally far more literal than P. C. [3]), the work as a whole, however, is much more freely treated: apparently Æ. now understands, as he ought, the Latin much better, while his omissions make the first approach to the perfect freedom of adaptation which separates Oros., and still more Boet., from the other works.

In adopting the order given we have, unfortunately, but gained a basis for our consideration; the Laws have not been included in any actual investigations; in the 'Grundriss' alone are they given a definite place in a list of Æ.'s works. The reason is, of course, that this code has not, heretofore, been generally considered except in its place among A.-S. laws. In attempting a consideration of the question we must confess at the outset that its results, like the material at hand for it, are likely to be meagre and unsatisfactory. This work differs from those discussed in being for the most part original; it lacks too any allusions that might help to determine the date. We are confined, then, to general observations as to the subject of the work, to a search for possible allusions to it in other works, and to the comparison of its fragment of translation (in the Introduction) and its general literary tenour with the conditions noted in the other works.

No value can be attached to W^{m.} of Malmesbury's statement that Æ. made laws amid the tumults of war. [4]) As Pauli and others have said, this code cannot have been made during actual war; it is a work of peace and its provisions are for a people at peace. Nor was this Code published immediately after peace was declared: whether or not Æ. gave some laws

---

[1]) Cf. p. 46 in Schmidt's work.
[2]) Cf. pp. 15—19 in Schmidt.
[3]) Cf. Schmidt, pp. 47—56.
[4]) Ille inter fremitus armorum et stridores lituorum leges tulit. See p. 8, Hardy (II, 122).

in the interim, this code cannot have been made before he
began his literary labours, of which the extracts from the Vulgate
were a fruit. The beginning of these labours is set at Asser's
first visit in 887. To be sure, the Decalogue had probably
been rendered into A.-S. before Æ., but the rest was certainly
made by Æ. for these laws. This is shown [1]), for example, by
omissions in XXI, 22, XXIII, 3 and 5, by alterations in XXI, 2
and 30, XXII, 1, XXIII, 1, 2, etc.; indeed the whole character
of the translation attests this beyond peradventure. Such a
work of translation cannot have been undertaken by Æ. before
Asser's visit.

This conclusion brings us to the consideration of the by
no means insignificant argument from the subject of the work,
viz: that a code of laws ought properly to precede any other
of Æ.'s works, because of the much greater need of it, a need
that Æ., alive to less evident wants of his kingdom, should
have been the first to feel. This argument, in its bearing on
our code, is somewhat modified in effect by the fact just adduced that this work could not have been completed until some
years of peace had passed. If Æ. had waited so long, a year
more or less could hardly matter to him. Still when once Æ.
set himself to literary tasks, a law-code should still have been
his first thought, and we may with propriety resolve to put
the code as near the beginning as other considerations permit.
On this ground, we take it, Wülker [2]) gives our code a place
between the Handbook and the P. C., thus making it the first
of Æ.'s extant works.

Our search for allusions to the Laws in Æ.'s other works
yields but little. In the oft-quoted Preface to P. C., Æ. dwells
at length upon the various translations of the Law (*sio œ*, the
Pentateuch): how it and the other books were translated from
Hebrew into Greek and Latin and how afterwards many other
Christian (i. e. Germanic) nations rendered them into their own
tongue. This seems to show that Æ.'s mind was then on such
work as he did for our Code, but it must he remembered that
the translations lately made in the Handbook may well have

---

[1]) Cf. pp. 36—37, and Text.
[2]) Grundriss, p. 398, foot-note.

covered similar ground. Moreover, we can hardly say whether this would point to earlier or later work on the Laws, though we should incline to consider it indicative of the formation of the plan merely; were our Code with its Introduction already completed, it might well have received more definite notice in this place. Another possible allusion is brought forward by Schmidt's work. Having previously shown how Æ. was accustomed to alter statements introduced in the original by *usque hodie, hactenus,* and the like, to conform them to the facts as in his time, Sch. finds certain such passages literally translated.[1]) This he believes to have been done in many cases because the statement was still true in Æ.'s time: among these "Fälle, in welchen man mit ziemlicher Sicherheit behaupten kann, dass Æ. wörtlich übersetzte, weil er aus eigener Kenntnis oder durch Mitteilungen anderer wusste, dass die geschilderten Verhältnisse noch fortbestanden", appears the following: *Qui (Aedilberct) inter cetera bona, quae genti suae consulendo conferebat, etiam decreta illi iudiciorum, iuxta exempla Romanorum, cum consilio sapientium constituit; quae conscripta Anglorum sermone hactenus habentur et obseruantur ab ea.* II, 5. — *Se cyning (Æþelbyrht) betwih ða oþre god ðe he his leodum ðurh geþeaht gefremede, eac swylce he rihtra doma gesetnesse mid snotera geþeahte gesette æfter Romana bysena ond ða het on englisc awritan ða nu gena oþ ðis mid him hæfde ond gehealdene synd.* 506[25]. — If we concur, as there is every reason to do, in Schmidt's view that Æ. intentionally translated this as it stood, then it seems to indicate not only that Æ. was acquainted with Æb.'s laws, but that he knew them to be still in use, a fact well explained by the existence of our code, with its adaptation of a great part of them. This conjecture would, of course, put the Code before Beda.

Both these possible allusions would place the Laws near the beginning of Æ.'s literary labours, thus agreeing with the conclusion reached at the outset by a consideration of the subject and nature of the work. We must now endeavour to bring the matter, so far as possible, to a final determination by a consideration of the general literary character of the work,

---

[1]) Cf. Schmidt, p. 57.

and of the results of our comparison of the translated part
with its original. At the close of the preceding chapter and
at various points throughout it [1]), we have drawn attention to the
skill with which Æ. handles the component parts of his code,
shaping and adapting them to his purpose, and welding them
together in a coherent whole. The work done here is far in
advance of anything in other A.-S. codes. It leads us to look
for a man of some literary experience, as well as natural talent.
Extensive as it is, the P. C. exhibits little, if anything, of this
sort. Though, of course, the author of P. C. might at that time
have been in a position to do such work as this, still Æ. appears
on the face of the matter to have been working then on a
somewhat lower plane. Not until the Preface, written after the
translation was completed, does he give proof of any literary
skill, and here too there is nothing that can be said to excel
the Introduction to the Laws, which might well have followed
after a short time.

The condition of matters with regard to the translation is
much the same. We find here a clear advance toward the
Beda. There are discernible in our Introd. the two marks that
distinguish that work from P. C., viz: general adherence to
the words of the text, and occasional freedom in adapting the
matter. As to the first point, the beginning of Chap. XXI and
many other passages may be compared with Schmidt's instances from Beda [2]), which they at least approach. Here and
in regard to the next point, we must not forget the great
difference in size between the two translations. To show
occasional adaptation, however, the changes [3]) in XXI, 2, 30,
in XXII, 1, 7—8, and in XXIII, 4, and as well the omissions
in XXI, 9—10, in XXII, 8, and in XXIII, 3, 5, may be put in
evidence. They differ only in number and variety from those
cited from the greater work [4]); the spirit is the same in both.
In respect of augmentation, indeed, our work [5]) shows little

---

[1]) Cf. pp. 31, 32, 33, 36, 42.
[2]) Cf. Schmidt, pp. 50 seqq.
[3]) Cf. pp. 36—37 and Text.
[4]) Cf. Sch., pp. 19—24.
[5]) Cf. p. 37.

more than the same use of synomyms with P. C.[1]), exhibiting no
independent additions; Beda[2]), however, is little in advance
here. In other respects we have certainly been able to note
a difference between the Laws and P. C. Other causes than
increase in experience might explain such a change; in the
absence, however, of any other evident reason, we cannot but
ascribe it to some difference in time.

The conclusion from our literary examination is, then, that
the Laws come after P. C. In adopting this result, we follow
other indications at the expense of the argument that the Laws,
as the most necessary work, should naturally have come first.
But as we have already shown, the weight of this argument
is not great, when a small difference of time is in question.
Then too, Æ. had Ine's Laws and probably some of his own
already at hand. In the Introduction (49, 9 and 10) he tells
us he prefers the old Laws, and shows that he regards his
own work as one of compilation and revision, saying nothing,
moreover, as Ine does, of the need for laws in his kingdom.
On the other hand, in P. C. he speaks most seriously of the
great demand for such a work to enlighten the shepherds of
his people. In view of all this, perhaps our Law-book seemed
at the time no more pressing a necessity than the other —
the code that was to help spiritual leaders in guiding men
aright.

We have no wish to put the Laws any later than this.
Not to mention the possible allusion to the Code in Beda, there
is no evidence which, in view of the consideration just discussed, should place it farther from the beginning of Æ.'s
labours, to the earlier stages of which it no doubt belongs.
Evidently Æ. had much of this work already at hand. The
plan of the Introd. he may have had in mind when he wrote
the Preface to P. C.; at all events, as already remarked[3]), it
is a result of the same educational purpose that animates the

---

[1]) Cf. Sweet (I, F), p. XLI.
[2]) Cf. Sch., pp. 30 seqq., also 37.
[3]) Cf. p. 33.

earlier work and is so earnestly expressed in the Preface. If we suppose the Introd. to have been prepared shortly after this, the publication of the completed Code may be set in the year 890. This seems a fair conclusion from the facts before us: it must, however, be remembered that the materials gathered for this work are inadequate to its final accomplishment, and that our conclusion is at best but a careful conjecture.

PART SECOND.

TEXT.

MANUSCRIPT E.

I. Be ðon þæt mon ne scyle oþrum deman buton swa
he wille þæt him mon deme.

II. Be aþum 7 be weddum.

III. Be circena socnum.

IIII. Be borᵹ bryce.

V. Be hlaford searwe.

VI. Be circena friðe.

VII. Be circan stale.

VIII. Be ðon þe mon on cynᵹes healle feohte.

VIIII. Be nunnan hæmede.

X. Be bearn eacnum wife ofslæᵹenum.

XI. Be twelfhyndes monnes wife forleᵹenum.

XII. Be cirliscre fæmnan onfenᵹe.

XIII. Be wudu bærnette.

XIIII. Be dumbera monna dǣdum.

XV. Be þam monnum þe beforan biscopum feohtað.

XVI. Be nunnena onfenᵹe.

XVII. Be ðam monnum þe heora wæpen to monslyhte lænað.

XVIII. Be ðam þe munecum heora feoh buton leafe befæstað.

XVIIII. Be preosta ᵹefeohte.

XX. Be eofetes andetlan.

XXI. Be hundes slite.

XXII. Be nietena misdædum.

XXIII. Be ceorles mennenes niedhæmede.

In red above: þis syndon þa domas ðe ælfred cyncᵹ ᵹeceas H |
I. ðam H | man GH | scule H | dēman H | butan GH | man him GH |
III. cyricena G | IV. *borh* Ot, burh GH | V. over searwe small but old
swice H | VI. cyricena G | fryþe G | VII. cyricena G, circean H | VIII. þon
þæt G, þam ðe H | man G | cyninᵹes OtG, kyninᵹes H | ᵹefeohte, ᵹe
above H | X. eac-num H | ofsleᵹenum Ot, ofslaᵹenum GH | XI.
.XII. hyndes G | mannes GH | XII. *cirilscre* Ot, cyrliscre G | an-

MANUSCRIPT B.

(These Headings are found on the margins of B,
which begins in the middle of IIII.)

Be cyninczes swicdome.
Be ciricene friðe.
Be ðam ðe steleð on ciricean.
Be ðam þæt man feohteð on kyninzes healle.
Be ðam þe nunnan of mynstre utalædeð.
Be ðam ðæt man ofslea wif mid cilde.
Be hæmed ðinzum.
Eft.
Be wude benete 7 Gif man afylled bið on zemænum weorce.
Be dumbra manna dædum.
Be ðam þæt man toforan bisceope feohteð.
Be ðam zif man of myran folan adrifþ oððe cu cealf.
Đe oðrum his unmazu ætfæsteð.
Be nunnena andfenczum.
Be þam þe heore wepna lænað to manslihte.
Be þam þe munecan heore feoh befæstað.
Be preosta zefeohte.
Be cyninczes zerefan ðyfðe.
Be hundes slite.
Be nytena misdædum.
Be ceorles mennenes nydhemede.

---

fenze G, onfænze H | XIII. wuda H | XIV. dumbra OtGH, r above
H | manna GH | XV. ðan G | mannum GH | bisceopum OtG, biscope
H | XVI. anfenzum H | XVII. mannum GH | biora, hi ab. Ot, hyra G |
wæpn G, wæpna H | monslihte G, manslyhte H | XVIII. þe man above
H | butan GH | befestað G | XX. ðeofes H | 7 detlan G, andettan II |
XXI. slyte Ot | XXII. nytena GH | XXIII, in H XXVI. ciorles H |
mennen H | niedhæmde G, nydhæmede H |

5*

XXIIII. Be twyhyndum men æt bloþslyhte.

XXV. Be syx hyndum men.

XXVI. Be .XII. hyndum men.

XXVII. Be unᵹewintredes wifmonnes ned hæmde.

XXVIII. Be swa ᵹerades monnes sleᵹe.

XXVIIII. Be folcleasunᵹe ᵹewyrhtum.

XXX. Be ᵹod borᵹum.

XXXI. Be ciepe monnum.

XXXII. Be cierlisces monnes byndellan.

XXXIII. Be speres ᵹemeleasnesse.

XXXIIII. Be bold ᵹetale.

XXXV. Be ðon ðe mon beforan caldormen on ᵹemote ᵹe-feohte.

XXXVI. Be cierlisces monnes flet ᵹefeohte.

XXXVII. Be bôclondum.

XXXVIII. Be fæhðe.

XXXVIIII. Be mæsse daᵹa freolse.

XL. Be heafod wunde.

XLI. Be feax wunde.

XLII. Be ear sleᵹe.

XLIII. Be monnes eaᵹwunde 7 oðerra missenlicra lima.

XLIIII. Be ines domum.

XLV. Be ᵹodes ðeowa reᵹole.

XLVI. Be cildum.

XLVII. Be sunnan dæᵹes weorcum.

XLVIII. Be ciric sceattum.

XLVIIII. Be ciric sôcnum.

L. Be ᵹefeohtum.

LI. Be stale.

LII. Be ryhtes bene.

LIII. Be ðam wrecendan ær *he* him ryhtes bidde.

LIIII. Be reaflace.

XXIV, in H XXIII. twyhindum Ot | slihte GH | — End of p. 65 in E |
XXV, in H XXIV | XXVI, in H XXV. *twelf* Ot | XXVII. tynᵹewintredes
H | monnes wif Ot, wifmannes GH | niedhæmde G, nydhæmede H | XXVIII.
mannes GH ; sleᵹes G, slæᵹe H | XXIX. leasunᵹa G | XXXI. cypemannum
G, cyp-mannum H | XXXII. cyrlisces OtG | mannes GH | byndelan H |
XXXIII. ᵹymeleasnesse GH | XXXV. þam GH | man GH | ealder H |
ᵹemôte H | feohte H | XXXVI. cyrlisces G | mannes GH | flett H |

Be twyhyndum men æt bloðslihte.
Be sixhyndum men.
Be twylfhendum men.
Be unȝewintrede wif mannes slaȝe.

Be ȝodborhȝum.
Be cypmannum.
Be ceorlisces mannes bindelan.
Be speres ȝymeleaste.
Be bold ȝetale.
Be ðam ðe beforan aldormen on ȝemote feohtc.
Eft.
Be cyrlisces monnes flette ȝefeohte.
Be burhbryce.
Be boclande.

(Leaf wanting.)

Be heafodwunde 7 oðre liman.

Ines Laȝe.

Be ciric sceatte.
Be ciric socnum.
Be ȝefeohtum.
Be stale.
Be rihtes bene.
Be þam wrecendan.
Be reaflace.

XXXVII. boclandum GH | XXXVIII. fæhðum G, fahþum H | XXXIX.
freolsum H | XLII. earslæȝe H | XLIII. mannes GH | eaȝena wunde,
ena above H | oððera Ot, oðra G, oðre H | mislicra G, mistlicra, t above
H | XLIV. ines G | XLV. reȝule H | XLVII. wyrcum G | XLVIII.
cyricsceatum G | XLIX. cyric G | — End of p. 66 in E — | LII. rihtes
GH | LIII. he above line, appar. new E | man rihtes, vac. him G, hine
man ryhtes H | — End of first fragment of Ot — |

LV. Be ðam monnum þe hiora ʒelondan bebycʒʒað.

LVI. Be ʒefonʒenum ðeofum.

LVII. Be ðam ðe hiora ʒewitnessa beforan biscope âleoʒað.

LVIII. Be hloðe.

LVIIII. Be heriʒe.

LX. Be þeofsleʒe.

LXI. Be forstolenum flæsce.

LXII. Be cirliscum ðeofe ʒefonʒenuni.

LXIII. Be cyninʒes ʒeneate.

LXIIII. Be feorran cumenum men butan weʒe ʒemctton.

LXV. Be swa ofsleʒenes monnes were.

LXVI. Be ðon ðe monnes ʒeneat staliʒe.

LXVII. Be elðeodies monnes sleʒe.

LXVIII. Be wite ðeowes monnes sleʒe.

LXVIIII. Be ciepe monna fore uppe on londe.

LXX. Be fundenes cildes fostre.

LXXI. Be þon þe mon dearnenʒa bearn ʒestriene.

LXXII. Be ðeofes onfenʒe æt ðiefðe.

LXXIII. Be ðon þe mon sweordes onlæne oðres ðeowe.

LXXIIII. Be ðon þe cierlisc mon flieman feormiʒe.

LXXV. Be ðon ðe mon wîf bycʒe 7 þonne sio ʒift tostande.

LXXVI. Be wilisces monnes lond hæfene.

LXXVII. Be cyninʒes horsweale.

LXXVIII. Be monslihte.

LXXVIIII. Be þeof slihte þæt he mote aðe ʒecyðan.

LXXX. Be ðeofes onfenʒe 7 hine ðonne forlæte.

LXXXI. Be cirlisces monnes ontyʒnesse æt ðiefðe.

LXXXII. Be þon ðe ryhtʒesamhiwan bearn hæbben 7 þonne se
wer ʒewite.

LV. þan G | mannum GH | hira G, heora, o above | ʒelandan GH, ʒe
above H | bebicʒað GH | LVI. ʒefanʒenum GH | þeofe G | LVII. þan
G | hyra G, heora, o above H | ʒewitnesse GH | bisceope G, biscope H | LIX.
herʒe G, hereʒe, second e above H ! LXII. cyrliscum G, cirliescum, e above H |
ʒefanʒenum GH | LXIII. kyninʒes H ! LXIV. cumenan H | ʒemettan G, ʒemet-
tuin, ʒe above H | LXV. ofslaʒenes GH, first e above H mannes GH | LXVI.
þan G, þam H | mannes ʒestaliʒe, vac. neat G | LXVII. ælþeodiʒes GH,
æ over erasure H | mannes GH | LVIII. mannes GH ; LXIX. cypmanna
G, cypemanna H | fôre G, fâre H | ûp G, upp H | land G, land stryne H |
LXXI. ðan G, þam H | man GH | dearnunʒa GH | ʒestriene, second e appar.
new G, ʒestri-ne H | LXXII. þeowes mannes, w over eras., mannes above

Be landbyʒene.
Be ʒefanʒenum ðeofum.
Be þam þe heore ʒewitnessc ʒeleoʒað.
  hloðe.
Be herʒe.
Be ðeofslæʒe.
Be forstolenum flæsce.
Be ceorliscum ðeofum ʒefanʒenum.
Be cinʒes ʒeneate.
Be feorran cumenan men.
Be swa ofslaʒenes mannes were.
Be ðam þe mannes ʒeneat staliʒe.
Be ælðeodiʒes mannes slæʒe.

Be cypmanna fare uppe land.
Be fundenes cildes fostre.
Be ðam þe dearnunʒe bearn stryneð.
Be ðeowes mannes onfenʒe æt ðyfðe.
Be ðam þe his sweord alæne oðres ðeowan.
Be þam þe cyrlisc man feormiʒe flyman.
Be þam þe man wif bycʒe 7 seo ʒift wiðstande.
Be wylisces mannes londhæfene.
Be cininʒes horswale.
Be manslihte.
Be ðeofslihte.
Be ðeofes andfenʒe 7 hine swa forlæte.
Be ceorlisces monnes betoʒenesse.
Be ðam ðe rihtʒesamhiwan bearn habban.

H | ðyfðe GH | LXXIII. þan G, þam II | man GH | his above sweord H ⦙
alæne H | ðeowan, n above H | .LXXIV. þan G, þam H | cyrlisc G | man
GH | flyman GH | LXXV. þan G | þam above H | man GH | bicʒe G,
bycʒe H | seo GH | ʒyft G | LXXVI. wylysces G | mannes GH, nes above
H | land GH | — End of p. 67 in E — | LXXVII. kyninʒes H | LXXVIII.
man G, mann, last n above H | slyhte H | LXXIX. slyhte H | he þæt
môte aðe G, he mott þæt mid aðe, þæt above H | LXXX. þænne G, hine
man ðonne H | LXXXI. cyrlisces G, cierlisces H | mannes GH | ðyfðe G |
æt þyfðe betoʒenisse H | LXXXII. ðan G, ðam H | riht GH | ʒesamhiwon
G | habben G, habban H |

LXXXIII. ûnalyfedum G, unazelyfedum H | fram GH | LXXXIV. ciorles H | weorðize, first e above H | LXXXV. andsæce GH | LXXXVI. ciorles H | LXXXVIII. wudu H | anfenze H | LXXXIX. burh GH | brece G | XC. stal GH | tihlan G | XCI. þam H | man GH | befehþ cêap H | XCII. mannum H | XCIII. unalyfedes GH | mæstenes GH | XCIV mannes GH | XCV. þan G, þam H | man GH | fyrd G, fyrde, e above H | XCVI. dyrnum GH | XCVII. mannes GH | forefenze G, forfenze H | XCVIII. werfæhte G | tihtlan GH | XCIX. eowes GH | C. zehwylces

Be unalyfedum fare fram his laforde.
Be ceorles worðiʒe.

(Included with above in B)

Be ðam þæt ceorlas habbað land ʒemæne 7 ʒærstunas.
Be wude bærnete.
Be wude andfenʒe.
Be burhbryce.
Be staltihlan.

Be witeðeowum mannum.
Be unalefedum mæstenum andfencʒe.
Be ʒesiðcundes mannes ʒeðinʒe.
Be þam þe ʒesiðcund man fyrde forsitte.
Be dyrnun ʒeþincðe.
Be forstolenes mannes forfenʒe.
Be werfæhðe tyhlan.
Be eowe wyrðe.
Be ʒehwylces ceapes wyrðe.
Be cyrlisces mannes stale.

Be hyr oxan.
Be ciricsceatte.
Be þam þe man to ceace fordræfe.
Be ʒesiðcundes mannes fare.
Be ðam þe hafð .XX. hida.
Be tyn hidum.
Be ðreom hidum.
Be ʒyrde.
Be ʒesiðcundes mannes drafe of lande.
Be sceapes ʒanʒe.

GH | anʒilde GH | CI. cyrlisces G, cirlisces H | mannes tale G | mannes H | —
End of p. 68 of E — | CIII. cu G, cû- H | CIV. hyreʒeohte H | CV. cyric
G, ciric H | sceatum G, sceattum H | CVI. ðan G, ðam H | man GH |
ceace GH | CVII. mannes GH | CVIII. ðan þe G, þam ðe H | landes
GH | CX. hidum, d like cl H | CXI. ʒirde H | landes GH | CXII.
siðcundes G | mannes GH | lande G | CXIII. sceapes, a above H | ʒanʒe
GH, perh. orig. o H | flesc G, flysc H |

CXIV. Be twyhyndum were.

CXV. Be wertyhtlan.

CXVI. Be werȝeld ðeofes forefonȝe.

CXVII. Be anre nihtes ðiefðe.

CXVIII. Be ðon ðe ðeowwealh frione mon ôfslea.

CXIX. Be forstolenes ceapes forefonȝe.

CXX. Be þon ȝif mon oðres ȝodsunu slea oððe his ȝodfæder.

CXV. tihlan G, tihtlan H | CXVI. werȝild GH | forefenȝe GH | CXVII. anra G | nihtæ G | ðyfðe GH | CXVIII. þan G, ðam above H | þeofwealh G | freonne m. G, friȝne man H | CXIX. forefenȝe G, forfenȝe H | CXX. ðan G, þam H | man GH | ofslea H | Added in H: CXXI. Be blaserum 7 be morðslihtum. | — Last 8 lines of p. 69 and all p. 70 blank in E — |

Be twyhindum were.
Be wertyhlan.
Be werzild ðeofes forefenze.
Be anre nihte ðyfte.
Be þam þe þeowwalh frizne man ofslca.
Be forstolene ceape.
Be zodfæderes oððe zodsunes slæhte.

———

MANUSCRIPT E.

1.   RYHTEN WÆS SPRECENde ðas word to
1, 1.   moyse 7 þus cwæð: Ic êom dryhten ðin ʒod;
          Ic ðe utʒelædde of eʒipta londe 7 of hiora ðeow-
1, 2. dome.   Ne lufa ðu oþre fremde ʒodas ofer me.
2.   Ne minne noman ne ciʒ ðu on idelnesse, forðon þe
         ðu ne bist unscyldiʒ wið me, ʒif ðu on idelnesse ciʒst
3.   minne noman.   Ʒemyne þæt ðu ʒehalʒiʒe þone ræste-
3, 1. dæʒ;   wyrceað eow .VI. daʒas 7 on þam siofoðan
3, 2. restað eow: forðam on .VI. daʒum crist ʒeworhte
         heofonas 7 eorðan, sæs 7 ealle ʒesceafta þe on him
         sint, 7 hine ʒereste on þone siofoðan dæʒ, 7 forðon
4.   dryhten hine ʒehalʒode.   Ara ðinum fæder 7 þinre
         medder ða þe dryhten sealde þæt ðu sie þy lenʒ libbende
5. 6.   on eorþan.   Ne sleah ðu;   ne liʒe ðu dearnenʒa.
7. 8.   Ne stala ðu;   ne sæʒe ðu lease ʒewitnesse.
9.   Ne wilna ðu þines nehstan ierfes mid unryhte.
10. 11. Ne wyrc ðe ʒyldne ʒodas oððe sylfrene.   Ðis sint
11, 1. ða domas þe ðu him settan scealt: Ʒif hwa ʒe-
         byccʒe cristenne þeow, .VI. ʒear ðeowiʒe he, ðy siofo-
11, 2. ðan beo he frioh ôrceapunʒa;   mid swelce hræʒle

1. rihten, blank for D, G || **1, 1.** eam H | drihten G ¦ ic G | utt ʒelæ
-de H | eʒypta GH | lande GH | hyra G, heora H || **1, 2.** mê G || **2.** naman
GH | ydelnesse H | forðam, vac þe H | byst GH | ʒecyʒst, ʒe above H |
naman GH || **3.** ʒemune G, ʒemun H ¦ ʒehalʒie GH | restedæʒ G, resten-
dæʒ H || **3, 1.** wyrceað GH | syx H | ðone G | seofoðan GH | After eow
added ðu 7 ðin sunu 7 ðine dohter 7 ðin ðeowe 7 ðine wylne 7 ðin weorcnyten 7 se cuma þe biþ binnan ðinan durum Lamb, tu, et filius tuus
et filia tua, servus tuus et ancilla tua, jumentum tuum et advena qui est
intra portas tuas Ve Vulg. || **3, 2.** forðan H | syx H | heofenas H | sæ
G, 7 sæ H | hym G, heom H | sindon GH | seofoðan GH | forðan G, forðam
H | drihten G || **4.** meder GH | drihten GH | sy H | þe H || **6.** dearnunʒa
G, deornunʒa H || **8.** seʒe G | ʒewitnessea G | added wiþ ðinum nehstan

EXTRACTS FROM THE VULGATE AS USED BY ÆLFRED.

From the Book of Exodus.

XX, 1. 2.   Locutus*que* est Dominus *cunctos* sermónes hos: Ego
      sum Dominus Deus tuus, qui eduxi te de terra Aegypti,
    3. de *domo* servitutis.   Non habebis deos alienos coram
(2) 7. me . . . . .   Non assumes nomen *Domini Dei tui* in
      vanum; nec enim habebit insontem *Dominus* eum,
(3) 8. qui assumpserit nomen *Domini Dei sui* frustra.   Me-
    9. mento ut diem sabbati sanctifices.   Sex diebus
  10. operaberis et *facies omnia opera tua.*   Septimo
      autem die sabbatum Domini Dei tui est; non facies
  11. omne opus *in eo* . . . . .   Sex enim diebus fecit
      Dominus coelum et terram *et* mare et omnia, quae
      in eis sunt, et requievit in die septimo; idcirco *bene-
      dixit* Dominus *diei sabbati et* sanctificavit eum.
(4) 12.   Honora patrem tuum et matrem tuam, ut sis
      longaevus super térram, quam Dominus *Deus tuus*
13. 14. 15. dabit tibi.   Non occides.   Non moechaberis. Non
 (8) 16. furtum facies.   Non loqueris *contra proximum tuum*
 (9) 17. falsum testimonium.   Non concupisces *domum* pro-
(10) 23. ximi tui, *etc.* . . Non facietis deos argenteos, nec *deos*
XXI, 1. aureos *facietis* vobis.   Haec sunt iudicia quae pro-
(11) 2. pones eis: Si emeris servum *Hebraeum,* sex annis
    3. serviet *tibi,* in septimo egredietur liber gratis.   Cum

---

Lamb, contra proximum tuum Ve Vulg. || 9. ʒewylna H | niehstan G,
nyhstan H | yrfes H ¦ unrihte G || 10. wyce G | wyrc ðu þe H | ʒyldene
GH || 11. sindon G, synt H | heom H || 11, 1. ʒebicʒe G, ʒebycʒe H |
cristene H ¦ syx H | þeowie H | ði G | seofoðan G | 7 on þam seofoðan
H | freoh G, freo H | ðrceapunʒe G, on ceapunʒe H ¦ 11, 2. swilce G,
7 mid swylce reafe H ¦ inneode H | swilce G, swylce H | ʒa G | flt G,
utt H.

70

11, 3. he ineode, mid swelce ʒanʒe he ût.   Ʒif he wîf self
11, 4. hæbbe, ʒanʒe bio ut mid him; ʒif se hlaford him þonne
11, 5. wif sealde, sie bio 7 hire bearn þæs hlafordes; ʒif se
þeowa þonne cweðe: Nelle ic from minum hlaforde ne
from minum wife ne from minum bearne, ne from minum
11, 6. ierfe; brenʒe hine þonne his hlaford to ðære dura þæs
temples 7 þurhþyrliʒe his eare mid æle, to tâcne þæt
12. he sie æfre siððan þeow.   Ðeah hwa ʒebycʒʒe his
dohtor on þeowenne, ne sie hio ealles swa ðeowu swa
12, 1. oðru mennenu.   Nage he hie ût on elðeodiʒ folc to
12, 2. bebycʒʒanne.   Ac ʒif he hire ne recce, se ðe hie bohte,
12, 3. læte hie freo on elðeodiʒ folc.   Ʒif he ðonne alefe his
12, 4. suna mid to hæmanne, do hiere ʒyfta,   lociʒe þæt hio
hæbbe hræʒl 7 þæt weorð sie hiere mæʒðhades, þæt
12, 5. is se weotuma aʒife he hire þone; ʒif he hire þara
13. nan ne do, þonne sie hio frioh.   Se mon se ðe his
13, 1. ʒewealdes monnan ôfslea, swelte se deaðe.   Se ðe
hine þonne nedes ôfsloʒe oððe unwillum oððe unʒewealdes
swelce hine ʒod swa sende on his honda, 7 he hine ne
ymbsyrede, sie he feores wyrðe 7 folcryhtre bote, ʒif
13, 2. he friðstowe ʒesece.   Ʒif hwa ðonne ôf ʒiernesse 7
ʒewealdes ôfslea his þone nehstan þurh searwa, aluc ðu
hine from minum weofode to þam þæt he deaðe swelte.
14. Se ðe slea his fæder oððe his modor, se sceal deaðe
15. sweltan.   Se ðe frione forstele 7 he hine bebycʒʒe 7
hit onbestæled sie þæt he hine bereccean ne mæʒe,
15, 1. swelte se deaðe.   Se ðe werʒe his fæder oððe his
16. modor, swelte se deaðe.   Ʒif hwa slea his ðone neh-

11, 3. habbe sylf G | silf H | heo GH | ût G || **11, 4.** Gyf H | þonne
him H | si G, sy H | hêo G, heo H | hyre GH | ðas G || **11, 5.** Gyf H |
— þonne End of p. 71 of E — cwæþe H | fram 4 times GH | yrfe GH ||
11, 6. Brynʒe G, Brinʒe H | æt ðas temples dura G | ðurhðirliʒe G, þurh-
þyrlie H | âle G, ane æle H | sy H | syððan G || **12.** ʒebicʒe GH | dohter
H | ôn ðeowenne G, to þeowte H | beo H | he G, heo H | alles H | þeow
H | oðre mennenu G, oðer þeow wifman H || **12, 1.** hî G, hy H | utt H |
ælðeodiʒ GH | bebycʒanne G, syllanne H || **12, 2.** hyre GH | by H | hie
faran freo G Lamb, hy friʒe H | ælðeodig GH || **12, 8.** alyfe GH | hys
H | sunea G, sune H | hæmenne H | dô G | hyre GH | ʒifta GH || **12, 4.** locie
G, 7 locie H | heo GH | habbe G | sy wurð H | hyre G, hire H | þæt his
H | sie wituma G, se wituma H | aʒyfe GH, vac. he H | hyre G, hire H |

quali veste intraverit, cum tali exeat; si habens
4. uxorem, *et uxor* egredietur simul. Sin autem dominus
dederit illi uxorem, *et perpererit filios et filias,* mulier
et liberi ejus erunt domini sui, *ipse vero exibit*
5. *cum vestitu suo.* Quod si dixerit servus: *Diligo*
dominum meum et uxores ac liberos, *non egre-*
6. *diar liber, offeret eum dominus diis, et* applicabitur ad ostium et postes, perforabitque aurem ejus
(12) 7. subula, et erit *ei* servus in saeculum. Si quis
vendiderit filiam suam in famulam, non *egredietur,*
8. sicut ancillae *exire consueverunt.* Si displicuerit
oculis *domini sui,* cui tradita fuerat, dimittet eam:
populo *autem* alieno vendendi non habebit potestatem,
9. *si spreverit eam.* Sin autem filio suo desponderit eam,
10. *iuxta morem filiarum faciet illi. Quod si alteram ei*
acceperit, providebit *puellae* nuptias, et vestimenta,
11. et pretium pudicitiae non negabit. Si *tria* ista non
(13) 12. fecerit, egredietur *gratis absque pecunia.* Qui percusserit hominem volens occidere, morte moriatur.
13. Qui autem non est insidiatus, sed Deus illum
tradidit in manus ejus, constituam tibi locum in quem
14. fugere debeat. Si quis per industriam occiderit
proximum suum et per insidias, ab altari meo evelles
(14) 15. eum, ut moriatur. Qui percusserit patrem suum
(15) 16. aut matrem, morte moriatur. Qui furatus fuerit
hominem et vendiderit eum, convictus noxae, morte
17. moriatur. Qui maledixerit patri suo vel matri,
(16) 18. morte moriatur. Si *rixati fuerint viri et* percusserit

---

þene H ‖ **12, 5.** hyre H | nanne ne dô H | sy H | heo GH | freoh GH |
13. man G | man þe, vac. se H | hys H | man GH ‖ **18, 1.** hyne G | nydes G,
neades H | ofslea H | unƺewylles H | swylcc GH | hyne H | sende swa H |
hys G | handa GH | byne ymbe ne sierede G Lamb, him ne syrwde ymbe,
ne above H | sy GH | rihtere H | fryðstowa G ‖ **18, 2.** Gyf GH | ƺeorn-
nesse GH | hys H | nyehstan G, nyhstan H | syrwunƺe H | alûc H | hyne
H | fram GH | minan G ‖ **14.** swyltan G | moder, swelte se deaþe
H ‖ **15.** freonne GH | forsteleþ H | 7 hine, vac. he GH | bebycƺe GH |
vac. 7 hit . . . . mæƺe Lamb | hit hym G | sy H | bereccan GH | mæƺ H ‖
15, 1. wyrƺe G, wyrie H | modor, vac. his G, moder H ‖ **16.** — slea End
of p. 72 of E — hys H | nyhstan H | ûtƺanƺen G, uttƺanƺan H | maƺe G |
be GH | stæfe GH | beƺyte GH | hwyle H | sylf GH.

stan mid stane oððe mid fyste 7 he þeah utჳonჳan
mæჳe bi stafe, beჳite him læce 7 wyrce his weorc ða
17. hwile þe he self ne mæჳe. Se ðe slea his aჳenne
þeowne esne oððe his mennen 7 he ne sie idæჳes dead,
ðeah he libbe twa niht oððe ðreo, ne bið he ealles
17, 1. swa scyldiჳ, forþon þe hit wæs his aჳen fioh. Ჳif
he ðonne sie idæჳes dead, ðonne sitte sio scyld on him.
18. Ჳif hwa on cease êacniende wif ჳewerde, bete þone
18, 1. æwerdlan swa him domeras ჳereccen. Ჳif hio dead
19. sie, selle sawle wið sawle. Ჳif hwa oðrum his eaჳe
oððo, selle his aჳen fore, toð fore têð, honda wið honda,
fet fore fet, bærninჳ for bærninჳe, wund wið wunde,
20. læl wið læle. Ჳif hwa âslea his ðeowe oððe his
ðeowenne þæt eaჳe ût 7 he þonne hie ჳedo âniჳჳe,
20, 1. ჳefreoჳe hie for þon. Ჳif he þonne ðone toð ôfaslea,
21. do þæt ilce. Ჳif oxa ofhnite wer oððe wîf þæt hie dead
sien, sie he mid stanum ofworpod 7 ne sie his flæsc eten;
21, 1. se hlaford bið unscyldiჳ. Ჳif se oxa hnitol wære
twam dagum æ̂r oððe ðrim 7 se hlaford hit wisse
7 hine inne betynan nolde, 7 he ðonne wer oððe
wîf ofsloჳe, sie he mid stanum ofworpod, 7 sie se
hlaford ôfsleჳen oððe forჳolden, swa ðæt witan toryhte
21, 2. finden; sunu oððe dohtor ჳif he ofstinჳe, ðæs ilcan
21, 3. domes sie he wyrðe; ჳif he ðonne ðeow oððe ðeowmennen ôfstinჳe, ჳeselle þam hlaforde .xxx. scill.
22. seolfres, 7 se oxa sie mid stanum ofworpod. Ჳif hwa

17. his aჳenne slea þeowne esne oððe his wifman H | sy GH | lybbe G |
nyht H | byþ H | scyldyჳ G ; ðan G, ðam, vac. þe H | hys G | feoh G, þeow
H | 17, 1. ჳyf ðonne he idæჳes sie G, ჳif he þonne byþ H | seo GH ;|
18. Gyf G | ceaste GH | ჳewyrde G | ჳebete G | æ̂wyrdlan G, æwyrdlan,
vac. þone H | hym G | demeras H | ჳetæcan GLamb, ჳereccan H || 18, 1. ჳyf
G | heo GH | sy GH | sylle GH || 19. ჳyf G | hwâ G | hys GH | oðdô G,
ofdo H | sylle GH | for toð GH | handa twice GH | for st. wið G | fett
twice H | for GH | bærninჳe twice G, bærnunჳ, bærnunჳe H | læle G || 20.
ofslea H | þeowan H | þeowene H | ût G, utt H | hy H | ჳedô GH | âneaჳe G,
aneჳede H | freoჳe, ჳe above H | hi G, heo H | ðan G || 20, 1. ჳyf G |
toð, vac. ðone H | ofâslea G | dô GH | sylfe G || 21. Gyf G | hi G, hy
H | deade H | syn H | sy H | oftorfod H | sy H | êten G, ჳeeten H | byþ
H || 21, 1. oððe þrim æ̂r G, ær oððe þrym H | sê G | nyste, ჳif he hit
ðonne wiste GLamb | wiste H | betynan, vac. inne G, innan H | sy GH |

alter proximum suum lapide vel pugno, et ille *mor-*
19. *tuus non fuerit, sed iacuerit in lectulo: si sur-*
rexerit et ambulaverit foris super baculum suum,
innocens erit, qui percusserit, ita tamen, ut operas
(17) 20. ejus et impensas in medicos restituat. Qui percusserit servum suum vel ancillam *virga,* et mortui fuerint
21. in manibus ejus, criminis reus erit; sin autem *uno*
die vel duobus supervixerit, non subiacebit poenae,
(18) 22. quia pecunia illius est. Si rixati *fuerint viri et*
percusserit quis mulierem praegnantem, *et abortivum*
quidem fecerit, sed ipsa vixerit: subiacebit damno,
quantum *maritus mulieris expetierit et* arbitri iudica-
23. verint. Sin *autem* mors ejus fuerit subsecuta, reddet
(19) 24. animam pro anima, oculum pro oculo, dentem pro
25. dente, manum pro manu, pedem pro pede, adusti-
onem pro adustione, vulnus pro vulnere, livorem pro
(20) 26. livore. Si percusserit quispiam oculum servi sui
aut ancillae et luscos eos fecerit, dimittet eos liberos
27. pro *oculo, quem eruit.* Dentem quoque si excusserit
servo vel ancillae suae, similiter *dimittet eos liberos.*
(21) 28. Si bos cornu percusserit virum aut mulierem, et
mortui fuerint, lapidibus obruetur et non comedentur
carnes ejus; dominus *quoque bovis* innocens erit.
29. *Quod* si bos cornupeta fuerit ab heri et nudiustertius, et contestati sunt dominum ejus, nec recluserit
eum, occideritque virum aut mulierem: *et* bos lapidibus
30. obruetur, et dominum ejus occident. *Quod si*
pretium fuerit ei impositum, dabit *pro anima sua*
31. quidquid fuerit postulatus. Filium *quoque* et filiam
si cornu percusserit, simili sententiae subiacebit.
32. Si servum ancillamque invaserit, triginta siclos
argenti domino dabit, bos vero lapidibus opprimetur.
(22) 33. Si quis aperuerit cisternam et foderit et non

---

ofworpen H, oftorfod Lamb | sy H | ofslaʒen G | se man forʒolden H |
wytan H | rihte GH | findan G, fyndaþ H || 21. 2. dohter H | ʒyf G | stynʒe
H | sy he þæs ylcan domes G | sy H || 21, 3. Gyf H | þeowan H | þeowne G,
þeowene H | ofstynʒe H | ʒesylle GH | þryttiʒ scll. H | — scill. End p. 73
in E — | sie from G, sy se oxa H | ofworpad G, ofworpen H, oftorfod
Lamb.

adelfe wæter pŷt oððe betynedne ontyne 7 hine eft ne
betyne, ʒelde swelc neat swelc ðæron befealle, 7 hæbbe

23.   him ðæt deade.   Ʒif oxa oðres monnes oxan ʒewundiʒe 7 he ðonne dead sie, bebycʒʒen þone oxan 7 hæbben
him þæt weorð gemǣne 7 êac ðæt flǣsc swa ðæs deadan.

23, 1.   Ʒif se blaford þonne wisse þæt se oxa hnitol wære
7 hine healdan nolde, selle him oðerne oxan fore 7

24.   hæbbe him eall ðæt flæsc.   Ʒif hwa forstele oðres
oxan 7 hine ôfslea oððe bebycʒʒe, selle tweʒen wið 7

24, 1.   feower sceap wið anum; ʒif he næbbe hwæt he selle,

25.   sie he self beboht wið ðam fio.   Ʒif ðeof brece mannes
hûs nihtes 7 he weorðe þær ofsleʒen, ne sie he na

25, 1. mansleʒes scyldiʒ.   Ʒif he siððan æfter sunnan up-
ʒonʒe þis deð, he bið mansleʒes scyldiʒ 7 he ðonne

25, 2. self swelte buton he nieddæda wære.   Ʒif mid him
cwicum sie funden þæt he ǣr stæl, be twyfealdum

26.   forʒielde hit.   Ʒif hwa ʒewerde oðres monnes winʒeard
oððe his æcras oððe his landes awuht, ʒebete swa

27.   hit mon ʒeeahtiʒe.   Ʒif fyr sie ontended rŷt to
bærnanne, ʒebete þone æfwerdelsan se ðæt fŷr ontent.

28.   Ʒif hwa oðfæste his friend fioh: ʒif he bit self

28, 1. stæle, forgylde be twyfealdum; ʒif he nyte hwa hit
stæle, ʒeladiʒe hine selfne þæt he ðær nân facn ne

28, 2. ʒefremede.   Ʒif hit ðonne cucu feoh wære 7 he secʒʒe
þæt hit here name oððe hit self âcwæle 7 ʒewitnesse

28, 3. hæbbe, ne þearf he þæt ʒeldan; ʒif he ðonne ʒewitnesse næbbe 7 he him ne ʒetriewe, sweriʒe be þonne.

---

22. delfe G | pitt H | ontŷne G, untyne H Lamb | ʒylde GH | swylc
GH | swylc G, swa H | habbe H ‖ **23.** ôxa G | mannes GH | ʒewundie
H | sy GH | bebicʒan GH | ôxan G | habbon G, habben H | hîm G, heom
H ‖ **23, 1.** wiste GH | he hyne G | sylle GH | eal H ‖ **24.** bebycʒe G,
bebicʒe H | sylle GH | tweʒen, vac. wið G | IIII. G | wyþ H ‖ **24. 1.** ʒyf
G | nite H | hwet G | sylle GH | sy GH | sylf H | þan H | feo GH ‖ **25.**
wurðe H | ofslaʒen G | sy GH | he, vac. na G ‖ **25, 1.** ʒyf G | syððan
H | upʒanʒe G, uppʒanʒe H | sylf swelte G, þonne swylte, vac. self H |
butan GH | nyddæde H ‖ **25, 2.** ʒyf G | cwycum H | sy H | forʒylde be
G, forʒylde H ‖ **26.** hwâ G | ʒewyrde G, awyrde H | mannes GH | wynʒeard
H | hys G | æceras GH | awiht G, awyht H | man GH | ʒeæhtie H ‖ **27.** fir
H | sy H | rŷt G, ryht H, ryp Lamb | bærnenne H | æwyrdlan G, æwyrdlan
H | ontende G, ontendeþ, vac. fyr H ‖ **28.** hys G | frynd G, freond· H |
feoh GH | ʒyf G | hyt G | sylf H | stele GH ‖ **28, 1.** ʒyf G | nite H | hyt

operuerit eam, cecideritque bos aut asinus in eam,
34.   reddet *dominus cisternae* pretium iumentorum;
(23) 35. quod autem mortuus est, ipsius erit.   Si bos *alienus*
bovem alterius vulneraverit et ille mortuus fuerit,
vendent bovem *vivum* et dividant pretium, cadaver
36. autem mortui *inter se dispertient*.   Sin autem sciebat,
quod bos cornupeta esset *ab heri et nudiustertius,* et
non custodivit eum dominus suus, reddet bovem pro
XXII, 1. bove, et cadaver integrum accipiet.   Si quis furatus
(24)   fuerit bovem *aut ovem* et occiderit vel vendiderit,
quinque boves pro *uno bove* restituet et quatuor oves
(25) · 2. pro una *ove*.   Si effringens fur domum *sive suffodiens*
fuerit inventus, et *accepto vulnere* mortuus fuerit,
3. *percussor* non erit reus sanguinis.   Quod si orto
sole hoc fecerit, homicidium perpetravit et ipse mo-
rietur. Si non habuerit quod *pro furto* reddat, ipse
4. venundabitur.   Si inventum fuerit apud eum, quod
furatus est, vivens, *sive bos sive asinus sive ovis,* du-
(26) 5. plum restituet. Si laeserit quispiam agrum vel vineam
et dimiserit iumentum suum, ut depascatur aliena, quid-
quid optimum habuerit in agro suo vel in vinea pro dam-
(27) 6. ni aestimatione restituet.   Si egressus ignis *invenerit*
spinas et comprehenderit acervos frugum sive stantes se-
getes in agris, reddet damnum qui ignem succenderit.
(28) 7.   Si quis commendaverit amico pecuniam *aut vas*
in custodiam, et ab eo qui susceperat furto ablata
8. *fuerint: si invenitur fur,* duplum reddet; *si latet fur,*
dominus domus applicabitur ad deos, et iurabit quod
9. non extenderit manum in rem proximi sui ad per-
10. petrandam fraudem. . . . . . . *Si quis commendaverit*
proximo suo asinum, bovem, ovem, et omne iumentum
ad custodiam, et mortuum fuerit, aut debilitatum, vel
11. captum ab hostibus, nullusque hoc viderit: Iusiur-
andum erit *in medio, quod non extenderit manum ad*

G, hitt H | stele H | ȝâ ladiȝe G, ȝeladie H | sylfne H | facen G, fanc H | ôn ne ȝefremede G, on ne fremede H ‖ 28, 2. ȝif ðonne, vac. hit G | — ðonne End of p. 74 in E. — | cwicu G | seecȝe G, sæcȝe H | hyt G, þæt hit H | sylf GH | he ȝewitnesse GH | ȝyldan GH ‖ 28, 8. ȝyf G | ne ȝetrywe G, ȝetreowe ne sy H | swerȝe G, swerie H | ðænne G ‖

29.   Ʒif hwa fæmnan beswice unbeweddode 7 hire mid-
slæpe, forʒielde hie 7 hæbbe hi siððan him to wife.

29, 1.   Ʒif ðære fæmnan fæder hie ðonne sellan nelle, aʒife

30.   he ðæt feoh æfter þam weotuman.   Ða fæmnan þe
ʒewuniað onfön ʒealdorcræftiʒan 7 scinlæcan 7 wiccan

31.   ne læt þu ða libban;   7 se ðe hæme mid netene, swelte

32.   he deaðe;   7 se ðe ʒodʒeldum önsecʒe ofer ʒod anne,

33.   swelte se deaðe.   Utancumene 7 elðeodiʒe ne ʒeswenc
ðu no, forðon ðe ʒe wæron ʒiu elðeodiʒe on eʒipta londe.

34.   Ða wuduwan 7 þa stiopcild ne sceððað ʒe, ne hie

34, 1. nawer deriað.   Ʒif ʒe þonne elles doð, hie cleopiað
to me 7 ic ʒehiere hie, 7 ic eow þonne slea mid minum
sweorde, 7 ic ʒedö þæt eowru wif beoð wydewan 7

35.   eowru bearn beoð steopcild.   Ʒif ðu fioh to borʒe selle
þinum ʒeferan þe mid þe eardian wille, ne niede ðu hine
swa swa niedling 7 ne ʒehene þu hine mid ðy eacan.

36.   Ʒif mon næbbe buton anfeald hræʒl hine mid to wreonne
7 to werianne 7 he hit to wedde selle, ær sunnan setlʒonʒe

36, 1. sie hit aʒifen.   Ʒif ðu swa ne dest, þonne cleopað he to
me 7 ic hine ʒehiere for ðon ðe ic eom swiðe mildheort.

37.   Ne tæl ðu ðinne dryhten ne ðone hlaford þæs folces

38.   ne werʒe þu.   Ðine teoðan sceattas 7 þine frum ripan

39.   ʒonʒendes 7 weaxendes aʒif þu ʒode.   Eal ðæt flæsc
þæt wildeor læfen ne eten ʒe þæt ac sellað hit hundum.

40.   Leases monnes word ne rec ðu no þæs to ʒehieranne,
ne his domas ne ʒeðafa ðu, ne nane ʒewitnesse æfter

41.   him ne saʒa ðu.   Ne wend ðu ðe no on þæs folces
unræd, 7 unryht ʒewill on hiora spræce 7 ʒeclysp ofer

---

29. beswyce GH | unbeweddude G | hyre G | slepe G | forʒylde GH |
heo H | habbe G | hî G, hy H | syððan H ‖ **29, 1.** ʒyf G | hie, e above
G, heo H | syllan GH | ðæm witoman weotuman G ‖ **30.** ʒewilniað H |
ânfön G | ʒaldorcræft G Lamb, ʒaldercræftiʒan H | scinlacan H | þu hi libban
H ‖ **31.** nictene G, nytene H | se GH ‖ **32.** ʒyldum G, ʒyltum H | on-
sæcʒe H | of G | ænne H ‖ **33.** Ûtan G | ælðeodiʒe G, ælþeodiʒe H | ʒe-
swænc H | þa st. nö G, ðone H | for þam H | íu G, vac. H Lamb | ælðeo-
diʒe GH | ön G | eʒypta GH | lande GH ‖ **34.** wydwan G, wydewan H |
steopcild, vac. þa G, steopcyld H | sceaððan ʒe hie nahwer nê ne deriað
G, scyþþað 7 ne hy nawer deriað H | **34, 1.** hy H | clipiað H | ʒehyre
G, ʒebire H | hy H | ʒedö G | eow ʒedö H | eowre GH | wudewan H |
eowre GH | steopcyld, vac. beoð H ‖ **35.** feoh GH | ʒesylle G Lamb, sylle
H | wylle H | nyd H | swa once GH Lamb | nydling H | ʒehyne G, ʒehyn

rem proximi sui: suscipietque dominus iuramentum, et
ille reddere non cogetur. . . . .

(29) 16.   Si seduxerit quis virginem necdum desponsatam,
dormieritque cum ea: dotabit eam, et habebit eam

17. uxorem.   Si pater virginis dare noluerit, reddet pe-

(30)   cuniam iuxta modum dotis, *quam* virgines accipere

18. 19. consueverunt.   Maleficos non patieris vivere.   Qui

(32) 20. coierit cum iumento, morte moriatur.   Qui immolat

(33) 21. diis, occidetur, praeterquam Domino soli.   Advenam
non contristabis, neque affliges eum: advenae enim

(34) 22. et ipsi fuistis in terra Aegypti.   Viduae et pupillo

23. non nocebitis.   Si laeseritis eos, vociferabuntur ad

24. me, et ego audiam *clamorem* eorum: Et *indigna-*
bitur furor meus, percutiamque vos gladio, et *erunt*

(35) 25. uxores vestrae viduae, et filii vestri pupilli.   Si pecuniam mutuam dederis *populo meo pauperi* qui
habitat tecum, non urgebis eum quasi exactor, nec

(36) 26. usuris opprimes.   Si pignus a proximo tuo acceperis

27. vestimentum, ante solis occasum reddes ei.   Ipsum
enim est solum, quo operitur *indumentum carnis*
eius, nec habet aliud in quo dormiat: si clamaverit

(37) 28. ad me, exaudiam eum, quia misericors sum.   *Diis*
non detrahes, et principi populi tui non maledices.

(38) 29.   Decimas tuas et primitias tuas non tardabis red-

30. dere: *primogenitum filiorum tuorum dabis mihi.*   De

31. *bobus quoque, etc.* . . . . *Viri sancti eritis mihi:*

(39)   carnem, quae a bestiis fuerit praegustata, non come-

XXIII, 1. ditis, sed proiicietis canibus.   Non suscipies vocem

(40)   mendacii: nec *iunges manum tuam ut* pro *impio*

(41) 2. dicas *falsum* testimonium.   Non sequeris turbam

H | hyne G | eâcan G ‖   **36.** man GH | butan GH | hræʒl, h above H |
oððe st. 7 GH | sylle GH | ʒanʒe GH | sy GH | hyt G | aʒyfen G ‖ **86, 1.**
clypiað H | hyne G, hy H | ʒehyre H | ðam H | eam H | swyþe H ‖   **87.**
— tæl ðu End of p. 75 of E — | drihten G | wyrʒ G, weriʒ H ‖
38. sceattas, tas above H | þinne H | ʒanʒendes GH | aʒyf G ‖ **39.** êal G, eall
H | wylddeor H | læfan H | nê H | etan H | syllað GH ‖ **40.** mannes GH |
rece G, recce H | na to ʒehyranne, vac. þæs G, þæs to ʒehiranne, vac. no
H | seʒe G ‖ **41.** ʒewend, ʒe above H | nâ G, na H | folces, ol over
longer eras. H | ûnræd G | unriht G, on unriht H | hyra G, hiora, o above
H | spæce G | ʒeclæsp G, ʒeclebs H, ʒeclebs Lamb | riht G | 7 on þæs G,

ðin ryht 7 ðæs unwisestan lare ne him ne ʒeðafa.

42. Ʒif ðe becume oðres mannes ʒiemelêas fioh on hond,
43. þeah hit sie ðin feond ʒecyðe hit him. Dem ðu swiðe emne. Ne dem ðu oðerne dôm þam weleʒan, oðerne ðam earman; ne oðerne þam liofran 7 oðerne þam
44. 45. laðran ne dem ðu. Ônscuna ðu â leasunʒa. Soð fæstne man 7 unscyldiʒne ne âcwele ðu þone næfre.
46. Ne onfoh ðu næfre mêdsceattum, for ðon hie ablendað ful ôft wisra monna ʒeðoht 7 hiora word onwendað.
47. Ðam elðeodeʒan 7 utancumenan ne læt ðu no uncuðlice wið hine ne mid nanum unryhtum þu hine ne
48. drece. Ne swerʒen ʒe næfre under hæðne ʒodas ne on nanum ðinʒum ne cleopien ʒe to him.
49. Ðis sindan ða domas þe se ælmihteʒa ʒod self sprecende wæs to moyse 7 him bebead to healdanne 7 siððan se âncenneda dryhtnes sunu ure ʒod þæt is hælend crist on middanʒeard cwom, he cwæð ðæt he ne come no ðas bebodu to brecanne ne to forbeodanne, ac mid eallum godum to ecanne, 7 mildheortnesse 7 eaðmod-
49, 1. nesse he lærde. Ða æfter his ðrowunʒe ær þam þe his apostolas tofarene wæron ʒeond ealle eorðan to læranne, 7 þa ʒiet ða hie ætʒædere wæron, moneʒa hæðena ðeoda hie to ʒode ʒecerdon; þa hie ealle ætsomne wæron, hie sendan ærendwrecan to antiohhia
49, 2. 7 to syrie cristes æ to læranne; þa hie ða onʒeaton þæt him ne speow, ða sendon hie ærendʒewrit to him. Ðis is ðonne þæt ærendʒewrit þe ða apostolas sendon ealle to antiohhia 7 to syria 7 to cilicia, ða sint nu

---

and þæs unwisestan lare þu ne ʒeþafa, un above, dot and long eras. after lare H ǁ **42.** becyme G | ʒymeleas GH | feoh G | handa, a crossed G, hand H | hyt G | sy H | fiond H | ʒecyþ H | hym G ǁ **43.** ðû G | swiðe rihte 7 swiðe emne G Lamb, swiþe ryhtne dom H | 7 above ne H | dôm G | ðæm G | earm-an H | leofran G, leofan over eras. H | laðan H | dæm H | ðû G ǁ **44.** þu âleasunʒa G, also E, ða leasunʒa H ǁ **45.** mann G | âcwelle G, acwel- H | ðæne, o above æ G ǁ **46.** þu above H | metsceattum H | ðon þe H | ht G, hy H | âblendað G | manna GH | hyra G, heora H | awendaþ H ǁ **47.** ælþeodeʒan G, ælþeodiʒan H | utancymenan G | ðû G | nâ GH | ûncuðlice G | wiþ ðone G | nânum G | ûnrihtum ʒê G | drecce G ǁ **48.** sweren ʒê G, sweriʒen ʒe, i ab. H | hæðene GH, first e ab. H | ôn G | næneʒum G | clypiʒen G, clipien H | ʒê H | hym G, heom H ǁ **49.** syndan G, sindon H | ælmihtiʒa GH | sylf GH | heald-

ad faciendum malum: nec in iudicio plurimorum

3. acquiesces sententiae, ut a vero devics.　*Pauperis*

(42)　4. *quoque non misereberis in iudicio.*　Si occurreris bovi

5. inimici tui *aut asino* erranti, *reduc ad eum.*　*Si*

videris asinum odientis te iacere sub onere, non per-

(43)　6. *transibis, sed sublevabis cum eo.*　Non declinabis in

(44)　7. iudicium pauperis. Mendacium fugies. Insontem et

(46)　8. iustum non occides, *quia aversor impium.*　Nec ac-

cipies munera, quae etiam excaecant prudentes, et

(47)　9. subvertunt verba *iustorum.*　Peregrino molestus non

eris, *scitis enim advenarum animas: quia et ipsi pere-*

10. *grini fuistis in terra Aegypti.*　*Sex annis seminabis*

12. 13. *etc. . . . . Sex diebus operaberis etc. . . . . Omnia*

(48)　*quae dixi vobis, custodite.*　*Et* per *nomen* externorum

deorum non iurabitis, neque audietur ex ore vestro.

---

ende G, healdenne H | syððan G | acenneda GH | drihtnes G, ʒodes H
fire G | vac. ure ʒod H | ys G | hælende GH | côm G, on woruld becom H | —
cwæð End of p. 76 in E — | nâ G, na H | word, bebodu new above H |
icanne G, ʒeecenne H | and, d ab. H ‖ **49,1.** ðâ G | tô G | lærranne G | ʒyt
GH | by H | ætʒædere, first e ab. H | mæniʒe G, maneʒa H | hæðena, e ab. H |
hy H | ʒecyrdon G, ʒecirdon to ʒode H | ðâ G | hî G, hy H | Hy H | sendon
GH | ærendracan H | tô G | antiochia GH | tô G | siria G, syria H | æ
GH ‖ **49, 2.** hî G, hy onʒeaton, a ab., vac. ða H | þæt him belampe Lamb,
quid inter eos ageretur Ve | hî G, hy over eras. H | ærendʒewrit . . . þæt
on margin H | tô G | hîm G | Paragraph G | ys þæt vac. þonne G | færend-
ʒewritt, f crossed, last t from e, H | sendan H | tô G | antiochia GH | 7 siria,
vac. to G | cilitia H | sind GH | nû G | æðenum G, hæðenum, e ab. H | tô
G | cryste H | ʒecyrred G, ʒecyrrede H.

80

49, 3. of hæðenum ðeodum to criste ʒecirde: ða apostolas
7 þa eldran broðor bælo cow wyscað, 7 we eow cyðað
þæt we ʒeascodon þæt ure ʒeferan sume mid urum
wordum to eow comon 7 eow hefiʒran *wisan budan* to
healdanne þonne we him budon 7 eow to swiðe ʒe-
dwealdon mid ðam manniʒfealdum ʒebodum, 7 eowra
sawla ma forhwerfdon, þonne hie ʒeryhton. Ða ʒe-
somnodon we us ymb ðæt 7 ûs eallum ʒelicode ða,
þæt we sendon paulus 7 barnaban, ða men wilniað
49, 4. hiora sawla sellan for dryhtnes naman;   mid him
we sendon iudam 7 silam þæt eow þæt ilce secʒʒen:
49, 5.   þæm halʒan ʒaste wæs ʒeðuht 7 ûs þæt we nane
byrðenne on eow settan noldon ofer þæt ðe eow ned-
ðearf wæs to healdanne, þæt *is* ðonne þæt ʒe forberen
þæt ʒe deofolʒeld ne weorðien, ne blod ne ðicʒʒen ne
asmorod, 7 from diernum ʒeliʒerum, 7 þæt ʒe willen
þæt oðre men êow ne don, ne doð ʒe ðæt oþrum
monnum.
.I.
49, 6.   Of ðissum anum dome mon mæʒ ʒeðencean þæt
he æʒhwelcne onryht ʒedemeð. Ne ðearf he naura
domboca oþerra. Ʒeðence he þæt he nanum men ne
deme þæt he nolde ðæt he him demde, ʒif he ðone
49, 7. dôm ofer hine sohte. Siððan ðæt þa ʒelamp þæt moneʒa ðeoda cristes ʒeleafan onfenʒon, þa wurdon moneʒa
seonoðas ʒeond ealne middanʒeard ʒeʒaderode, 7 eac
swa ʒeond anʒelcyn, siððan hie cristes ʒeleafan onfenʒon, haleʒra biscepa 7 êac oðerra ʒeðunʒenra witena;
hie ða ʒesetton for ðære mildheortnesse þe crist lærde
æt mæstra hwelcre misdæde þætte ða weoruld blafordas
moston mid hiora leafan buton synne æt þam forman

49, 3. and, d ab. H | ieldran G, yldran H | broþra H | wyrcað G |
ʒeahsodon G, ʒeaxodon H | ûre G | tô G | coman H | hefiʒran wisan budan
GH Lamb, Vulg. text in Ve (mistake in E here) | healdonne H | hym G |
tô G, vac. H | swyðe H | ʒedwe-ldon H | moniʒfealdum G | mà H | forh-
wyrfdon GH, h ab. H | heo H | rihton G, ʒerihton H | Parag. G | ʒesamnodan
G, ʒesamnoden H | wè G | ûs G | ûs ða eallum ʒelicode G, us eallum ða
ʒelicode þa, þa ab. H | sendan G | willað G, ða ʒewilniað, vac. men H |
hyra G, hira H | saula G | to above syllanne H | drihtnes G ‖ 49, 4. hym
G | sendað G, sendon, on ab. H | hy above eow H | secʒað G, secʒan
H ‖ 49, 5. þam GH | hyrþene GH | ðeow niedþearf is G, nydðearf H |

From the Acts of the Apostles.

XV, 23. Apostoli et seniores fratres *his qui sunt Antiochiae et Syriae et Ciliciae fratribus ex gentibus* salutem.
24. Quoniam audivimus quia quidam ex nobis exeuntes, turbaverunt vos verbis, evertentes animas vestras,
25. quibus non mandavimus: placuit nobis collectis in unum, *eligere viros, et* mittere *ad vos cum claris-*
26. *simis nostris* Barnaba et Paulo, hominibus, qui *tradiderunt* animas suas pro nomine Domini *nostri*
27. *Jesu Christi.* Misimus *ergo* Judam et Silam, qui
28. et ipsi vobis verbis referent eadem. Visum est *enim* Spiritui sancto et nobis nihil ultra imponere
29. vobis oneris quam haec necessaria: ut abstineatis vos ab immolatis simulacrorum, et sanguine, et suffocato, et fornicatione, [et quod vobis non vultis fieri, non faciatis aliis,] *a quibus custodientes vos, bene agetis. Valete.*

MS. H.   .I.

49, 6. On ðyssum anum dome man mæᵹ ᵹeþencan ðæt he æᵹhwylcne dom on ryht ᵹedeme. Ne þearf he nanre domboca oþera cêpan. Ʒeðænce he ðæt he nanum men ne deme þæt he nolde ðæt man him
49, 7. demde, ᵹif he þone dom ofer hine ahte. Syþþan ðæt þa ᵹelamp ðæt maneᵹa ðeoda cristes ᵹeleafan underfenᵹon, Ða wurdon maniᵹe synoðas ᵹeond ealne middaneard ᵹeᵹaderode, and eac swylce on anᵹelcynne syððan hy cristes ᵹeleafan onfenᵹon, haliᵹra biscopa and eac oðerra ᵹeðunᵹenra witena. Hy þa ᵹesetton for ðære mildheortnesse ðe crist lærde æt mæstra ᵹehwylcere misdæde ðæt ða woruld hlafordas moston mid heora leafan butan synne æt þam forman ᵹylte ðæra fiohbota onfon butan æt hlaford

49, 6. ðyssum, first s above | dom above | ᵹedeme, ᵹe above | cêpan above || 49, 7. cynnesyððan Ms. | ᵹeleafan, ᵹe ab. | eras. before haliᵹra | -heornesse Ms. | ᵹehwylcere, second e ab. | eras. after ðæt | heora, o ab. | leafan, n ab. | æt hlaford ab. | mildheortnesse above ne ᵹedemde.

healdenne G, healde-ne H | is from GH | forberan GH | deofolᵹyld G, diofolᵹyld H | weorðian G, wurðian H | ðieᵹan GH | fram GH | — from End p. 77 of E — | dyrnum GH | willan H | do H | — ðæt End of Ms. G — | mannum H || 49, 6. sohte, soh new over flaw E ||

ʒylte þære fiohbote ônfon þe hie ða ʒesettan, buton æt
hlaford searwe hie nane mildheortnesse ne dorston ʒecweðan, forþam ðe ʒod ælmihtiʒ þam nane ne ʒedemde
þe hine oferhoʒdon, ne crist ʒodes sunu þam nane ne ʒedemde þe hine to deaðe sealde, ⁊ he bebead þone hlaford

49, 8. lufian swa hine; hie ða on moneʒum senoðum mo-
neʒra ,menniscra misdæda bote ʒesetton, ⁊ on moneʒa
senoð bêc hie writan hwær anne dom hwær oþerne.

49, 9.   Ic ða ælfred cyninʒ þâs toʒædere ʒeʒaderode ⁊
awritan het, moneʒe þara þe ure foreʒenʒan heoldon
ða ðe me licodon ⁊ maneʒe þara þe me ne licodon ic
âwearp mid minra witena ʒeðeahte ⁊ on oðre wisan
bebead to healdanne, forðam ic ne dorste ʒeðristlæcan
þara minra awuht fela on ʒewrit settan, forðam me
wæs uncuð hwæt þæs ðam lician wolde ðe æfter ûs
wæren, ac ða ðe ic ʒemette awðer oððe on ines dæʒe
mines mæʒes oððe on offan mercna cyninʒes, oððe on
æþelbryhtes þe ærest fulluhte onfenʒ on anʒelcynne þa
ðe me ryhtoste ðuhton ic þa heron ʒeʒaderode ⁊ þa

49, 10. oðre forlêt.   Ic ða ælfred westseaxna cyning eallum
minum witum þas ʒeeowde, ⁊ hie ða cwædon þæt him
þæt licode eallum to healdanne.

.II.

1.   Æt ærestan we lærað þæt mæst ðearf is þæt æʒhwelc

1, 1. mon his að ⁊ his wed wærlice healde. ʒif hwa to hwæðrum
þissa ʒenied sie onwoh oððe to hlaford searwe oððe to
ænʒum unryhtum fultume, þæt is þonne ryhtre to âleo-

1, 2. ʒanne þonne to ʒelæstanne. *ʒif he þonne ðæs weddie*
þe him ryht sie to ʒelæstanne ⁊ þæt aleoʒe, selle mid
eaðmedum his wæpn ⁊ his æhta his freondum to ʒe-
healdanne ⁊ beo feowertiʒ nihta on carcerne on cyninʒes
tune, ðrowiʒe ðær swa biscep him scrife ⁊ his mæʒas

1, 3. hine feden ʒif he self mete næbbe. ʒif he mæʒas
næbbe oððe þone mete næbbe, fede cyninʒes ʒerefa

1, 4. hine. ʒif hine mon to ʒenedan scyle ⁊ he elles nylle,

.   49, 9. âwearp End of p. 7S in E | mercna, erc new over flaw || **1, 2.**
ʒif . . . ʒelæstanne, line skipped by E; revised from H.

searwe ðe hy ða ʒesetton, ðam hy nane mildheortnesse ne dorston ʒecweðan, for ðam ðe ʒod ælmihtiʒ
ðam nane mildheortnesse ne ʒedemde ðe hine ofer-
hoʒodon, Ne crist ʒodes sunu ðam nane ne ʒedemde
ðe hyne to deaðe ʒesealde, and he bebead þone
49, 8. hlaford lufian swa hine selfne.   Hy ða on maniʒum
synoþum maneʒa menniscra misdæda bote ʒesettan, and
on maneʒra synoþbec hy writon hwær ænne dóm, hwær
49, 9. oþerne.   Ic ða ælfred cyninʒ ðas toʒædere ʒeʒaderode, and awriten het maniʒe ðara þe ure foreʒenʒan
heoldon þara ðe me lycedan, and moniʒe ðara ðe
me ne lycedon ic awearp mid minre witena ʒeðeahte,
and on oðre wisan bebead to healdenne. Forðam
ic ne dorste ʒeðristlæcan ðara minra awuht feola
on ʒewrit settan. Forðon me wæs uncuþ hwæt ðæs
þæm lician wolde þe æfter us wæron. Ac þa ða
ic ʒemette aþær oððe on Ines dæʒe mines mæʒes,
oððe on offan myrcena cyninʒes, oþþe on æþelberhtes
þe æres fulluht onfenʒ on anʒelcynne, ða ðe me ryhtest
þuhton, ic ða heron ʒeʒaderode, and ða oþre forlett.
49, 10.   Ic þa ælfred westseaxena cynʒ eallum minum
witum þas ʒeowde, 7 hy þa cwædon, þæt heom
þæt licode eallum wel to healdene.

.II.

1.   Æt ærestan we lærað ðæt mæst þearf is, þæt
1, 1. æʒhwilc man his að 7 his wedd wærlice healde. Ʒif
hwa to hwæðerum þisra ʒenyd sy onwoh, oþþe to
hlaford searwe, oððe to æniʒum unrihtum fultume,
þæt þonne rihtre is to aleoʒenne þonne to ʒelæstanne.
1, 2.   Ʒif he þonne ðæs weddie þe hym riht sy to ʒelæstanne 7 þæt aleoʒe, sylle mid eadmedum hys wæpn
7 his æhta his freoudum to ʒebealdenne 7 beo .XL.
nihta on carcerne æt cyninʒes tune, þrowie ðær swa
biscop him scrife, 7 his maʒas hine fedan, ʒif he
1, 3. sylf mete næbbe.   Ʒif he maʒas næbbe oððe þone
1, 4. mete, fede cyninʒes ʒerefa hine.   Ʒif hine man to

49, 8. synoþum ab. ‖ 49, 9. ðælfred Ms. | þara ab. ðe | lycedon, y
ɔw | awearp, a ab. | on ab. oðre | feola, o ab. | Ines, I over i | myrcena, e
ɔ. | ryhtest, est over eras. | forlett, ett over eras.

ʒif hine mon ʒebinde, þoliʒe his wæpna 7 his ierfes;

1, 5. 6.   ʒif hine mon ôfslea, licʒʒe he orʒilde.   Ʒif he ût

oðfleo ær þam fierste 7 hine mon ʒefô, sie he feowertiʒ

1, 7. nihta on carcerne swa he ǽr sceolde.   Ʒif he losiʒe,

sie he âfliemed 7 sie âmænsumod ôf eallum cristes

1, 8. ciricum.   Ʒif þær ðonne oþer mennisc borʒ sie, bete

þone borʒ bryce swa him ryht wisie 7 ðone wed bryce

swa him his scrift scrife.

.III.

2.   Gif hwa þara mynster hama hwelcne for hwelcere

scylde ʒesece þe cyninʒes feorm to belimpe oððe oðerne

frione hiered þe ârwyrðe sie, aʒe he þreora nihta fierst

2, 1. him to ʒebeorʒanne, buton he ðinʒian wille.   Ʒif

hine mon on ðam fierste ʒeyfliʒe mid sleʒe oððe

mid bende oððe þurhwunde, bete þara æʒhwelc mid

ryhte ðeodscipe, ʒe mid were ʒe mid wite, 7 þam hiwum

hundtwelftiʒ scill. ciric friðes to bote 7 næbbe his aʒne

forfonʒen.

.IIII.

3.   Gif hwa cyninʒes borʒ abrece, ʒebete þone tyht

swa him ryht wisie 7 þæs borʒes bryce mid .V. pundum

mærra pæninʒa; ærcebiscepes borʒes bryce oððe his

mund byrd ʒebete mid ðrim pundum; oðres biscepes

oððe ealdormonnes borʒes bryce oððe mund byrd

ʒebete mid twam pundum.

.V.

4.   Gif hwa ymb cyninʒes feorh sierwe ðurh hine oððe

ðurh wreccena feormunʒe oððe his manna, sie he his

4, 1. feores scyldiʒ 7 ealles þæs ðe he aʒe;   ʒif he hine

selfne triowan wille, do þæt be cyninʒes werʒelde:

4, 2.   swa we êac settað be eallum hadum, ʒe ceorle ʒe eorle,

se ðe ymb his hlafordes fiorh sierwe, sie he wið ðone

his feores scyldiʒ 7 ealles ðæs ðe he aʒe oððe be his

hlafordes were hine ʒetriowe.

1, 6. nihta End of p. 79 in E | 4, 1. werʒelde End of p. 80 in E.

Continuation of Variants from p. 85.

4, 2. settað, vac be | ymbe, e above | hys | syrwie, i ah | ʒetreowie, new s
betw. w and i B, ʒetrewsie II.

ᵹenydan scyle 7 he elles nylle, ᵹif hine man ᵹebinde,

1, 5. þolie his wæpna and his yrfes; ᵹif hine man ofslea,

1, 6. lecᵹe orᵹylde. Ᵹif he ut oðfleo ær þan fyrste 7 hine man ᵹefô, sy he .XL. nihta on carcerne, swa he ær

1, 7. sceolde. Ᵹif he þonne losie, sy he aflymed, 7 sy he

1, 8. amansemod, of eallum cristes cyricum. Ᵹif ðær ðonne oþer mennisc borh sy, bete þone borh brice swa him riht wisie, 7 þone wed brice swa him his scrift scrife.

.III.

2. Ᵹif hwa þæra mynster hama hwylcne ᵹesece for hwylcere scylde þe cyninᵹes feorm to belimpe, oþþe oðerne freonne hyred þe arwyrðe sy, aᵹe he ðreora nihta fyrst him to ᵹebeorᵹanne, butan he þinᵹian wille.

2, 1. Ᵹif hine man on þam fyrste ᵹeyflie mid slæᵹe, oððe mid bende, oððe þurh wunde, bete ðæra æᵹhwylc mid rihte þeowscipe, ᵹe mid were ᵹe mid wite, 7 þam hiwum .CXX. scll. cyric friðes bote, 7 hæbbe his aᵹen forfanᵹen.

.IIII.

3. Ᵹif hwa cyninᵹes borh abrece, ᵹebete þone tihtlan swa him riht wisie, 7 þæs borᵹes bryce mid .V. pundum mærra peninᵹa. Ercebiscopes borᵹes bryce oððe his

*MS. B. mund byrd ᵹebete mid .III. pundum. *Oþres bisceopes oððe ealdormannes borᵹes bryce oððe mundbyrd, ᵹebete mid .II. pundum.

4. Gyf hwâ ymb cyninᵹes feorh syrwie, ðurh hine oððe wrecena feormunᵹe, oððe his manna, sy he his

4, 1. feores scyldiᵹ, 7 ealles ðæs þe he aᵹe; ᵹyf he hine sylfne treowsian wylle, do þæt be cyninᵹes werᵹylde.

4, 2. Swa we eac settað be eallum hadum, ᵹe ceorle ᵹe eorle: Se ðe ymbe his hlafordes feorh syrwie, sy he wiþ ðone his feores scyldiᵹ, 7 ealles þæs þe he aᵹe, oððe be his hlafordes were hine ᵹetreowie.

1, 5. sceolde, first e above ‖ Oþres begins B; now given in full, with notes on B and Variants from H. H has generally ᵹif, scll., always the chapter number. — ‖ 3. biscopes | ealder- | brice | his mundbyrd | Eras. bef. II in B, twam H ‖ 4. All or most of first line of chapters caps in B | eard new ab. wrecena B, þurh wrecena H ‖ 4, 1. treowan | dô ‖

.VI.

5.   Eâc we settað æȝhwelcere cirican ðe biscep ȝehal-
ȝode ðis frið, ȝif hie fáh mon ȝeierne oððe ȝeærne þæt
hine seofan nihtum nan mon ût ne teo; ȝif hit þonne
hwa dô, ðonne sie he scyldiȝ cyninȝes mundbyrde 7
þære cirican friðes, mare ȝif he ðær mare ôfȝefo,
ȝif he for hunȝre libban mæȝe, buton he self ûtfeohte.

5, 1.   Ȝif hiwan heora cirican maran þearfe hæbben, healde
hine mon on oðrum ærne 7 ðæt næbbe ðon ma dura

5, 2. þonne sio cirice;   ȝewite ðære cirican ealdor þæt

5, 3. him mon on þam fierste mete ne selle.   Ȝif he self
his wæpno his ȝefan utræcan wille, ȝehealden hi hine

5, 4. .XXX. nihta 7 hie hine his mæȝum ȝebodien.   Eac
cirican frið, ȝif hwelc mon cirican ȝesece for ðara ȝylta
hwylcum þara ðe ær ȝeypped nære 7 hine ðær on

5. 5. ȝodes naman ȝeandette, sie hit healf forȝifen.   Se ðe
stalað on sunnan niht oððe on ȝehhol oððe on eastron
oððe on ðone halȝan þunres dæȝ on ȝanȝdaȝas, ðara
ȝehwelc we willað sie twy bote swa on lencten fæsten.

.VII.

6.   Gif hwa on cirican hwæt ȝeðeofiȝe, forȝylde þæt
anȝylde 7 ðæt wite swa to ðam anȝylde belimpan wille

6, 1. 7 slea mon þa hond ôf ðe he hit mid ȝedyde;   ȝif
he ða hand lesan wille 7 him mon ðæt ȝeðafian wille,
ȝelde swa to his were belimpe.

.VIII.

7.   Gif hwa in cyninȝes healle ȝefeohte oððe his wæpn
ȝebrede 7 hine mon ȝefô, sie ðæt on cyninȝes dome,

7, 1. swa deað swa lif swa he him forȝifan wille;   ȝif he
losiȝe 7 hine mon eft ȝefô, forȝielde he hine self â
be his wereȝilde 7 ðone ȝylt ȝebete swa wer swa wite
swa he ȝewyrht aȝe.

5, 5. twy bote, wy new over rubbed place |:   **6, 1.** ȝif he End of
p. 81 in E.

Continuation of Variants from p. 87.

ciric-an | wîte | belimpan | wille | 7, poss. s. crossed and erased B | man | on
marg. æt oþrum cerre, new B | mid dyde, stæl above || **6, 1.** alysan, first
a ab. | wille | ȝeðafyan | wille || **7.** healle | ȝefeohte, ȝe ab. | wæpen, vac
his | ȝebrède perhaps B | ȝefô, ȝe ab. | dôme | wille || **7, 1.** man eft ȝefô,
eft ub. | sylfne, ne ab. | werȝilde.

5.   Eác we settað æghwylcere cyricean ðe bisceop
zehalzode ðis frið. Gif zefahmon ciricean zeyrne, oððe
zeærne, þæt hine seofon nihtum nan man ut ne têo;
zyf hit ðonon hwa do, ðonne sy he scyldiz cyninzes
mundbyrde, 7 ðære cyricean friðes, mare zyf he ðær
mare ofzefô, zyf he for hunzre libban mǽz, buton he

5, 1. sylf ut feohte.   Gyf hiwan hêora ciricean mare ðearfe
hæbben, healde hine mon on oðrum huse 7 þæt næbbe

5, 2. ðon ma dura ðonne seo cyrice;   zewite ðær cyricean

5, 3. ealdor, þæt him mon on fyrste mete ne sylle.   Gyf
he sylf his wæpno his zefân utrǽcan, zehealdan hi
hine ðrittiz nihta, 7 hi hine his mazum zebeoden.

5, 4.   Eac cyricean frið zyf hwylc man cyricean zesêce,
for ðara zylta hwylcum þæra ðe ær zeypped nære, 7
hine ðær on zodes naman zeandette, sy hît healf for-

5, 5. zyfen.   Se ðe stalað ôn sunnan niht, oðð on zeol,
oððe on eastron, oððe on ðone halzan þunres dǽz, 7
on zanz dazas, ðara zehwylc we willað, sy twy bote,
swa on lencten fæsten.

6.   Gyf hwâ on cyricean hwæt zeþeofize, forzylde þæt
anzylde, 7 þæt wite swa to ðam anzylde zelimpan
wylle, 7 slea mon ða hand ôf, ðe he hit mid zedyde.

6, 1.   Gyf he ða hand lysan wylle, 7 him mon þæt zeþafian
wylle, zylde swa to his were belimpe.

7.   Gyf hwa on kyninzes halle zefeohte, oððe his wæpne
zebrede 7 hine mon zefo, sy þæt on cyninzes dome,

7, 1. swa deað, swa lif, swa he him forzyfan wylle;   zyf
he losize 7 hine mon eft zefô, forzylde he hine sylfne
be his werzylde, 7 þone zylt zebête, swa wer swa wite,
swâ he zewyrht aze.

---

5. æghwylcere, first e ab. | cirican | biscop | fazman | ciricean above,
but old B, hy H | utt, last t above | ðonon, ne ab. on B, ðonne H | dô |
vac ðonne bef. sy | cirican | ofzefô | mǽz, e above new B, mæze H | butan |
utt, t ab. ‖ **5, 1.** heora, o ab. | cirican | ærne for huse | ðonne, ne ab. | seo
above circe ‖ **5, 2.** þære | cirican | on þam fyrste mete, mete above ‖ **5, 3.** —
sylf, end of p. 13 in B — wæpna | zefân | wylle above lighter B, wille H |
.XXX. | zebodie ‖ **5, 4.** cyric-an | is new ab. B | ciric-an | þæra | þæra ab. ðe |
forzifen ‖ **5, 5.** oþþe | zeol in text, al. zeohhol on margin | hal-zan | 7 new
BH | æghwylc | swa, al above new B | swa lencten, eras. betw. words H ‖ **6.**

88

.VIIII.

8. Gif hwa nunnan of mynstere utâlede buton kyning-
es lefnesse oððe bisc*epes* ʒeselle hundtwelftiʒ. scill.
healf cyninʒe, healf biscepe 7 þære cirican blaforde ðe

8, 1. ðone munuc aʒe; ʒif hio lenʒ libbe ðonne se ðe hie

8, 2. utlædde, naʒe hio his ierfes owiht; ʒif hio bearn
ʒestriene, næbbe ðæt ðæs ierfes ðon mare ðe seo

8, 3. modor; ʒif hire bearn mon ofslea, ʒielde cyninʒe þara
medren mæʒa dæl, fædren mæʒum hiora dæl mon
aʒife.

.X.

9. Gif mon wîf mid bearne ôfslea þon*ne* þæt bearn
in hire sie, forʒielde ðone wifman fullan ʒielde 7 þæt

9, 1. bearn bc ðæs fædren cnosles were healfan ʒelde; â
sie þæt wite .LX. scill. oð· ðæt anʒylde ârise to .XXX.
scill., siððan hit to ðam ârise þæt anʒylde, siððan sie

9, 2. þæt wite .CXX. scill.; ʒeo wæs ʒoldðeofe 7 stodðeofe
7 beoðeofe 7 maniʒ witu maran ðon*ne* oþru, nu sint
ealʒelic buton manðeofe .CXX. scill.

.XI.

10. Gif mon hæme mid twelfhyndes monnes wife, hundtwelftiʒ. scill. ʒebete ðam were, syxhyndum men hundteontiʒ. scill. ʒebcte, cierliscum men feowertiʒ. scill.
ʒebete.

.XII.

11. Gif mon on cirliscre fæmnan breost ʒefô, mid .V.

11, 1. scill. hire ʒebete; ʒif he hie oferweorpe 7 mid ne

11, 2. ʒehæme, mid .X. scill. ʒebete; ʒif he mid ʒehæme,

11, 3. mid .LX. scill. ʒebete; ʒif oðer mon mid hire læʒe

11, 4. ær, sie be healfum ðæm þon*ne* sio bot; ʒif hie mon
teo, ʒeladieʒe hie be sixteʒum hida oððe ðoliʒe be

8, 3. ʒielde, e over i ‖ 10. wife hund End of p. 82 in E ‖
11, 4. ʒeladieʒe (ʒe apart in Ms.), confusion of -die and -diʒe.

Continuation of Variants from p. 89.
but 7 þæt sy ... sylle 18, 1. added Lamb ‖ 11. cyrliscre ǀ fæmnan above ǀ
ʒefð ǀ .V. ǀ hire ab. ʒebete B ǀ Before 11,1 appears: ʒyf he mid ʒehæmede,
tyn scill. ʒebete in B, underlined and partially erased ‖ 11, 1. — Gyf End
of p. 15 in B — oferweorpe hy, hy ab. ǀ mid .X. ‖ 11, 2. mid .LX. ǀ hit
ʒebete ‖ 11, 3. ʒe on margin before læʒe ǀ ær ǀ healfum ðæm ðonne seo
bote, ðonne ab. ǀ 11, 4. hy ʒeladiʒe hy ǀ .LX. ǀ hida ǀ healfre ðære bote.

8.   Gyf hwa nunnan of mynstre utalæde butan cyninȝes
leafe oððe bisceopes, ȝesylle hundtwentiȝ scill., healf
cyninȝe, healf bisceope, ðære cyrice hlaforde, þe þa
8, 1. nunnan aȝe.   Gyf heo lenȝ libbe þonne se ðe heo
8, 2. utlæde, naȝe heo yrfer nawiht.   Gyf heo bearn ȝe-
stryne, næbbe þæt þæs yrfes na mare þonne seo moder.
8, 3.   Gyf man hire bearn ofslêa, ȝylde cyninȝe þæra
medra maȝa dæl; fædren maȝum hêora dæl man aȝyfe.

9.   Gyf man wif mid bearne ofslea, ðonne þæt bearn
in hire sy, forȝylde ðone wifman fullan ȝylde, 7 þæt
9, 1. bearn be ðæs fædren cnosles were halfan ȝylde;   a
sy þæt wite syxti scill. oþ þæt anȝylde arise to ðrittiȝ
scill.; syððan hit to ðæm arîse þæt anȝylde, syþþan
9, 2. sy þæt wite hundtwelftiȝ;   hwilon wæs ȝoldþeofe 7
stodðeofe 7 beoþeofe, 7 maniȝ witu maran þonne
oðru; nu synd ealle ȝelice, butan manþeofe hundtwelftiȝ
scill.

10.   Gif mon hæme mid twelfhyndes mannes wîfe,
hundtwelftiȝ scill. ȝebete man were. Syxhyndum men
hundteontiȝon scill. ȝebete. Ceorliscum men feowertiȝum
scill. ȝebete.

11.   · Gyf man on ceorliscne fænan breost ȝefo, mid fif
11, 1. scill. ȝebete..... Gyf he hiȝ oferweorpe 7 mid ne
11, 2. ȝehæme, tyn scill. ȝebete;   ȝyf he mid ȝehæme, syxti
11, 3. scill. ȝebete.   Gif oðer man mid hire læȝe ǽr, sy be
11, 4. healfum seo bot;   ȝyf hi man teo, ȝehladiȝe hî be
11, 5. sixtiȝum hidum, oððe þolie be healfere bote;   ȝyf

8. ûtalæde | biscopes | .CXX. | —cyninȝe healf End of p. 14 in B —
biscope 7 ciric-an, vac. ðære || 8, 1. se þe, þe ab. | ûtlædde | his yrfes
awuht || 8, 2. ȝestri-ne | naȝe | þes | irfes | ðe for na | ðe modor || 8, 3.
hire bearn man | þam cyninȝe, þam ab. | ðara | meddren, last d ab. | mæȝa |
mæȝum { hiora, o ab. | aȝife || 9. hwa wif ofslea mid bearne | hyre sy,
sy ab. | forȝilde | ðone, e over eras. B | heo for ðone wifman | healfân || 9, 1.
.LX. | .XXX. | siððan | .CXX. scill. || 9, 2. ȝeo | 7 beo þeofe, vac. B, from
marg. and H | maneȝu | sint | ealle ȝelice, 2nd and 4th e above | man, a
second n above B | .CXX. || 10. man | .XII. | hyndes, y out of u B |
.CXX. | ȝebete man þam were, man ab. | Syx hyndum, both y's out of u
B | .C. | scill, 1 made into y B | Cyrliscum | .XL. | ȝebete above | vac. ȝebete,

90

11, 5. healfre þære bote; ʒif borenran wifmen ðis ʒelimpe, weaxe sio bôt be ðam were.

.XIII.

12. Gif mon oðres wudu bærneð oððe heaweð unalief-edne, forʒielde ælc ʒreat treow mid .V. scill. 7 siððan æʒhwylc sie, swa fela swa hiora sie, mid .V. pæninʒum,

13. 7 .XXX. scill. to wite; ʒif mon oðerne æt ʒemænan weorce ôffelle unʒewealdes, aʒife mon þam mæʒum þæt treow, 7 hi hit hæbben ær .XXX. nihta of þam lande oððe him fô se to se ðe ðone wudu aʒe.

.XIIII.

14. Ʒif mon sie dumb oððe dêaf ʒeboren þæt he ne mæʒe synna onsecʒʒan ne ʒeandettan, bete se fæder his misdæda.

.XV.

15. Gif mon beforan ærcebiscepe ʒefeohte oððe wæpne

15, 1. ʒebreʒde, mid .L. scill. 7 hundteonteʒum ʒebete; ʒif beforan oðrum biscepe oððe ealdormen ðis ʒelimpe,

16. mid hundteonteʒum .scill. ʒebete. Ʒif mon cu oððe stod-myran forstele 7 folan oððe cealf ôfadrife, forʒelde mid

17. .scill. 7 þa moder be hiora weorðe; ʒif hwa oðrum his unmaʒan oðfæste 7 he hine on ðære fæstinʒe forferie, ʒe-triowe hine facnesse ðe hine fede, ʒif hine hwa hwelces teo.

.XVI.

18. Gif hwa nunnan mid hæmeð þinʒe oððe on hire hræʒl oððe on hire breost butan hire leafe ʒefô, sie

18, 1. hit twybete swa we ær be læwdum men fundon; ʒif beweddodu fæmne hie forlicʒʒe, ʒif hio sie cirlisc, mid .LX. scill. ʒebete þam byrʒean 7 þæt sie on cwic æhtum feoʒodum 7 mon næniʒne mon on ðæt ne selle.

18, 2. Ʒif hio sie syxhyndu, hundteontiʒ .scill. ʒeselle

14. he, e old over i ‖ 16. cu oððe End of p. 83 in E.

Continuation of Variants from p. 91.

underlined and feowertiʒum written above prob. new B, mid scyllinge H ∣ moder ∣ weorðe ‖ 17. 7 he hine, he ab. ∣ ʒetreowiʒe, new s before iʒe B, ʒetreowsie, sie ab. H ∣ facnes ∣ ðe, se before it new B, se ðe H ∣ ʒif hine hwa ‖ 18. on before hire hræʒl ∣ butan ∣ ʒefð ∣ twybote ∣ mannum ‖ 18, 1. beweddo, eras. at end B, beweddod H ∣ hy ∣ cierlisc ∣ mid .LX. ∣ ðam þe ʒebyrie, vac. hit ∣ næniʒne ‖ 18, 2. syx ∣ .C. ∣ ʒesylle ðam ðe, ðe above, also hit lighter B, ʒebete ðam þe hit ʒebyrie H.

borenran wifmen þis ʒelimpe, wexe seo bôt be ðam were.

12. Gyf man oðres wudu bærneð oððe heaweþ unalyf-
edne, forʒylde ælc ʒreat treow mid fif scill. 7 syþþan
æʒhwylc sy, swa feola swa heora sy, mid fif peneʒum
13. 7 þrittiʒ scill. to wite. Gyf man oðerne æt ʒemænan
weorce offealle unʒewealdes, aʒyfe man þam maʒon
þæt treow, 7 hî hit hæbben ær þrittiʒ nihta of ðæm
lande, oððe him fo to se ðe ðone wudu aʒe.

14. Gyf mon sy dumb oððe deaf ʒeboren þæt he ne
mæʒe his synna ʒeandettan ne ætsacan, bete se fæder
his misdæda.

15. Gyf man beforan ercebisceope ʒefeohte, oððe wæpne
15, 1. ʒebrede, mid fiftiʒum scill. 7 hundteontiʒum ʒebete. Gyf
beforan oðrum bisceope oððe ealdormen ðis ʒelimpe,
16. mid hundteontigum scill. ʒebete. Gyf man cu oððe
stodmære forstele 7 folan oððe cealf ofadrife, forʒylde
17. mid sixtiʒ scill. 7 þa modor be heora wyrðe. Gyf
hwâ oðrum his unmaʒan oðfæste, 7 he hine on ðære
fæstinʒe forferie, ʒetreowiʒe hine facnesse ðe hine fede,
ʒyf hwâ hine hwylces têo.

18. Gyf hwa nunnan mid hæmed ðinʒe, oððe hire
hræʒl, oððe on hire breost, buton hire leafe ʒefô, sy
18, 1. hit twibote, swa we ær be læwedum men fundon. Gyf
beweddo fæmne hêo forlicʒe, ʒyf hêo sy ceorlisc, syxtiʒ
scill. ʒebete ðam þe hit ʒebyriʒe 7 þæt sy on cwycæhtum
feoʒodum 7 man næninʒne man on þæt ne sylle.
18, 2. Gyf hêo sy sixhynde, hundteontiʒ scill. ʒesylle

11, 5. borenran, æðel ab. B | ʒif þis bett bor. wifmen ʒelimpe, bett ab. | weaxe || 12. .V. | siþþan | ælc swa, vac. sy | moniʒ for feola | þær for heora | .V. | peninʒum | .XXX. || 13. weorce ab. | aʒife | maʒum | hy | .XXX. | fð | se þe, þe ab. || 14. man | vac. his bef. synne | onsæcʒan ne ʒeandettan H, ʒeondettan ne onsecʒan Lamb. || 15. ærcebiscope | .L. scll. ʒebete 7 .C. || 15, 1. biscope | ealdormenn | .C. || 16. cû | — cu oððe End of p. 16 in B — | stodmyran | ofadrifeð | forʒilde | sixtiʒ

7*

18, 3. þam byrȝean; ȝif hio sie twelfhyndu, .CXX. scill.
ȝebete þam byrȝean.

.XVII.

19. Gif hwa his wæpnes oðrum onlæne þæt he mon
mid ôfslea, hie moton hie ȝesomnian, ȝif hie willað, to

19, 1. þam were; ȝif hi hie ne ȝesamnien, ȝielde se ðæs
wæpnes onlah þæs weres ðriddan dæl 7 þæs wites

19, 2. ðriddan dæl; ȝif he hine triewan wille þæt he to

19, 3. ðære læne facn ne wiste, þæt he mot; ȝif sweord
hwita oðres monnes wæpn to feormunȝe onfô oððe
smið monnes andweorc, hie hit ȝesund beȝen aȝifan,
swa hit hwæðer hiora ær onfenȝe, buton hiora hwæðer
ær þinȝode þæt he hit anȝylde healdan ne ðorfte.

.XVIII.

20. Gif mon oðres monnes munuce feoh oðfæste butan
ðæs munuces hlafordes lefnesse 7 hit him losiȝe, þoliȝe
his se ðe hit ær ahte.

.XVIIII.

21. Ȝif preost oðerne mon ôfslea, weorpe mon to handa
7 eall ðæt he him hames bohte 7 hine biscep onhadiȝe
þonne hine mon of ðam mynstre aȝife, buton se hlaford
þone wer forðinȝian wille.

.XX.

22. Gif mon on folces ȝemote cyninȝes ȝerefan ȝeyppe
eofot 7 his eft ȝeswican wille, ȝestæle on ryhtran hand
ȝif he mæȝe; ȝif he ne mæȝe, ðolie his anȝyldes.

.XXI.

23. Gif hund mon toslite oððe abite, æt forman misdæde ȝeselle .VI. scill., ȝif he him mete selle, æt æfteran

23, 1. cerre .XII. scill., æt ðriddan .XXX. scill. Ȝif æt ðissa
misdæda hwelcere se hund losiȝe, ȝa ðeos bôt hwæðre

---

20. Ends with p. 84 in E.

Continuation of Variants from p. 93.

hande underlined and him over it B, handa H | 7 part. erased B | eal, 2nd
new l B | mid him | onhadiȝe | mon | þæm | aȝife | forðinȝian | wille || 22.
man | folces, es ab. | ȝe eofot yppe, cf. E | ryhtran | maȝe | maȝe | anȝildes |
and fô to ðam wite added || 23. abîte | mysdæde | æt æfterran ci-rre | þriddan
ci-rre || 23, 1. ȝyf, here prob. he erased B | ðissa | hweþere, 2nd e ab.

93

18, 3. ðam ðe to ʒebyrian. Gyf heo sy twelfhynde, hundtwelftiʒ scill. ʒebete ðam ðe to ʒebyriʒe.

19.   Gyf hwa his wæpne oðrum læne þæt he mid man
ofslea, hi moton hi ʒesanian, ʒyf hi wyllað, to ðæm
19, 1. were;   ʒyf heo hi ne ʒesamnian, ʒylde se ðæs wæpnes
onlænde þæs weres ðridda dæll, 7 þæs *wites ðriddan*
19, 2. *dæl*;   ʒyf he hine triwian wylle þæt he to ðære læne
19, 3. facne nyste, þæt he mot. Gyf sweord hwita oðres
mannes wepen to feormunʒe underfð, oððe smið mannes
andweorc, hi hit ʒesund beʒen aʒyfen, swa hit hwæðer
heora ær underfenʒe, buton heora hweðer ær ðinʒode
þæt he hit anʒylde healdan ne þorfte.

20.   Gyf mon oðres monnes muneke feoh befæste, buton
þæs munekes hlafordes hleafe, 7 hit him losiʒe, þolie
his se ðe ær ahte.

21.   Gyf preost oðerne man ofslêa, weorpe man to
hande 7 eal þæt he him mid hâmes brohte, 7 hine
biscop unhadie ðonne hine man of ðem mynstre aʒyfe,
buton se hlaford ðone wer foreðinʒian wylle.

22.   Gyf mon on folces ʒemote cyninʒes ʒerefan ʒeyppe
þeofðe, 7 his eft ʒeswican wille, ʒestæle on rihtran
hand, ʒyf he mæʒe; ʒyf he ne mæʒe, þoliʒe his anʒyldes.

23.   Gyf hund man toslite oððe abite, æt forman misdæde ʒesylle .VI. scill., ʒyf he him mete sylle, æt ðam
23, 1. oðran cyrre .XII. scill., æt ðriddan .XXX. scill.; ʒyf
æt ðisra misdæda hwylcere se hund losiʒe, ʒa ðeos

18, 3. hio | .XII. | .CXX. | hit lighter above ʒebyriʒe B, hit ʒebyrie
H ‖ 19. wæpn | man mid | by | hy | ʒesam-nian | willað ‖ 19, 1. hy heo
ʒesamni-an nellen | ʒilde | onlan | ðriddan | dæl | 7 þæs wites ðriddan dæl
vac. B Lamb., from H ‖ 19, 2. triwian, new s betw. wi B, trywan H |
wille | to ðære fore 7 to ðære læne | facn ‖ 19, 8. wæpn | onfð H, underfð
Lamb. | hy | — beʒen End of p. 17 in B | — aʒifen | heora hwæðer,
o ab. | onfenʒe H, underfenʒe Lamb. | heora, o ab ‖ 20. hlafordes under-
lined and aldres over it B | Ʒif man oþres mannes munuce butan his hla-
fordes leafe feoh befæste, mannes and his above | losie | ðoliʒe ‖ 21. to

23, 2. forð.   Ʒif se hund ma misdæda ʒewyrce 7 he hine
hæbbe, bete be fullan were swa dolʒbote swa he wyrce.

.XXII.

24.   Gif neat mon ʒewundiʒe, weorpe ðæt neat to
honda oððe foreðinʒie.

.XXIII.

25.   Gif mon ceorles mennen to ned hæmde ʒeðreatað,
mid .V. scill. ʒebete þam ceorle 7 .LX. scill. to wite;

25, 1.   ʒif ðeow mon þeowne to ned hæmde ʒenede, bete
mid his eowende.

.XXIIII.

26*.   Gif mon twyhyndne mon unsynniʒne mid hloðe
ofslea, ʒielde se ðæs sleʒes andetta sie wer 7 wite 7 æʒhwelc mon ðe on siðe wære ʒeselle .XXX. scill. to bloð bote.

.XXV.

27.   Gif hit sie syxhynde mon, ælc mon to hloð bote
.LX. scill. 7 se slaʒa wer 7 fulwite.

.XXVI.

28.   Gif he sie twelfhynde, ælc hiora hundtwelftiʒ

28, 1. scill., se slaʒa wer 7 wite;   ʒif hloð ðis ʒedô 7 eft
oðswerian wille, tio hie ealle 7 þonne ealle forʒielden
þone wer ʒemænum hondum 7 ealle ânwite swa to
ðam were belimpe.

.XXVII.

29.   Gif mon unʒewintrædne wifmon to niedhæmde
ʒeðreatiʒe, sie ðæt swa ðæs ʒewintredan monnes bot.

30.   Ʒif fædren mæʒa mæʒleas mon ʒefeohte 7 mon ôfslea 7 þonne, ʒif medren mæʒas hæbbe, ʒielden ða
þæs weres ðriddan dæl, *ðriddan dæl ða ʒeʒildan* 7 for

30, 1. *ðriddan dæl* he fleo;   ʒif he medren mæʒas naʒe,
ʒielden þa ʒeʒildan healfne, for healfne he fleo.

---

26. ofslea, eras. of er? betw. of & slea. ‖ **28.** scill. End of p. 85 in
E. ‖ **30.** words skipped in E supplied from H, where and in Lamb.
full sense is to be got. *Thorpe-Schmid put 29, 30, 31 before 26.

Continuation of Variants from p. 95.

28, 1. ʒedô | oþswerian | wille | teo man hy, man ab. | forʒilden | wær |
ʒemænum | ân wite | bef. belimbe new to B | belimpe ‖ **29.** ʒewintredan ‖
30. fæddren, second d ab. | maʒa, æ new ab. B, mæʒa H | mæʒleas | 7
man | he new ab. meddren B | meddren, first d ab. | mæʒas | ʒilden | —
ʒeʒilden End of p. 19 in B — | words supplied from H ‖ **30, 1.** after
ʒyf new he B | maʒes, es over eras. | naʒe | ʒilden | healfne and for.

23, 2. bôt ðeah hwæðere forð.   Gyf se hund ma misdæda
zewyrce 7 he hine hæbbe, bete be fullan were swa
dolhbote swa he zewyrce.

24.   Gyf neat man zewundize, weorpe þæt neat to
handa oððe foreðinzie.

25.   Gyf man ceorles mennen to nyd hæmede zeðreataþ,
mid fif scill. zebete ðam ceorle 7 syhtiz scill. to wite.

25, 1.   Gyf ðeow man ðeowne to nyd hæmede zenyde,
bete mid his eowende.

26.   Gyf man twyhynde man unsynnizne mid hloþe
ofslêa, zylde se ðæs slæzes andetta sy wer 7 wite 7
ælc mon ðe on syþe wære zesylle ðrittiz scill. to loð bote.

27.   Gif hyt sy syxbynde man, ælc to hloð bote feo-
wertiz 7 se slaza were 7 fulwite.

28.   Gyf he sy twelfhynde, ælc heora hundtwelftiz
28, 1. scill., se slaza wer 7 wite;   zyf hloð ðis zedô, 7 eft
ætswerian wylle, teo hi ealle 7 ðonne ealle forzylden
ðone wer zemæne handum 7 ealle anwite swa to ðam
were belimbe.

29.   Gyf man unzêwintredne wifman to nyd hæmede
zeþreatize, sy þæt swa ðæs zewintredes mannes bot;

30.   zyf fædren maza mæizleas mon zefeohte 7 mon
ofslêa 7 ðonne, zyf meddren mazas hæbbe, zylden þa
ðæs weres ðriddan dæl, *ðriddan dæl ða zezyldan* 7 for
30, 1. ðriddan dæl he flêo;   zyf medren mazas næbbe, zylden
ða zezylden heafne, for healfne he fleo.

23, 2. dolhbote, on marg. oððe new B, after swa, hwætt new above
B, both in Lamb. ‖   **24.** mannes neat | — þæt neat End of p. 18 in B — |
fore zeþinzie, ze ab. ‖   **25.** as .XXVI. put after 26, 27, 28 in H, 29 follows
it in Ve. Lamb. | ciorles ! .V. | ciorle | .LX. ‖   **25, 1.** zenide | hyde for
eowende ‖   **26.** ofslea mid hloþe | zilde | se ðe þæs slezes, ðe ab. | wer,
second new r | æzhwylc for ælc | ðara for mon | on ðæm syþe | zeselle |
.XXX. | hloþbote ‖   **27.** ælc man | feowertiz, scill. ab. new B, .LX. scll.
H | wer | full, last 1 ab. ‖   **28.** .XII. | .CXX. | 7 new bef. se B, and H |

.XXVIII.

31.   Gif mon swa ʒeradne mon ofslea, ʒif he mæʒas
næʒe, ʒielde mon healfne cyninʒe healfne þam ʒeʒildan.

.XXVIIII.

32.   Gif mon folc leasunʒe ʒewyrce 7 bio on hine ʒeresp
weorðe, mid nanum leohtran ðinʒe ʒebete þonne him
mon aceorfe þa tunʒon ôf, þæt hie mon na undeorran weorðe moste lesan ðonne hiè mon be þam were ʒeeahtiʒe.

.XXX.

33.   Gif hwa oðerne ʒodborʒes oncunne 7 tion wille
þæt he hwelcne ne ʒelæste ðara ðe he him ʒesealde,
aʒife þone foreað on feower ciricum, 7 se oðer, ʒif he
hine treowan wille, in .XII. ciricum do he ðæt.

.XXXI.

34.   Eâc is ciepe monnum ʒereht, ða men ðe hie up
mid him læden ʒebrenʒen beforan kyninʒes ʒerefan on
folc ʒemote 7 ʒerecce hu maniʒe þara sien, 7 hie
nimen þa men mid him þe hie mæʒen eft to folc ʒe-

34, 1. mote to ryhte brenʒan,   7 þonne him ðearf sie ma
manna ûp mid him to habbanne on biora fore, ʒecyðe
symle swa ôft swa him ðearf sie in ʒemotes ʒewitnesse
cyninʒes ʒerefan.

.XXXII.

35.   Ʒif mon cierliscne mon ʒebinde unsynniʒne, ʒebete
35, 1. mid .X. scill.; ʒif hine mon beswinʒe, mid .XX. scill.
35, 2. ʒebete; ʒif he hine on henʒenne alecʒʒe, mid .XXX.
35, 3. scill. ʒebete; ʒif he hine on bismor to homolan be-
35, 4. scire, mid .X. scill. ʒebete; ʒif he hine to preoste
35, 5. bescire unbundenne, mid .XXX. scill. ʒebete; ʒif he
35, 6. ðone beard ôfascire, mid .XX. scill. ʒebete; ʒif he
hine ʒebinde 7 þonne to preoste bescire, mid .LX. scill.
ʒebete.

34, 1. swa him ðearf sie End of p. 86 in E.

Continuation of Variants from p. 97.

simle | him bef. ðearf | on for in | ʒewitnesse || **85.** man ab. cierliscne |
man | — ʒebinde End p. 20 in B — | unsynniʒne | .X. || **35, 1.** .XX. ||
85, 2. henʒenne | .XXX. scillinʒa || **85, 8.** on bysmer above | bescire ||
85, 5. new on marg. of B | ofascyre || **85, 6.** to above new B, to preoste
H | syxtig, new feowertiʒ above B, .LX. H.

31. Gyf mon swa ʒeradne man ofslêa, ʒyf he maʒas
naʒe, ʒylde man healfe kyninʒe, healfne þam ʒeʒyldan.

32. Gyf mon folc leasunʒe ʒewyrce, 7 heo on hine
ʒeræf weorðe, mid nanum leohtran ðinʒe ʒebete þonne
him mon aceorfe ða tunʒan ôf, þæt heo mon na undeorran wurde moste lesan þonne hêo mon be ðæm
were ʒeehtiʒe.

33. Gyf hwâ oþerne ʒodborʒes oncunne 7 teon wylle
þæt he hwylcne ne ʒelæste ðara ðe he him ʒesealde,
aʒŷfe ðone foreað on feower cyricum, 7 se oþer ʒyf
he hine treowian wylle, innan twelf cyricum do he þæt.

34. Eac is cypemonnum ʒereht ða men þe hi up
mid heom lædað ʒebrinʒan beforan cyninʒes ʒerefan
on folc ʒemote 7 ʒerecca hu monie ðæra syn, 7 hi
nimen þa men mid heom ðe hiʒ maʒon eft to folc ʒe-
34, 1. mote *to ryhte* brinʒan, 7 þonon heom þearf sy *ma
manna* up mid heom to habbanne on heora fôre, ʒecyðe
symble swa oft swa ðearf sy in ʒemotes ʒewitnysse
cyninʒes ʒerefan.

35. Gyf mon ceorliscne mon ʒebinde unscyldiʒne, ʒe-
35, 1. bete mid tyn scill.; ʒyf hine man beswinʒe, mid twentiʒ
35, 2. scill. ʒebete; ʒyf he hine on henʒene ʒebrinʒe, mid
35, 3. ðrittiʒ scill. ʒebete. Gyf he hine on bismor to homelan
35, 4. bescyre, mid .X. scill. ʒebete. Gyf he hine to preoste
35, 5. bescyre unbundenne, mid .XXX. scill. ʒebete. *Gif he
35, 6. þone beard ofascere, mid .XX. scill. ʒebete.* Gyf he
hine ʒebinde, 7 þonne preoste bescyre, mid syxtiʒ scill.
ʒebete.

---

31. ʒilde | healfne were þam cyninʒe, were þam ab. | ʒeʒildan |; **32.**
wêorðe ʒeræf H, ʒeræ fLamb. | bef. ʒebete new ne B | man | hy | môn nâ |
wurde, ð uncrossed B, weorðe H | alysan | vac. hêo | man | þæm, m ab. |
ʒeeahtiʒe || **33.** wille | aʒife | for-âþ | ciricum, 2d i above | treowan | wille ;
on .XII. | ciricum | do þæt on margin || **34.** mannum | bef. ða men new
þæt inserted B | hy | lædan | ʒebrinʒe | ʒerecce | moniʒe | hy | up mid
him | hy | to ryhte vac. B, from H, where ʒemote to above | brenʒan ||
34, 1. þonne | him | ma manna from H | him | to for on | heora, o ab. |

98

.XXXIII.

36.　　　Eac is funden, ȝif mon hafaÞ spere ofer eaxle 7
hine mon on asnaseÞ, ȝielde þone wer, butan wite;

36, 1.　　ȝif beforan eaȝum asnase, ȝielde þone wer; ȝif hine
mon tio ȝewealdes on Þære dæde, ȝetriowe hine be
þam wite 7 mid Þy þæt wite afelle, ȝif se ord sie

36, 2. ufor þonne hindeweard sceaft;　　ȝif hie sien bu ȝelic,
ord 7 hindeweard sceaft, þæt sie butan pleo.

.XXXIIII.

37.　　　Gif mon wille of boldȝetale in oÞer boldȝetæl
hlaford secan, do Þæt mid Þæs ealdormonnes ȝewitnesse

37, 1. þe he ær in his scire folȝode;　　ȝif he hit butan his
ȝewitnessc do, ȝeselle se þe hine to men feormie .CXX.
scill. to wite: dæle he hwæÞre Þæt, healf cyninȝe in
Þa scire Þe he ær folȝode, healf in þa Þe he oncymÞ;

37, 2.　　ȝif he hwæt yfla ȝedon hæbbe Þær he ær wæs,
bete Þæt se Þe hine Þonne to men onfo 7 cyninȝe .CXX.
scill. to wite.

.XXXV.

38.　　　Gif mon beforan cyninȝes ealdormen on ȝemote
ȝefeohte, bete wer 7 wite swa hit ryht sie 7 beforan

38, 1. þam .CXX. scill. Þam ealdormen to wite; ȝif he folcȝemot
mid wæpnes bryde ârære, Þam ealdormen hund twelftiȝ

38, 2. scill. to wite;　　ȝif Þises hwæt beforan cyninȝes ealdormonnes ȝinȝran ȝelimpe oÞÞe cyninȝes preoste, .XXX.
scill. to wite.

.XXXVI.

39.　　　Gif hwa on cierlisces monnes flette ȝefeohte, mid

39, 1. syx scill. ȝebete Þam ceorle;　　ȝif he wæpne ȝebrede

---

87. in above his scire, but old ‖ **87, 2.** Ends with p. 87 in E; page
rough, causing large spaces betw. syllables.

Continuation of Variants from p. 99.

to men under on fÞ, þonne on marg., under above | .CXX. ‖ **88.** man |
ealder | feohtaþ, aþ out of æh B, ȝefeohte H | wer, second r added new
B | ryht | .CXX. | ealdermen | to wite etc. from H ‖ **88, 1.** before hundt-
welftiȝ new 7 B | .CXX. ‖ **88, 2.** First difference in chapters betw. B and
EH | Þyses | ealder | ȝi-nȝran | .XXX. | scillinȝas ‖ **89.** ciorlisces | ȝebete
mid .VI. scll. Þam ciorle ‖ **89, 1.** ȝebre-de.

36.　　　Eac is funden, ʒyf mon hæfð spere ofer eaxle 7
36, 1. hine man onsnǽseþ, ʒylde þone wer buton wite. *Gif
beforan eaʒum, ʒylde þone wer.* Gyf hine man teo
ʒewealdes on þære dæde, ʒetreowie hine be ðam wite
7 mid ðam þæt wite afylle, ʒyf se ord ufor ðonne
36, 2. hindeweard sceaft; ʒyf hi syn buta ʒelice, ord 7
hindeweard sceaft, þæt sy butan pleo.

37.　　　Gyf mon wylle of bold ʒetæle in oðer bold ʒetæl
hlaford secan, do þæt mid ealdormannes ʒewitnysse
37, 1. þe he ær in his scire folʒode.　Gyf he hit buton his
ʒewitnysse dô, ʒesylle *se ðe* hine to men feormie, bund-
twelftiʒ scill. to wite; dæle he hwæðere þæt, healf cyninʒe in þam scire þe he ær folʒode, healf in þa þe
37, 2. he cymð.　Gyf he hwæt to yfele ʒedon hæfð ðær
he ær wæs, bete þæt se ðe hine ðonnon to men underfo,
7 cyninʒe hundtwelftiʒ scill. to wite.

38.　　　Gyf mon beforan cyninʒes ealdormen on ʒemote
feohtaþ, bete wer 7 wite, swa hit riht sy, 7 beforan
38, 1. ðam hundtwelftiʒ scill. ðam ealdormen *to wite; ʒif
he folces ʒemot mid wæpnes bryde arære, þam ealdermen*
hundtwelftiʒ scill. to wite.
38, 2.　　　Gyf ðisses hwæt beforan cyninʒes ealdormannes
ʒinʒran ʒelimpe, oððe cyninʒes preoste, ðrittiʒ scill. to
wite.

39.　　　Gyf hwa on ceorlisces mannes flette ʒefeohte, mid
39, 1. .VI. scill. ʒebete ðam ceorle; ʒyf he wæpne ʒebrede

---

36. ʒefunden, ʒe ab. | man | hafað | eaxlen, n ab. | on asnæseð, on
above | ʒilde | butan ‖　36, 1. words new on margin B | eaʒum asnæse |
ʒilde | ʒetreowie, betw. wi new s B, ʒetrywe H | ðæm | þy for ðam | 7
þis beo new ab. ʒyf B | after ord new si B, sy H | þreo finʒre ufor ‖
36, 2. ac new ab. ʒyf B | hy | bû | ʒelic ‖　37. man of bold ʒetæle wille, wille
first l above | dô | ðæs ealdermannes | ʒewitnysse, ysse over eras. but old
B, ʒewitnesse H | ǽr | on for in ‖　37, 1. butan | ʒewitnesse | dô | ʒesylle,
ylle over eras. but old B | se ðe new ab. hine B, se þe H | hyne | feormiʒe |
.CXX. | þæt hweðere, 2nd e above | þam bef. cyninʒe new B, þam above
H | on for in | ða | folʒade | new 7 above | on for in | þonne oncymð, þonne
ab. H, on new B ‖　37, 2. —hæfð End of p. 21 in B — | bete ðætþonne se ðe hine

39, 2. ꝥ no feohte, sie be healfum ðam; ᵹif syxhyndum
þissa hwæðer ᵹelimpe, ðriefealdlice *arise be ðære cier-*
liscan bote, twelfhyndum men twyfealdlice be þæs syx-

40.   hyndan bote; cyninᵹes burᵹ bryce bið .CXX. scill.,
ærcebiscepes hundniᵹontiᵹ scill., oðres biscepes 7 ealdormonnes .LX. scill., twelfhyndes monnes .XXX. scill.,
syxhyndes monnes .XV. scill, ceorles edorbryce .V.

40, 1. scill.; ᵹif ðisses hwæt ᵹelimpe ðenden fyrd ute sie

40, 2. oððe in lencten fæsten, hit sie twybote; ᵹif mon in
lenctenne haliᵹ ryht in folce butan leafe alecᵹᵹe, ᵹebete mid .CXX. scill.

.XXXVII.

41.   Se mon se ðe bocland hæbbe 7 him his mæᵹas
læfden, þonne setton we þæt he hit ne moste sellan of
his mæᵹburᵹe, ᵹif þær bið ᵹewrit oððe ᵹewitnes ðæt
hit ðara manna forbod wære þe hit on fruman ᵹe-
strindon 7 þara þe hit him sealdon þæt he swa ne
mote 7 þæt þonne on cyninᵹes 7 on biscopes ᵹewit-
nesse ᵹerecce beforan his mæᵹum.

.XXXVIII.

42.   Eac we beodað se mon se ðe his ᵹefan hamsittendne
wite þæt he ne feohte ær ðam he him ryhtes bidde;

42, 1. ᵹif he mæᵹnes hæbbe þæt he his ᵹefân beride 7
inne besitte, ᵹehealde hine .VII. niht inne 7 hine ôn
ne feohte, ᵹif he inne ᵹeðolian wille 7 þonne ymb .VII.
niht, ᵹif he wille on hand ᵹan 7 wæpenu sellan, ᵹehealde hine .XXX. nihta ᵹesundne 7 hine his mæᵹum

42, 2. ᵹebodie 7 his friondum; ᵹif he ðonne cirican ᵹeierne,
sie ðonne be ðære cirican are, swa we ær bufan cwædon;

89, 2. Line skipped; revised from B ‖ **40.** hundniᵹontiᵹ begins 2nd
Ot. fragm. (cf. Ap. A) from which foll. variants: hundniᵹontiᵹ, d above
old ǀ bisceopes ǀ vac. monnes after syxhyndes? ǀ lenctenne haliᵹ, ne ha
over eras. but old E ǀ **41.** ᵹestryndon ǀ bisceopes ‖ **42.** sittende ǀ —
wite þæt End of p. 88 in E — ‖ **42, 1.** ᵹyf ǀ maᵹum ‖ **42, 2.** cirican ðonne?
cf. cyricean ðonne Lamb ǀ sie, i above.

39, 2. 7 ne feohte, sy be healfum ðam.   Gyf .VI. hyndum
       ðissa hweðer ʒelimpe, ðryfealdlice arise bæ ðære cyr-
       liscan bote, twelfhyndum men twifealdlice be ðæs syx-
40.   hyndum bote.   Cyninʒes burh bryce bið hundtwelftiʒ
       scill.   Ercebisceopes hundniʒonti scill.   Oþres bisceopes
       7 ealdormannes syxtiʒ scill.   Twelfhyndes mannes
       ðrittiʒ scill.   Syxhyndes mannes fiftene scyll.   *Ceorles*
40, 1. *eoderbryce fif scill.*   Gyf ðisses hwæt ʒelimpe ðonne
40, 2. fyrd ute sy oððe in lenctene, *si hit twibote.   Gif mann*
       on lenctene haliʒ riht in folce buton leafe alecʒe,
       ʒebete mid hundtwelftiʒum scillinʒum.

MS. H.   .XXXVII.
41.   Se man se þe bocland hæbbe 7 him þonne his
       yldran læfdan, þonne setton we ðæt he hit ne mot
       syllan of his mæʒburʒe, ʒif ðær bið ʒewritt oððe ʒe-
       witnesse ðæt hit ðara manna fodbod wære ðe hit on
       fruman ʒestrindon 7 ðara ðe hit him sealdon ðæt he
       swa ne mote 7 þæt þonne on cyninʒes ʒe on biscopes
       ʒewitnesse ʒerecce beforan his maʒum.

                               .XXXVIII.
42.   Eac we bedað, se man se ðe his ʒefân hamsitt-
       ende wite, ðæt he ne feohte, ær ðam ðe he him ryhtes ·
42, 1. bidde.   Ʒif he mæʒnes hæbbe, ðæt he his ʒefân berîde
       and hine inne besitte, ʒehealde hine seofan niht inne
       7 him on ne feohte, ʒif he inne ʒeðolian wille, 7 þonne
       ymbe seofan niht, ʒif he wille ond hand ʒan and his
       wæpnu syllan, ʒehealde hine .XXX. nihta ʒesundne 7
42, 2. hine his freondum 7 his maʒum bebeode.   Ʒif he þonne
       ciricean ʒyrne, sy ðonne be þære ciricean âre, swa we

39, 2. before .VI. new on B | syx | hynd, y out of u B | ðissa above
hwæðer | ðri-fealdlice, first e ab. | cierliscan | .XII. | twy- | syxhyndan ‖ **40.**
Cyninʒes, a bigger red C put before old C B | brice | .CXX. | Ercebiscopes |
.XC. | biscopes | ealder | .LX. | .XII. hyndes | .XXX. | .XV. | ceorles etc.
from margin of B, new | edorbrice | V. ‖ **40, 1.** þysses | lenʒten fæsten | si
hit etc. from margin B, new | hit sy twybote ‖ **40, 2.** man | lenʒten |
ryht H, haliʒrift Lamb | on for in | butan | leafe above | alecʒe, c above |
— scillinʒum End of p. 22 in B, next leaf lost — ‖ **41.** þonne above |
ʒewitnesse, se above | ʒestri-ndon ‖ **42, 1.** inne above besitte | feohte, o
above | ʒeðoli-an | ymbe, e ab. | his above wæpnu | 7 his maʒum above ‖
42, 2. ciricean, 2nd i ab. | ciricean, 2nd i ab.

42, 3. ȝif he ðon*ne* þæs mæȝenes ne hæbbe þæt he hine
inne besitte, ride to þam ealdormen, bidde hine fultumes;
ȝif he him fultuman ne wille, ride *to* cyninȝe ær he

42, 4. feohte. Eac swelce ȝif mon becume on his ȝefân ꝸ
he hine ǽr hamfæstne ne wite, ȝif he wille his wæpen
sellan, hine mon ȝehealde .XXX. nihta ꝸ hine his fre-
ondu*m* ȝecyðe; ȝif he ne wille his wæpenu sellan, þon*ne*
mot he feohtan on hine; ȝif he wille on hond ȝan ꝸ
his wæpenu sellan ꝸ hwa ofer ðæt on him feohte,
ȝielde swa wer swa wunde swa he ȝewyrce ꝸ wite ꝸ

42, 5. hæbbe his mæȝ forworht. Eac we cweðað þæt mon
mote mid his hlaforde feohtan orwiȝe, ȝif mon on ðone
hlaford fiohte, swa môt se hlaford mid þy men feohtan;

42, 6. æfter þære ilcan wisan mon mot feohtan mid his
ȝeborene mæȝe, ȝif hine mon on woh onfeohteð, buton

42, 7. wið his hlaforde, þæt we ne liefað, ꝸ mon mot feohtan ôrwiȝe, ȝif he ȝemeteð operne æt his æwum
wife betynedu*m* durum oððe under anre rêon, oððe æt
his dehter æwumborenre, oððe æt his swister borenre
oððe æt his medder ðe wære to æwum wife forȝifen
his fæder.

.XXXVIIII.

43. Eallum frioum monnu*m* ðas daȝas sien forȝifene
butan þeowum monnu*m* ꝸ esne wyrhtan: .XII. daȝas
on ȝehhol ꝸ ðone dæȝ þe crist ðone deofol oferswiðde
ꝸ scs. ȝreȝorius ȝemynd dæȝ ꝸ .VII. daȝas to eastron
ꝸ VII ofer, ꝸ an dæȝ æt sce. petres tide ꝸ sce. paules
ꝸ on bærfeste ða fullan wican ǽr sca. marian mæssan
ꝸ æt eallra haliȝra weorðunȝe anne dæȝ, ꝸ .IIII. wodnes-
daȝas on .IIII. ymbren wicum ðeowum monnum eallum
sien forȝifen þam þe him leofost sie to sellanne æȝ-
hwæt ðæs ðe him æniȝ mon for ȝodes noman ȝeselle
oððe hie on æneȝum hiora hwilsticcu*m* ȝeearniau mæȝen.

42, 3. ȝyf ‖ **42, 4.** after ȝecyþe, ȝyf ‖ **42, 5.** cwæðað ‖ **42, 6.**
lyfað ‖ **42, 7.** oððe æt his swister borenre, written above in E, yet prob.
same hand | sweoster borenre | forȝyfen | XXXVIIII, last I invisible E |
— 42, 7 ends with p. 89 in E — ‖ **43.** forȝyfene | oferswiþde, d above |
weorþun, End of second Ot. fragment, cf. Ap. A.

Continuation of Variants from p. 103.
marian | ænne | .IIII. | .IIII. | forȝifen | leofast | æniȝ man | heora, o above |
ȝeearni-an | maȝen.

42, 3. ær bufan cwædon.   Ʒif he ðonne ðæs mæʒnes næbbe
ðæt he hine inne besitte mæʒe, ride to ðam ealdormen·
7 bidde hine fultumes; ʒif he him fultomian nelle, ride

42, 4. to cyninʒe ær he feohte.   Eac swylce ʒif man becyme on his ʒefân 7 he hine ær þam fæstne ne wite,
ʒif he wille his wæpen syllan, hine man ʒehealde
.XXX. nihta 7 hine his freondum ʒecyðe 7 ʒif he nelle
his wæpen sellan, ðonne mot he feohtan on hine. Ʒif
he wille on hand ʒân 7 his wæpen sellan 7 ʒif hwa
ofer ðæt on hine feohte, ʒylde swa wer swa wite, swa
ðær he ʒewyrce 7 wite ðæt he hæbbe his mæʒ for-

42, 5. worht.   Eac we cweðaþ *þæt* man mote mid his hlaforde feohtan on wiʒe. Ʒif mon on þone hlaford feohte,

42, 6. swa mot se hlaford mid þam men feohtan. Æfter
ðære ilcan wisan man mot feohtan mid his ʒeborenum
mæʒe, ʒif him man on wôh onfeohteð, butan wið his

42, 7. hlaforde, ðæt we ne lyfað,   7 man mot feohtan orwiʒe ʒif he oðerne ʒemeteð mid his æwum wife be-
tynede durum oððe under anre reon, oþþe mid his
dehter æwum borenre, oððe mid his swister æwumborenre, oððe mid his meder þe wære to æwum wife
forʒifen his fæder.

.XXXVllll.

43.   Eallum freo mannum ðas daʒas syn forʒifenne
butan ðeowum mannum 7 esne wyrhtum: .XII. daʒas
on ʒehhol 7 ðone dæʒ ðe crist oferswiðde ðone deofol

*MS. B. 7 scs. ʒreʒorius ʒemynd dæʒ 7 seofon *daʒas to eastron
7 seofen ofer 7 an dæʒ æt sce. petres tide 7 sce.
paules 7 on herfeste ða fullan wucan ær sca. maria
mæssan. And æt ealra haliʒra weorðunʒe an dæʒ 7
feower wodnesdaʒas on feower ymbren wucum ðeowum
mannum eallum synd forʒyfen ðam ðe him leofest sy
to syllanne æʒhwæt ðæs ðe him man for ʒodes naman
ʒesylle oððe heo on æniʒum heora hwilstyccum ʒear-
nian maʒan.

42, 3. 7 above bidde | fultomian, i ab. ‖ 42, 4. 7 he hine, he above |
after ʒecyðe, 7 above ‖ 42, 7. betynede- | anre, n ab. | oððe mid his
swister æwumborenre on margin — cf. note on E. Lamb. has æwum ‖
43. freo- | above ʒehhol, ʒeol | ·seofon ends extract from H, now given
variant from B | eastrum | .VII. | to for æt | tide after paules | hærfest |

.XL.

44.   Heafod wunde to bote, ȝif ða ban beoð butu ðyrel,
44, 1. .XXX. scill. ȝeselle him mon; ȝif ðæt uterre ban bið
þyrel, ȝeselle .XV. scill. to bote.

.XLI.

45.   Gif in feaxe bið wund inces lanȝ, ȝeselle anne
45, 1. scill. to bote; ȝif beforan feaxe bið wund inces lanȝ,
tweȝen scill. to bote.

.XLII.

46.   Gif him mon âslea oþer earo of, ȝeselle .XXX.
46, 1. scill. to bote; ȝif se hlyst oðstande þæt he ne mæȝe
ȝehieran, ȝeselle .LX. scill. to bote.

.XLIII.

47.   Gif mon men eaȝe ofâslea, ȝeselle him mon .LX.
scill. 7 VI. scill. 7 VI. pæninȝas 7 ðriddan dǽl pæninȝes to
47, 1. bote; ȝif hit in ðam heafde sie 7 he noht ȝeseon ne
48. mæȝe mid, stande ðriddan dæl þære bote inne; ȝif
mon oðrum þæt neb ôfaslea, ȝebete him mid .LX. scill.;
49. ȝif mon oðrum ðone toð on foran heafde ôfaslea, ȝebete
49, 1. þæt mid .VIII. scill.; ȝif hit sie se wonȝtoð, ȝeselle
49, 2. .IIII. scill. to bote; monnes tux bið .XV. scill. weorð;
50.   ȝif monnes ceacan mon forslihð, þæt hie beoð fo-
50, 1. rode, ȝebete mid .XV. scill. Monnes cinban, ȝif hit
51. bið toclofen, ȝeselle mon .XII. scill. to bote. Ȝif
52. monnes ðrotbolla bið þyrel, ȝebete mid .XII. scill. Ȝif
monnes tunȝe bið of heafde oþres monnes dædum dôn,
53. þæt biþ ȝelic 7 eaȝan bot; ȝif mon bið on eaxle
wund þæt þæt lið seaw ûtflowe, ȝebete mid .XXX.
54. scill. Ȝif se earm bið forad bufan elmboȝan, þær
55. sculon .XV. scill. to bote. Ȝif ða earm scancan beoð
56. beȝen forade, sio bot bið .XXX. scill.; ȝif se ðuma

---

47. after .LX. scill. at end of line appar. ȝes erased E || 49, 2. tux
bið End of p. 90 in E || 50. ceacan, first c above.

Continuation of Variants from p. 105.

.XV. scll. || 50, 1. Mannes | cinn, last n ab. | .XII. || 51. byð | þyrel |
ȝebete ðæt | .XII. || 52. mannes | dedum | ȝedôn, ȝe ab. | Here 1½ in.
erased in B; prob. þæt bið ȝelic was written twice | eaȝan || 53. man bið
on ða eaxle | ȝewunded, ȝe, ed above | .XXX. || 54. forod | þæm above
el-boȝan | .XV. || 55. .XXX. || 56. se þuma | aslæȝen | sceal, a above |
.XXX.

44.   Heafod wunde to bote, ȝyf ða ban beoð butu þyrle,
44, 1. .XXX. scill. ȝesylle him mon;   ȝyf þæt uttre ban biþ
ðyrl, ȝesylle fihtyne scill. to bote.

45.   Gyf in feaxe bið wund ynces lanȝ, ȝesylle anne
45, 1. scill. to bote;   ȝyf he beforan feaxe bið wund, ynces
lanȝ, tweȝen scillinȝas to bote.

46.   Gyf him man ofaslea þæt oðer eare of, ȝesylle
46, 1. him ðrittiȝ scill. to bote;   ȝyf se lyst ætstande, ðæt
he ne mæȝ ȝehyran, ȝesylle syxti scill. him to bote.

47.   Gyf mon men eaȝe ofaslea, ȝesylle him mon syxti
scill. 7 syx scill. 7 syx peneȝas 7 ðriddam dæl peniȝes
47, 1. to bote;   ȝyf hit in ðan heafde sy 7 he noht ȝeseon
ne mæȝe mîd, stande driddan dæl ðære bote inne.

48.   *Gif mann oðrum þæt nebb ofaslea, ȝebete hit mid*
49.   *feowertiȝ scill.* Gyf man oðrum ðone toð on foren
49, 1. heafde ofslea, ȝebetað þæt mid eahta scill.   Gyf hit sy
49, 2. ðe wonȝtoð, ȝesylle feower scill. to bote;   monnes tux
50. biþ syxtyne scill. weorð.   Gyf man mannes ceacan
forslea, þæt heo beon forede, fiftyne scill. ȝebete.
50, 1.   Monnes cinban ȝyf hit bið toclofen, ȝesylle mon
51. twelf scill. to bote.   Gyf mannes ðrotbolla bið ðyrl,
52. ȝebete mid twelf scill.   Gyf mannes tunȝe bið of
heafde oðres monnes dædum ȝedon, þæt bið ȝelic 7
53. eaȝon bot.   Gyf mon on eaxle bið ȝewunded, þæt
54. þæt liðseaw utflowe, ȝebete mid ðrittiȝ scill.   Gyf
se earm bið forad bufan ðam elboȝan, ðær sculon
55. fiftyne scill. to bote.   Gyf ða earmscancan beoð
56. beȝen forade, seo bot bið ðrittiȝ scill.   Gyf ðe ðuma

---

44. butu beoð | butu þyrle X written over eras. in same hand B |
ðyrle, e ab. | ȝesylle .XXX. scll. him mon ‖ 44, 1. utre | byð | .XV. ‖
45. wund bið ynces | 45, 1. vac. he | .II. ‖ 46. asclea | þæt above oðer |
of well erased B, vac. of H | .XXX. ‖ 46, 1. hlyst | oþstande | mæȝe |
ȝehiran | .LX. scll. him to bote ȝesylle ‖ 47. his eaȝe | .LX. | .VI. | .VI.
peninȝas ‖ 47, 1. on ðam | mæȝe End of p. 23 in B | se þriddan ‖ 48.
from margin of B, new | man | ðfaslea him for hit | .LX. ‖ 49. oþrum of-
aslea on foran heafde ðone toð | ȝebete | .VIII. ‖ 49, 1. wanȝ toþ ȝebete
mid .IIII. scll. ‖ 49, 2. mannes | .XV. ‖ 50. mannes ceacan man | for-
slea, erasure at end B, forslyhð H | hy | forede, last e above | ȝebete mid

56, 1. bið ôfaslæʒen, þam sceal .XXX. scill. to bote. ʒif se
57. næʒl bið ôfasleʒen, ðam sculon .V. scill. to bote. ʒif
     se scytefinʒer bið ôfasleʒen, sio bôt bið .XV. scill.,
58. his næʒles bið .III. scill; ʒif se midlesta finʒer sie
     ôfasleʒen, sio bot bið .XII. scill. 7 his næʒles bot bið
59. .II. scill. ʒif se ʒoldfinʒer sie ôfasleʒen, to þam sculon
     .XVII. scill. to bote, 7 his næʒles .IIII. scill. to bote.
60.   ʒif se lytla finʒer bið ôfasleʒen, ðam sceal to bote
     .VIII. scill. 7 an scill. his næʒles, ʒif se sie ôfasleʒen.
61.   ʒif mon bið on hrif wund, ʒeselle him mon .XXX.
61, 1. scill. to bote. ʒif he ðurhwund bið, æt ʒehweðerum
62. muðe .XX. scill. ʒif monnes ðeoh bið þyrel, ʒeselle
62, 1. him mon .XXX. scill. to bote; ʒif hit forad sie, sio
63. bot eac bið .XXX. scill.; ʒif se sconca bið þyrel be-
63, 1. neoðan cneowe, ðær sculon .XII. scill. to bote. ʒif he
     forad sie beneoðan cneowe, ʒeselle him .XXX. scill.
64. to bote; ʒif sio micle ta bið ôfasleʒen, ʒeselle him
64, 1. .XX. scill. to bote; ʒif hit sie sio æfterre ta, .XV.
64, 2. scill. to bote ʒeselle him mon; ʒif seo midleste ta
64, 3. sie ôfasleʒen, þær sculon .VIIII. scill. to bote; ʒif hit
64, 4. bið sio feorþe ta, ðær sculon .VI. scill. to bote. ʒif
65. sio lytle ta sie ôfasleʒen, ʒeselle him .V. scill. ʒif
     mon sie on þa herðan to ðam swiðe wund þæt he ne
     mæʒe bearn ʒestrienan, ʒebete him ðæt mid .LXXX. scill.
66.   ʒif men sie se earm mid honda mid ealle ofâcorfen
66, 1. beforan elmboʒan, ʒebete ðæt mid .LXXX. scill.; æʒ-
     hwelcere wunde beforan feaxe 7 beforan aliefan 7 bene-
67. oðan cneowe, sio bot bið twy sceatte mare. ʒif sio
     lendenbræde bið forsleʒen, þær sceal .LX. scill. to bote;
67, 1.   ʒif hio bið onbestunʒen, ʒeselle .XV. scill. to bote;
67, 2.   ʒif hio bið ðurhðyrel, ðonne sceal ðær .XXX. scill.

64, 2. midleste ta End of p. 91 in E — || **65.** ʒestrienan from H ||

Continuation of Variants from p. 107.

.XXX. || **64.** miccle, first c above | tâ | ofaslazen | man | .XX. || **64, 1.** ʒif seo æftere tâ sy ofaslæʒen, ʒesylle him man .XV. || **64, 2.** tâ | ofaslæʒen | sculon | .IX. | **64, 3.** tâ | ðær | .VI. || **64, 4.** tâ bið | ofaslæʒen | him.V., vac. mon || **65.** man | herðan | ʒewunded, ʒe, ed above | ʒestrienan for beʒytan | .LXXX. scillinʒum || **66.** after earm, mid handa mid ealle | ofâcorfen | el-boʒan | .LXXX. || **66, 1.** æʒhwylcre | slyfan | bið | twy sceatte mare || **67.** bræde | .LX. || **67, 1.** — onbestunʒen End of p. 25 in B — | .XV. scll. to bote ||

56, 1. bi& ofaslaʒen, &æm sceall &rittiʒ scill. to bote.   Gyf
57.   se næʒel bi& ofaslaʒen, seo bot bi& fif scill.   Gyf se
       scytefinʒer bi& ofaslaʒen, seo bot bi& fiftyne scill. 7
58.   his næʒles beo& .IIII. scill.   Gyf se midleste finʒer
       sy ofaslaʒen, seo bot bi& .XII. scill. 7 his næʒles .II.
59.   scill.   Gyf se ʒoldfinʒer sy ofaslæʒen, to &æm sculon
60.   seofentyne scill. to bote 7 his næʒles .IIII. scill.   Gyf
       se lytle finʒer sy ofaslaʒen, &am sceal to bote niʒon
61.   scill., 7 an scill. his næʒles, ʒyf he sy ofaslaʒen.   Gyf
61, 1. mon rif wund bi&, ʒesylle him mon &rittiʒ scill.   Gyf
62.   he &urhwund bi&, æt æʒ&ran mu&e twentiʒ scill.   Gyf
       monnes &eoh bi& &url, ʒesylle him man &rittiʒ scill. to
62, 1. bote;   ʒyf hit forad sy, seo bot bi& .XXX. scill.
63.   Gyf se scanca bi& &url beneo&an cweowe, &ær
63, 1. sculon twelf scill.;   ʒyf he forad sy beneo&an cnêowe,
64.   ʒesylle him &ritti scill. to bote.   Gyf mycle ta bi&
64, 1. ofaslaʒen, ʒesylle him mon twentiʒ scill. to bote.   Gyf
64, 2. hit sêo æftere tâ sy, fiftene scill. to bote.   Gyf seo
       midlæste tâ sy ofaslaʒen, &ær scylan niʒon scill. to
64, 3. bote.   Gyf hit bi& seo feor&e tâ, &ar sculon syx scill.
64, 4. to bote.   Gyf seo lytle tâ sy ofaslaʒen, ʒesylle him
65.   mon fif scill. to bote.   Gyf mon sy on &a hær&an to
       &an swiþe ʒewundod þæt he ne mæʒe bearn beʒytan,
66.   ʒebete him þæt mid hundeahtatiʒ scill.   Gyf men
       sy se earm ofacoruen beforan elmboʒan, ʒebete þæt
66, 1. mid hundeahtatiʒ scill.;   æʒhwylcere wunde beforan
       feaxe 7 beforan slefan 7 beneo&an cneowe, seo bot
67.   by& twyʒʒylde mare;   ʒyf seo lendenbreda bi& for-
67, 1. slæʒen, þær sceal syxtiʒ scill. to bote.   Gyf heo bi&
       onbestunʒen, fihtene scill.;

56. 1, næʒl | ofaslæʒen, &an sculon. V. scll. to bote | eras. after fif B ||
57. ofaslæʒen | .XV. | bi&. V. || **58.** midlæsta | bi& | ofaslæʒen | næʒles
bot bi& .II. || **59.** bi& for sy | .XVII. | his næʒles III in same hand over
eras. B | .IIII. End of p. 24 in B | scll. to bote || **60.** litla | bi& for
sy | ofaslæʒen | &æm above | sceal, a above | .IX. scll. | he, prob. orig.
hit, B, se H | bi& for sy | ofaslæʒen, .I. scll. | **61.** mon on rife ʒe-
wunded, on, e, ʒe, ed new above B, man bi& on hrife wund H | man |
.XXX. | scll. to bote || **61, 1.** æʒ&rum | .XX. || **62.** mannes | &url, y
stroke new B, þyrel H | .XXX. || **62, 1.** bi& eac | **68.** &url, y stroke
uew B, þyrel H | cneowe | .XII. | scll. to bote || **63, 1.** bi& for sy | man

108

68. to bote. Ʒif mon bi'ð in eaxle wund, ʒebete mid .LXXX.
69. scill., ʒif se mon cwic sie; ʒif mon o'ðrum 'ða hond
     utan forslea, ʒeselle him .XX. scill. to bote, ʒif hine
69, 1. mon ʒelacnian mæʒe; ʒif hio healf on weʒ fleoʒe,
70. þonne sceal .XL. scill. to bote; ʒif mon oþrum rib for-
     slea binnan ʒehaldre hyde, ʒeselle .X. scill. to bote.
70, 1. Ʒif sio hyd sie tobrocen 7 mon ban ôfâdo, ʒeselle
71. .XV. scill to bote. Ʒif monnes eaʒe him mon ôf-
     aslea, o'ð'ðe his hand o'ð'ðe his fot, 'ðær ʒæ'ð ʒelic bot
     to eallum, .VI. pæninʒas 7 .VI. scill. 7 .LX. scill. 7
72. 'ðriddan dæl pæninʒes. Ʒif monnes sconca bi'ð ôf-
     asleʒen wi'ð 'ðæt cneou, 'ðær sceal .LXXX. scill to bote.
73. Ʒif mon o'ðrum 'ða sculdru forslea, ʒeselle him mon
74. .XX. scill. to bote. Ʒif hie mon inbeslea 7 mon ban
75. ôfado, ʒeselle mon 'ðæs to bote .XV. scill. Ʒif mon 'ða
     ʒreatan sinwe forslea, ʒif hie mon ʒelacnian mæʒe
75, 1. þæt hio hal sie, ʒeselle .XII. scill. to bote; ʒif se
     mon healt sie for þære sinwe wunde 7 hine mon ʒe-
76. lacnian ne mæʒe, ʒeselle .XXX. scill. to bote; ʒif 'ða
     smalan sinwe mon forslea, ʒeselle him mon .VI. scill.
77. to bote; ʒif mon o'ðrum 'ða ʒeweald forslea uppe on
     þam sweoran 7 forwundie to þam swi'ðe þæt he naʒe
     þære ʒeweald 7 hwæ'ðre lifie swa ʒescended, ʒeselle
     him mon .C. scill. to bote, buton him witan ryhtre 7
     mare ʒereccan.

.XLIIII.

     Ic ine mid ʒodes ʒife wesseaxna kyninʒ mid
     ʒe'ðeahte 7 mid lare cenredes mines fæder 7 heddes
     mines biscepes 7 eorcenwoldes mines biscepes mid
     eallum minum ealdormonnum 7 þæm ieldstan witum
     minre 'ðeode 7 êac micelre ʒesomnunʒe ʒodes 'ðeowa
     wæs smeaʒende be 'ðære hælo urra sawla 7 be 'ðam

---

76. — ʒif 'ða End of p. 92 in E — |

Continuation of Variants from p. 109.
p. 26 in B — | sweoran | forwundiʒe | 'ðæra | vac. 'ðeah | hwæ'ðere, first e
above | libbe | ʒescynded | him .C. scll., vac. mon | butan | mare ʒereccan
7 ryhtre ‖ **Introd.** Here Ines cyninʒes asetnysse in H | ine appar. over
eras, but old B, yne H | westseaxena, second e above | cænredes | bis-
copes | eorcenwaldes | biscepes | ealder | witum | micelre | ʒesamnunʒe

67, 2. ȝyf heo biÐ ÐurhÐurl, Ðonne sceal Ðrittiȝ scill. to bote.

68.   Gyf mon biÐ on eaxle ȝewundad, ȝebete mid

69.   hundeahta*ti* scill., ȝyf se mon cwic sy. Gyf man on oÐru*m* Ða hand uton forslea, ȝesylle him .XX. scill. to bote. Gyf

69, 1. hine man ȝelacnian mæȝe. Gyf he healf on weȝ fleoȝe,

70.   Ðonne sceal syxtiȝ scill. to bote. Gyf man oÐru*m* ribb forslêa binnan ȝehalre hyde, ȝesylle tyn scill. to bote.

70, 1.   Gyf seo hyd sy tobrocen 7 man ban ofadô, ȝesylle

71.   fiftyne scill. Gyf mon him *eaȝe* ofslêa oþþe his hand oÐÐe his fott, Ðær ȝæÐ ȝelic bot tô eallum, syx peneȝas

72.   7 syx scill. 7 syxtiȝ scill. 7 driddan dæl peniȝes. Gyf mannes sceanca biÐ ofaslaȝen wiÐ þæt cneow, Ðær sceall

73.   hundeahtati scill. to bote. Gyf man oÐru*m* Ða sculdru

74.   forslea, ȝesylle him mon .XX. scill. to bote. Gyf hine mon inbeslêa 7 man ban ofadô, ȝesylle mon Ðæs to bote

75.   fiftyne scill.; ȝyf mon Ða ȝreatan synewe forslêa, ȝyf hine man ȝelacnian mæȝe þæt he hal sy, ȝesylle twelf

75, 1. scill. to bote. Gyf se mon healt sy for Ðære synewe wunde 7 hine mon ȝelacnian ne mæȝe, ȝesylle .XX.

76.   scill. to bote; ȝyf Ða *sma*l*an* synewan man forslêa,

77.   ȝesylle hi*m* man syx scill. to bote. Gyf man oÐrum Ða ȝewald forslêa uppe on Ðam sweore 7 forwundie to Ðam swiÐe þæt he naȝe þær ȝeweald 7 Ðeah hwæÐere lifiȝe swa ȝescend, ȝesylle him mon hund scill. to bote, buton him witan rihtre 7 mare ȝereccan.

    Ic ine mid ȝodes ȝyfe wessexena cyninȝ mid ȝe-Ðeahte 7 mid lare cenredes mines fæder 7 heddes mines bisceopes 7 erconwoldes mines bisceopes 7 mid eallu*m* minu*m* ealdormannu*m* 7 Ðam yldestan witan minre Ðeode 7 eac mycelre somnunȝe ȝodes þeowena

---

67, 2. Ðurl, y stroke new B, þyrel H | sceal, a ab. | þær above .XXX. ||
68. man | ȝewundod, ȝe, od above | hundeahta, ti added new above B,
.LXXX. H | man || 69. utan || 69, 1. heo for he | syxtiȝ, on marg. new
feowertiȝ B, .XL. H || 70. ribb, last b above | .X. || 70, 1. bân | ofadô |
.XV. scll. to bote || 71. eaȝe supplied in an eras. in B, mannes eaȝe him
man ofaslea H | fôt | ȝeÐ | .VI. | .VI. | .LX. | peni-ȝes || 72. scanca |
ofaslæȝen | sceal, a above | .LXXX. || 74. hine, n above | man | bân | ofadô |
.XV. || 75. man | sinwe | ȝelacni-an | he- B, heo H | .XII. || 75, 1. se
above man | sinwe | .XX., on marg. new .XXX. B, .XXX. H || 76. smalan,
s appar. new and l over eras. B | sinwe | .VI. || 77. — oÐrum End of

staþole ures rices þætte ryht æw 7 ryhte cynedomas
ðurh ure folc ʒefæstnode 7 ʒetrymede wæron þætte
næniʒ ealdormonna ne us underʒeðeodedra æfter þam
wære awendende ðas ure dômas.

.XLV.

1.   Ærest we bebeodað þætte ʒodes ðeowas hiora
ryhtreʒol on ryht healdan; æfter þam we bebeodað
þætte ealles folces æw 7 domas ðus sien ʒebealdene.

.XLVI.

2.   Cild binnan ðriteʒum nihta sie ʒefulwad; ʒif hit
swa ne sie, .XXX. scill. ʒebete; ʒif hit ðon*ne* sie dead
butan fulwihte, ʒebete he hit mid eallum ðam ðe he aʒe.

.XLVII.

3.   Ʒif ðeowmon wyrce on sunnandæʒ be his hlafordes bæse, sie he frioh 7 se hlaford ʒeselle .XXX.
3, 1. scill. to wite.   Ʒif þon*ne* se ðeowa butan his ʒe-
3, 2. witnesse wyrce, þolie his hyde; ʒif ðonne se friʒea
ðy dæʒe wyrce butan his hlafordes bæse, ðolie his
freotes.

.XLVIII.

4.   Ciricsceattas sin aʒifene be sce. martines mæssan;
ʒif hwa ðæt ne ʒelæste, sie he scyldiʒ. LX. scill. 7
be .XII.fealdum aʒife þone ciric sceat.

.XLVIIII.

5.   Gyf hwa sie deaðes scyldiʒ 7 he cirican ʒeierne,
5, 1. hæbbe bis feorh 7 bete swa him ryht wisiʒe; ʒif hwa
his hyde forwyrce 7 cirican ʒeierne, sie him sio swin-
ʒelle forʒifen.

.L.

6.   Gif hwa ʒefeohte on cyninʒes huse, sie he scyldiʒ
ealles his ierfes 7 sie on cyninʒes dome, hwæðer he
6, 1. lîf aʒe þe naʒe.   Ʒif hwa on mynster ʒefeohte, .CXX.

Introd. æfter þam wære begins Bu. fragm. (cf. App. B), now given
variant from E | **1.** healden | þæm | ʒehealdenne || **2.** .XXX. | nyhtum |
ʒefullod | buton | þæm || **3.** werce | freoh | **3, 1.** ʒewitnysse || **3, 2.** bu-
ton | vac. his before hlafordes | — 3, 2 ends with p. 93 in E — || **4.** sien |
scildiʒ || **5.** vac. he before cirican | ʒeænne | habbe | wisie || **5, 1.** for-
werce | ʒeirne || **6.** kininʒes | habbe for aʒe ||

Continuation of Variants from p. 111.
preost eras. and new si B || **4.** aʒifene | martines | .LX. | .XII. | aʒife |
ciric | sceatt | **5.** 7 cirican, vac. he. || **5, 1.** ciricean, second i ab. | ʒeirne |
forʒifen || **6.** on cyninʒes huse ʒefeohte | hweþer || **6, 1.** .CXX. ||

wæs smeaʒende be ðære hǽle ure sawla 7 be ðam staðole ures rices *þæt* riht ǽwe 7 rihte cynedomas þurh ure folc ʒefæstnode 7 ʒetrymede wæron *þæt* næniʒ ealdormanna ne us underʒeðeodendra æfter ðem wære awendende ðas ure domas.

1.   Ærest we bebeodað *þæt* ʒodas þeowas heora riht reʒol ʒyman 7 on riht healdon; æfter ðam we beodað *þæt* ealles folces æw 7 domas ðus syn ʒehealdene.

2.   Cild binnan .XXX. nihta sy ʒefullad; ʒyf hit swa ne sy, .XXX. scill. ʒebete; ʒyf hit ðonne sy dead butan fulluhte, ʒebete he hit mid eallum ðam ðe he aʒe.

3.   Gyf ðeowmon wyrce on sunnandæʒ be his hlafordes hæse, sy he freo 7 se hlaford ʒesylle .XXX. scill. to
3, 1. wite; ʒyf þonne se ðeowa butan his ʒewitnysse
3, 2. wyrce, þolie his hyde, oððe hydʒyldes; ʒyf ðonne se friʒea ðy dæʒe wyrce buton his hlafordes hǽse, ðolie his freotes, oððe sixtiʒ scill. 7 preost twyscyldi.

4.   Cyricsceattas syn aʒeuene be sce. martynes mæssan; ʒyf hwa *þæt* ne ʒelæste, sy he scyldiʒ feortiʒ scill. 7 be twelffealdum aʒyfe ðone cyricsceat.

5.   Gyf hwâ sy deaðes scyldiʒ 7 he cyricean ʒeyrne,
5, 1. hæbbe his feorh 7 bete swa him riht wisie; ʒyf hwâ his hyde forwyrce 7 cyricean ʒeyrne. Sy him seo swinʒle forʒyfen.

6.   Gyf hwa ʒefeohte on cyninʒes huse, sy he scyldiʒ ealles his yrfes 7 sy on cyninʒes dome hwæðer he lif
6, 1. aʒe ðe naʒe.   Gyf hwa on mynstre ʒefeohte, hund-

þeowa | þæt, te added above B, ðætte, te above H | ryht | ryhte | ʒetrymede, new m after y at end of line B | þætte, te ab., for þæt (næniʒ) | ealder | þam for ðem   **1.** heora, o ab. | ryht reʒol on riht healden, vac. ʒyman 7 H, found in Lamb. | þætte, te ab., for þæt | ǽw, w erased B, æw H ‖ **2.** Cyld | nihtum | ʒefullod | ʒebete hit, vac. he | âʒe ‖ **3.** man | — dæʒ be End of p. 27 in B — | freob ‖ **3, 1.** ʒewitnesse | on margin oððe hyd ʒyld H, found in Lamb ‖ **3, 2.** friʒea, ʒe above | butan | ðoliʒe | oððe .LX. scll. 7 preost twyscildiʒ on margin H, found in Lamb | after

6, 2. scill. ӡebete;   ӡif hwa on ealdormonnes huse ӡefeohte
oððe on oðres ӡeðunӡenes witan, .LX. scill. ӡebete he

6, 3. 7 oþer .LX. ӡeselle to wite.   Ӡif ðonne on ӡafol-
ӡeldan huse oððe on ӡebures ӡefeohte, .CXX. scill. to

6, 4. wite ӡeselle 7 þam ӡebure .VI. scill.   7 þeah hit sie
on middum felda ӡefohten, .CXX. scill. to wite sie

6, 5. aӡifen. Ӡif ðonne on ӡebeorscipe hie ӡeciden 7 oðer
hiora mid ӡeðylde hit forbere, ӡeselle se oðer .XXX.
scill. to wite.

.LI.

7.   Gif hwa stalie swa his wíf nyte 7 his bearn, ӡe-

7, 1. selle .LX. scill. to wite;   ӡif he ðonne stalie on ӡewitnesse ealles his hiredes, ӡonӡen hie ealle on ðeowot;

7, 2.   .X. wintre cniht mæӡ bion ðiefðe ӡewita.

.LII.

8.   Gif hwa him ryhtes bidde beforan hwelcum scirmen oððe oþrum deman 7 âbiddan ne mæӡe 7 him
wedd sellan nelle, ӡebete .XXX. scill. 7 binnan .VII.
nihton ӡedô hine ryhtes wierðne.

.LIII.

9.   Gif hwa wrace dô ær ðon he him ryhtes bidde,
þæt he him onnime aӡife 7 forӡielde 7 ӡebete mid
.XXX. scill.

.LIIII.

10.   Ӡif hwa binnan þam ӡemærum ures rices reaflâc
7 niednæme dô, aӡife he ðone reaflac 7 ӡeselle .LX.
scill. to wite.

.LV.

11.   Gif hwa his aӡenne ӡeleod bebycӡe ðeowne oððe
friӡne, ðeah he scyldiӡ sie, ofer sæ, forӡielde hine
his were.

.LVL

12.   Gif ðeof sie ӡefonӡen, swelte he deaðe oððe his
lif be his were man aliese.

6, 2. scll. | vac. he after ӡebete || 6, 3. mon for ðonne | ӡafolӡildan |
bure for ӡebure || 6, 4. middan | ӡefeohtan || 6, 5. við on ӡebeor-
scipe || 7, 1. ӡewitnysse | eallæs || 7, 2. beon | þeofðe | ӡewitæ or ӡe-
witte? || 8. hine | wed | mid .XXX. | nyhtum | weorðe || 9. wræce | him
on End of p. 94 in E | forӡylde || 11. bebycӡe | scildiӡ || 12. monna
liese or læse ||

6, 2. twelftiᵹ scill. ᵹebete.   Gyf hwâ in ealdormannes
     huse feohte, oððe on oðres ᵹeðunᵹenes witan, syxtiᵹ
6, 3. scill. ᵹebete hê 7 oðer syxtiᵹ ᵹesylle he to wite.   Gyf
     ðonne on ᵹafolᵹylden huse oððe on ᵹebures ᵹefeohte,
     hundtwelftiᵹ scill. to wite ᵹesylle 7 ðæm ᵹebures syx
6, 4. scill.   7 ðeah hit sy on middan felda ᵹefohtan, hund-
6, 5. twelftiᵹ scill. to wite sy aᵹyfen;   ᵹyf ðonne on ᵹebeor-
     scipe hi ᵹeciden 7 oðer heora mid ᵹeþyldê hit forbere,
     ᵹesylle se oðer .XXX. scill. to wite.
7.   Gyf hwâ staliᵹe swa his wif nyte 7 his bearn,
7, 1. ᵹesylle syxti scill. to wite;   ᵹyf he ðonne stalie on
     ᵹewitnysse ealles his hiredes, ᵹanᵹen heo ealle on
7, 2. ðeowet;   tynwintre cniht mæᵹ beon þyfðe ᵹewita.
8.   Gyf hwa him rihtes bidde beforan hwylcum scirmen
     oððe oðrum deman 7 abiddan ne mæᵹe, 7 him wed
     syllan nylle, ᵹebete .XXX. scill. 7 binnon seofen niht
     ᵹedo hine rihtes wyrðe.
9.   Gyf hwa wrace dô ær ðon he him rihtes bidde,
     þæt he him onnime aᵹyfe 7 forᵹylde 7 bete .XXX. scill.
10.   Gyf hwa binnan ðam ᵹemærum ures rices reaflac
     7 nydnæme dô, aᵹyfe he ðone reaflac 7 ᵹesylle syxti
     scill. to wite.
11.   Gyf hwa his aᵹene leodan bebicᵹe ðeowne oððe
     friᵹe, þeah he scyldiᵹ sy, ofer sǽ, forᵹylde hine be
     his wêre.
12.   Gyf ðeof sy ᵹefonᵹen, swylte he deaðe oððe his
     lif be his were mon alyse.

6, 2. on for in | ealder | huse oððe on oþres witan ᵹeþunᵹenan
ᵹefeohte, .LX. | oþer .LX. to wite, vac. ᵹesylle he ‖   6, 3. ᵹafolᵹildan |
.CXX. | ᵹebure | .VI. ‖   6, 4. ᵹefeohten on middan felda, ᵹefeohten, first
e above | .CXX. | aᵹifen ‖   6, 5. ᵹyf End of p. 28 in B | hy | .XXX. to
wite, scll. on marg. | 7. hit nyte, hit ab. | .LX. ‖   7, 1. ᵹewitnesse |
hyredes | ᵹân- | hy ‖   7, 2. .X. wintra ¦ beon above ‖   8. ryhtes |
vac. oðrum | 7 him ryht abiddan | wedd, last d above | nelle ¦ ᵹebete above
.XXX. | binnan | .VII. | nihtum | ᵹedô ‖   9. dô | ær he, vac. ðon | ryhtes ¦
aᵹife | forᵹilde | ᵹebete ‖   10. reaflac 7 nydnæme binnan þam ᵹemærum
ures rices ᵹedo | aᵹife | after aᵹyfe eras. in B | .LX. ‖   11. aᵹenne | leod
above | ᵹebycᵹe | friᵹne, 7 before ofer, sende after sǽ new in B, 7 ofer
sǽ ᵹesylle H | forᵹilde | 7 wið ᵹodd deoplice bete on marg. B, also
Lamb ‖   12. ᵹefanᵹen | vac. mon ‖

.LVII.

13.   Gif hwa beforan biscepe his ʒewitnesse 7 his wed
13, 1. aleoʒe, ʒebete mid .CXX. scill.;   ðeofas we hatað oð
.VII. men, from .VII. hloð oð .XXXV., siððan bið here.

.LVIII.

14.   · Se ðe bloþe betyʒen sie, ʒeswicne se hine be .CXX.
hida oððe swa bete.

.LVIIII.

15.   Se ðe hereteama betyʒen sie, he hine be his
15, 1. werʒilde âliese oððe be his were ʒeswicne;   se að
15, 2. sceal bion healf be huslʒenʒum;   þeof siððan he bið
on cyninʒes bende, nah he þa swicne.

.LX.

16.   Se ðe ðeof ofslihð, se mot ʒecyðan mid aðe þæt
he hine synniʒne ofsloʒe, nalles ða ʒeʒildan.

.LXI.

17.   Se ðe forstolen flæsc findeð 7 ʒedyrneð, ʒif he
dear, he mot mid aðe ʒecyðan þæt he hit aʒe; se
ðe hit ofspyreð, he ah ðæt meldfeoh.

.LXII.

18.   Cierlisc mon ʒif he ôft betyʒen wære, ʒif he æt
siðestan sie ʒefonʒen, slea mon hond oððe fot.

.LXIII.

19.   Cyninʒes ʒeneat ʒif his wer bið twelf hund scill., he
mot swerian for syxtiʒ hida, ʒif he bið huslʒenʒea.

.LXIIII.

20.   Gif feorcund mon oððe fremde butan weʒe ʒeond
wudu ʒonʒe 7 ne hrieme ne horn blawe, for ðeof he
bið to profianne oððe to sleanne oððe to âliesanne.

.LXV.

21.   Gif mon ðonne þæs ôfslæʒenan weres bidde, he
mot ʒecyþan þæt he hine for ðeof ofsloʒe, nalles þæs

---

13. biscope | hundtwelftiʒum ‖ **13, 1.** with 14 as .LVIII., so also in
H | hatað .VII. men, vac. oð ‖ **14.** he for se ‖ **15.** teame | betiʒen | wereʒilde | **15, 1.** byon ‖ **15, 2.** with 16 as .LX., so also in H | kininʒes |
swycne ‖ **16.** ofslehð | he for se | ʒeceþan mid aþe | þa (for þam?) ʒeʒildanum ‖ **17.** ʒederneð | ofspereð ‖ **18.** Cirlisc | betwyʒen ‖ **19.** sweriʒen |
sixtiʒ | huslʒenʒa | 19 ends with p. 95 in E ‖ **20.** forcund | buton | hrime |
lesanne ‖ **21.** ðeofðe for ðeof | ofslæʒenan ‖

13.   Gyf hwâ beforan bisceope his ȝewitnysse 7 his
13, 1. wcd aleoȝe, ȝebete mid hundtwelftiȝ scill.; þeofas we
batað oð seofen m*en*, *from* seofon hloð, oð fif an-
ðrittiȝ here.

14.   Se ðe bloðe betoȝen sy, ȝeclensie se hine be hund-
twelftiȝu*m* bida oððe swa ȝebete.

15.   Se ðe hereteama betoȝen sy, hine be his werȝylde
15, 1. alyse, oððe be his *were* ȝeclænsie; se að sceal beon
15, 2. *half* be huslȝenȝum; þeof syððan he hið on cyninȝes
bendum, nah he ða ȝeswicne.

16.   Se ðe ðeof ofslihð, se mot ȝecyþan mid aðe *þæt*
he hine scyldiȝ ofslôȝe, nalles ða ȝyldan.

17.   Se ðe forstolen flæsc findeð 7 ȝedyrneð, ȝyf he
dear, he mot mid aþe ȝecyðan *þæt* he hit âȝe; se þe
hit ofspyrað, he ah *þæt* meldfeoh.

18.   Cyrlisc mon ȝyf he oft betoȝen wære, ȝyf he æt
siþestan sy ȝefanȝen, slêa mân hand oððe fôt of.

19.   Cyninȝes ȝeneat ȝyf his wer bið twelf hund scill.,
he mot swerian for sixti bida, ȝyf he bið huslȝenȝa.

20.   Gyf feorcuman man oððe fremde butan weȝe ȝe
on wudu ȝonde 7 ne ryme ne horn blawe, for ðeof
he bið to profianne oððe to alysenne.

21.   Gyf man ðonne ðæs ofslæȝenan weres bidde, he
mot ȝecyþan *þæt* he hine for þeof ofsloȝe, nalæs ðæs

13. biscope | his above ȝewitnesse | wedd | ȝebete End of p. 29 in
B | **18,1.** with 14 as .LVIII., so also in Bu | þeofas, Ð new over
þ, B | seo erased bef. seofen B | fram seofon mannum hloð oþ
.XXXV. | 7 syððan, after fif anðrittiȝ, new B, siððan bið here H |' **14.**
ȝeswicne for ȝeclensie | .CXX. | oððe bete swa ‖ **15.** hereteame |
before hine new he above eras. B, he hine H | wereȝilde | þam uew over
his B, were from H | ȝeswicne for ȝeclænsie ‖ **15,1.** half new above
B, healf H ‖ **15,2.** with 16 as .LX., so also in Bu | þeof, Ð new over
þ, B :' **16.** synniȝne for scyldiȝ | nallæs ða ȝeȝildan ‖ **17.** ȝedirneð |
ofspyreð | **18.** Ciorlisc | man | of, t added uew B, oft H | siðmestan,
m above | sî | hand of oððe fot ‖ **19.** .CXX. | sweriȝan | .LX. ‖ **20.**
feorcund | ȝeond for ȝe on | ȝonde, d made new into ȝ, B, ȝanȝe H |
bryme | profianne oððe to sleanne oþþe | alysanne, a above | alysenne End
of p. 30 in B ‖ **21.** nallæs | ofslaȝenan | ȝeȝildan ‖

21, 1. ofslezenan zezildan ne his hlaford. Ʒif he hit ðonne
dierneð 7 weorðeð ymb lonʒ yppe, ðonne rymeð he
ðam deadan to ðam aðe þæt hine moton his mæzas
unsynzian.

.LXVI.

22.   Gif ðin zeneat stalie 7 losie ðe, ʒif ðu hæbbe
byrzean, mana þone þæs anzyldes;   ʒif he næbbe,
zyld ðu þæt anzylde 7 ne sie him no ðy ðinzodre.

.LXVII.

23.   Gif mon elðeodizne ôfslea, se cyninz ah twædne
23, 1. dæl weres, þriddan dæl sunu oððe mæzas.   Ʒif he
23, 2. ðonne mæzleas sie, healf kyninze, healf se zesið.   Ʒif
hit ðonne abbod sie oððe abbodesse, dælen on þa
23, 3. ilcan wisan wið þone kyninz;   wealhzafolzelda .CXX.
scill., his sunu .C., ðeowne .LX., somhwelcne fiftezum,
weales byd twelfum.

.LXVIII.

24.   Gif witeðeow enzliscmon hine forstalie, hô hine
24, 1. mon 7 ne zylde his hlaforde;   ʒif hine mon ofslêa,
ne zylde hine mon his mæzum, ʒif hie hine on .XII.
24, 2. monðum ne âliesden;   wealh ʒif he hafað .V. hida,
he bið syxhynde.

.LXVIIII.

25.   Gif ciepemon uppe on folce ceapie, do þæt beforan
25, 1. zewitnessum;   ʒif ðiefefíoh mon æt ciepan befo 7
he hit næbbe beforan zodum weotum zeceapod, zecyðe
hit be wite þæt he ne zewita ne zestala nære oððe
zielde to wite .VI. 7 .XXX. scill.

.LXX.

26.   To fundes cildes fostre, ðy forman zeare zeselle
.VI. scill., ðy æfterran .XII., ðy driddan .XXX., siððan
be his wlite.

21, 1. vac. ðonne | dirneð | wierðeð | remeð | þæm | þæm (aðe) | mæzes |
unsinzian || 22. habbe | berzan | manna | anzeldes | zeld | anzelde || 23.
kininz | mæzes End of Bu fragm. (cf. App. B.) || 25 and 25, 1. i in zewit-
nessum, e in beforan and e in þæt he, all at end of lines, dim || 25, 1.
.XXX. scill. ends p. 96 in E ||

- -
Continuation of Variants from p. 117.
tor ne wite | zilde | .VI. || 26. ðu, new y stroke B, ðy H | .VI. | 7 ðy
æfteran zeare .XII. | 7 þy | .XX. | 7 siððan ||

21, 1. ofslæᵹenan ᵹyldan, ne his hlaford;   ᵹyf he hit þonne
dyrneð 7 weorðeð emb lonᵹ yppe, ðonne rymeð he
ðam deadan to ðam aðe þæt hine moton maᵹos
unsynᵹian.

22.   Gyf ðin ᵹeneat stalie 7 losiᵹe ðe, ᵹyf ðu hæbbe
borᵹas, mana ðone ðæs anᵹyldas; ᵹyf he næbbe, ᵹyld
ðu þæt anᵹylde 7 ne sy him na þe ᵹeðinᵹodre.

23.   Gyf mon ælþeodiᵹne mon ofslea, se cynᵹ ah
tweᵹeu dælas þæs weres, ðriddan dæl sunu oððe maᵹas;
23, 1.   ᵹyf he ðonne mæᵹleas sy, half cyninᵹ, half se
23, 2. ᵹesið. Gyf hit ðonne abbud sy oððe abbudisse, dælon
23, 3. on ða ilcan wisan wið ðonne cyninᵹ. Wealhᵹafol-
ᵹylda hundtwelftiᵹ scill., his sunu hund, ðeow sextiᵹ
scill. Somhwylcne mid fiftiᵹ, weales hid mid twelfum.

24.   Gyf witeðeow enᵹliscmon hine forstalie, hô hine
24, 1. mon 7 ne ᵹylde his blaforde. Gyf hine mon ofslea,
ne ᵹylde hine man his maᵹum, ᵹyf hy hine on twelf
24, 2. monðum ne alysdon. Wealh ᵹyf he hæfð fif hida,
he bið syxhynde.

25.   Gyf cepeman uppe on folce ceapiᵹe, do þæt beforan
25, 1. ᵹewitnysse. Gyf ðeof mon feoh æt cyp men befô 7
he hit næbbe beforan ᵹodum witum ᵹeceapod, ᵹecyðe
hit be wite þæt he ne wite ne ᵹestala nære oððe
ᵹylde to wite syx 7 .XXX. scill.

26.   To fundenes cyldes fostre, ðu forman ᵹeare, ᵹesylle
syx scill., ðu æftran twelf, ðu þriddan .XXX., syððan
be his wlite.

21, 1. dirneð | wurð | ymbe, e above | lanᵹe | his before maᵹos and
a above o new B, his maᵹas unscyldiᵹne ᵹedôn H || 22. staliᵹe |
byrᵹean, e ab. | anᵹyldes | ᵹild | ᵹeðinᵹrode || 23. man first | cyninᵹ |
dælas þæs weres, as þæs ab. || 23, 1. mæᵹleas, a ab. | healf | cyninᵹe | healf ||
23, 2. ðone bef. cyninᵹ || 23, 3. .CXX. | red above eras. after hund, so
ne after ðeow B, .C. þeowne .LX. H | eras. aft. sextiᵹ B || 24. ænᵹliscman |
hô | man || 24, 2. byþ | hinde | syxhynde End of p. 31 in B || 25. ceap-
man || uppe above | dô | beforan ᵹewitnesse, foran ᵹe above || 25, 1. ðeof
erased, before feoh forstolen supplied new on marg., men new above
eras. B, ᵹif man forstolen feoh æt ceap men befô, ap above H | na ᵹewita

118

.LXXI.

27.   Se ðe dearnenʒa bearn ʒestrieneð 7 ʒehileð, nah se his deaðes wer, ac his hlaford 7 se cyninʒ.

.LXXII.

28.   Se ðeof ʒefehð ah .X. scill., 7 se cyninʒ ðone ðeof,

28, 1.   7 þa mæʒas him swerian aðas unfæhða; ʒif he ðonne oðierne 7 oriʒe weorðe, þonne bið he wites scyldiʒ;

28, 2.   ʒif he onsacan wille, do he ðæt be ðam fêo 7 be ðam wite.

.LXXIII.

29.   Ʒif mon sweordes onlæne oðres esne 7 he losie, ʒielde he hine ðriddan dæle; ʒif mon spere selle, healfne; ʒif he horses onlæne, ealne he hine ʒylde.

.LXXIIII.

30.   Gif mon cierliscne monnan flieman feorme teo, be his aʒnum were ʒeladiʒe he hine; ʒif he ne mæʒe, ʒielde hine his aʒne were 7 se ʒesiðmon swa be his were.

.LXXV.

31.   Gif mon wîf ʒebyccʒe 7 sio ʒyft forð ne cume, aʒife þæt feoh 7 forʒielde 7 ʒebete þam byrʒean swa his borʒbryce sie.

.LXXVI.

32.   Gif wilisc mon hæbbe hide londes, his wer bið .CXX. scill.; ʒif he þonne healfes hæbbe, .LXXX. scill.; ʒif he næniʒ hæbbe, .LX. scillinʒa.

.LXXVII.

33.   Cyninʒes horswealh, se ðe him mæʒe ʒeærendian, ðæs werʒield bið .CC. scill.

.LXXVIII.

34.   Se ðe on ðære fore wære þæt mon monnan ofsloʒe, ʒetriewe hine ðæs sleʒes 7 ða fore ʒebete be

34, 1.   ðæs ofsleʒenan werʒielde; ʒif his werʒield sie .CC. scill., ʒebete mid .L. scill. 7 ðy ilcan ryhte do man be ðam deorborenran.

34, 1. ðy ilcan End of p. 97 in E ‖

Continuation of Variants from p. 119.

n added B, man H | eras. bef. ofsloʒe | ʒetwywie, new r above B, ʒetriwe H | sleʒes 7 þa fore | ofslæʒnan | werʒylde,old l above r B, were H ‖ 34, 1. his, s over eras. B | werʒild | .CC. | .L. | ylcan | ryhte | dô | man, new n ab. B ‖

27.   Se ðe dearnunᵹa bearn ᵹestreonað 7 ᵹeheleð, nah
se his deaðes wêr, ac his blaford 7 se cynᵹ.

28.   Se ðe ðeof ᵹefehð, he ah tyn scill., 7 se cyninᵹ
ðone ðeof 7 ða maᵹas him swerian aðas unfæðða;

28, 1.   ᵹif he ðonne oðerna 7 oriᵹe weorðe, ðonne bið he

28. 2. wites scyldiᵹ;   ᵹyf he ætsacan wylle, do he þæt be
ðam feo 7 be ðam wite.

29.   Gyf mon sweordes onlæne oðrum esne 7 hit losiᵹe,
be ðriddan dæle he hit ᵹylde. Gyf mon spere sylle,
healfne; ᵹyf mon hors onlæne, ealne he hine ᵹylde.

30.   Gyf man cyrliscne mannan flyman feormienne têo,
be his aᵹenon were ᵹeladiᵹe hine; ᵹyf he ne mæᵹe,
ᵹylde he hine be his aᵹenum were 7 se ᵹesiþmon eac
swâ be his were.

31.   Gyf mon wif bycᵹe 7 seo ᵹyft forð ne cume, aᵹyfe
þæt feoh 7 forᵹylde 7 ᵹebête ðam byrᵹean swa his
borhbryce sy.

32.   Gyf wylisc man hæbbe hide landes, his wer bið
hundtwelftiᵹ scill.; ᵹyf he ðonne healfe hæbbe,
hundeahtati scill.; ᵹyf he næbbe nan land, sixti scill.

33.   Cyninᵹes horswealh, se ðe him mæᵹ ᵹeerendian,
ðæs werᵹyld bið twa hund scill.

34.   Se ðe on ðere fore wære ðær mon mon ofsloᵹe,
ᵹetwywie hine ðæs slæᵹes oððe fore ᵹebete be þæs

34, 1. ofslæᵹenan werᵹylde; ᵹyf his werᵹyld sy twa hund
scill., ᵹebete mid fiftiᵹ scill. 7 ða ilcan rihte dô man be
ðam deorborenran.

---

27. ᵹestryn-ð | cyninᵹ ‖ **28.** .X. | unfehþa ▌ **28, 1.** oðerna, so
new above B, oþyrne H | orriᵹe, first r above ‖ **28, 2.** onsacan | wille |
dô | were ab. and for feo ‖ **29.** man | oþres | êsne | 7 he | ᵹilde he hine ðriddan
dæle | man | healfne dæl hine ᵹilde, dæl above | man | horses | læne |
ᵹilde ‖ **80.** cierliscne | mannan, an erased B, man H | feormienne, nᵹe
new above enne B, feormie H | 7 hine man teo | aᵹenum | ᵹeladie | he
new above B, he hine H | ᵹilde | he above | be above | aᵹeuan, n ab. |
ᵹesiðman | eac above | were End of p. 32 in B ▌ **81.** man | ᵹift | aᵹife |
forᵹilde | byrᵹean, attempt to make o over y, on marg. borᵹan new B ‖
82. wilisc | .CXX. | healfes | .LXXX. | næniᵹ næbbe, .LX. scillinᵹa ‖
88. ᵹeærndi-an | ðes wereᵹild is .CC. hund scll., eᵹild above ‖ **84.**
þe above | þære | fôre | ðæt for ðær | man | mon (second), o into a and

.LXXVIIII.

35.   Se ðe ðeof slihð, he mot aðe zecyðan þæt he hine
flondne for ðeof sloze, 7 þæs deadan mæzas him
swerian unceasea âð; zif he hit þonne dierne 7 sie eft
35, 1. yppe, þonne forzielde he hine. Zif mon to þam men
feoh zeteme ðe his ær oðswaren hæfde 7 eft oðswerian
wille, oðswerize be ðam wite 7 be ðæs feos weorðe;
zif he oðswerian nylle, zebete þone mænan að twybote.

.LXXX.

36.   Se ðe ðeof zefehð oððe him mon zefonzenne azifð
7 he hine þonne âlæte oððe þa ðiefðe zedierne, for-
36, 1. zielde þone þeof his were;   zif he ealdormon sie,
ðolie his scire buton him kyninz arian wille.

.LXXXI.

37.   Se cirlisca mon se ðe oft betyzen wære ðiefðe 7
þonne æt siðestan synnizne zefð in ceape oððe elles
æt openre scylde, slea him mon hond ôf oððe fôt.

.LXXXII.

38.   Gyf ceorl 7 his wif bearn hæbben zemæne 7 fere
se ceorl forð, hæbbe sio modor hire bearn 7 fede;
azife hire mon .VI. scill. to fostre, cu on sumera, oxan
on wintra; healden þa mæzas þone frumstol oð ðæt
hit zewintred sie.

.LXXXIII.

39.   Gif hwa fare unâliefed fram his hlaforde oððe on
oðre scire hine bestele 7 hine mon zeahsize, fare þær
he ær wæs 7 zeselle his hlaforde .LX. scill.

.LXXXIIII.

40.   Ceorles worðiz sceal beon wintres 7 sumeres betyned; zif he bið untyned 7 recð his neahzebures ceap
in on his azen zeat, nah he æt þam ceape nan wuht,
adrife hine ut 7 ðolie æfwerdlan.

ðõe in oððe and (next it) LXX dim, XIII gone, below it e of zeahsize
gone, below this all but L of LXXXIIII dim ‖   **40.** ed zif and azen
dim | ut, clearer, ends p. 98 in E ‖

Continuation of Variants from p. 121.
wurðiz | wyntres | receþ | neahzebures ceap on his azen zeat in | ceape ab. |
nanwuht | hit for hine | æfwyrdlan ‖

35.   Se ðe ðeof slihþ, he mot mid aðe ʒecyðan þæt he hine fleondne for ðeof sloʒe, 7 ðes deadan maʒas him swerian unceases að. Gyf he hit ðonne dyrne 7

35, 1. sy eft yppe, ðonne forʒylde he hine; ʒyf mon to ðæm men feoh ʒetême þe his ætsworen hæfde 7 eft ætswerian wylle, sweriʒe be ðam wite 7 be ðæs feos wyrðe; ʒyf he ætswerian nylle, ʒebete ðone mænan að twyʒbote.

36.   Se ðe ðeof ʒefehð oððe him mon ʒefonʒene aʒyfð 7 he hine ðonne alæte oððe ða þyfþe ʒedyrne, forʒylde

36, 1. ðone ðeof be his were. Gyf he ealdorman sy, ðolie his scire, buton him cyninʒ arian wylle.

37.   Se ceorlisce man se ðe oft betoʒen were ðyfðe 7 ðonne æt siþestan synninʒne ʒefð in ceace oððe elles æt openre scylde, slea him mon handa of oððe fot.

38.   Gyf ceorl 7 his wîf bearn hæbben ʒemǽne 7 fære se ceorl forð, hæbbe seo modor hire bearn 7 fede; aʒyfe hire man syx scill. to fostre, cû on sumera, oxan on wintran; healdan ða maʒas ðone frumstol, oð þæt hit ʒewintrod sy.

39.   Gyf hwâ fare unalyfede fram his laforde, oððe on oðre scire hine bestele 7 hine man ʒeacsize, fare ðær he ær wæs 7 ʒylde his laforde syxtiʒ scill.

40.   Ceorles worði sceal beon wintres 7 sumeres betyned: ʒyf he bið untyned 7 recð his nehhebures ceap in on his aʒen ʒeat, nah he æt ðam ceape nan riht, adrife

---

35. mot aþe, vac. mid | fleonde | ðæs | unceastes | að | forʒilde ‖ **85, 1.** man | ær oþsworen | oðswerian | wille | oþswerie for sweriʒe | ʒif he þonne oþ-sweri-an nylle | twybote ‖ **36.** fehð | mon End of p. 33 in B | ʒefanʒenne | aʒifð | ða, a ab. | ʒedirne | forʒilde ‖ **36, 1.** ealderman | þoliʒe | bntan | se cyninʒ | wille ‖ **37.** ciorlisca | man þe | wære | þifðe | siðestan cyrre | synniʒne | man ʒefð | in ceace oþþe scylde elles | man hand oððe fot, vac. of ‖ **88.** ciorl | 7 se ciorl forðfære | moder | 7 above aʒife | man hire | .VI. | cû | wintra | healden | ʒewintred ‖ **39.** unalyfed | hlaforde | ʒeaxie | þær above he | wæs ær | ʒesylle for ʒylde | hlaforde | .LX. ‖ **40.** Ciorles |

.LXXXV.

41.   Borȝes mon môt oðsacan, ȝif he wât þæt he ryht deð.

.LXXXVI.

42.   Gif ceorlas ȝærstun hæbben ȝemænne oððe oþer ȝedâlland to tynanne 7 hæbben sume ȝetyned hiora dæl, sume næbben, 7 etten hiora ȝemænan æceras oððe ȝærs, ȝân þa þonne þe ðæt ȝeat aȝan 7 ȝebete þam oðrum þe hiora dæl ȝetynedne hæbben þone æwerdlan þe ðær ȝedon sie, abidden him æt þam ceape swylc

42, 1. ryht swylce hit kyn sie; ȝif þonne hryðera hwelc sie þe heȝas brece 7 ȝa in ȝehwær 7 se hit nolde ȝehealdan se hit aȝe oððe ne mæȝe, nime se hit on his æcere mete 7 ôfslea 7 nime se aȝenfriȝea his fel 7 flæsc 7 þolie þæs oðres.

.LXXXVII.

43.   Ðonne mon beam on wuda forbærne 7 weorðe yppe on þone ðe hit dyde, ȝielde he fulwite, ȝeselle

43, 1. .LX. scill., forþam þe fŷr bið þeof; ȝif mon afelle on wuda welmoneȝa treowa 7 wyrð eft undierne, forȝielde .III. treowu ælc mid .XXX. scill.; ne ðearf he hiora mâ ȝeldan, wære hiora swa fela swa hiora wære, forþon sio æsc bið melda, nalles ðeof.

.LXXXVIII.

44.   Gif mon þonne aceorfe an treow þæt mæȝe .XXX. swina underȝestandan 7 wyrð undierne, ȝeselle .LX.

44, 1. scill.; ȝafolhwitel sceal bion æt hiwisce .VI. pæninȝa weorð.

.LXXXVI*III*.

45.   Burȝbryce mon sceal betan .CXX. scill. kyninȝes 7 biscepes þær his rice bið, ealdormonnes .LXXX. scill., cyninȝes ðeȝnes .LX. scill., ȝesiðcundes monnes landhæbbendes .XXXV., 7 bi ðon ansacan.

43, 1. LXXXVIII, III not in Ms.

Continuation of Variants from p. 123.

o above | forðon | æx ‖ **44.** man | .XXX. | wyrð | undirne | .LX. ‖ **44, 1.** — hwitel End of p. 35 in B — | sceal beon æt hiwisce, a ab. | .VL | peninȝa | wyrð ‖ **45.** sceal, a above | mid .CXX. | Cininȝes, attempt to change C to c, B | biscepes | Ealder | .LXXX. | ðeȝnes | .LX. | .XXXV. : bið ofsacan, new am to make bi ðam B, byþ on ansacan H ‖

41. hine ut 7 ðolie ðone æfwyrlan. *Borges* mon mot ætsacan, ʒyf he wat *þæt* he riht deð.

42. Gyf ceorlas habban ʒærstun ʒemæne oþþe oðer ʒedalland to tynanne 7 hæbben sume ʒetyned heora dæl, sume næbben, 7 etten heora ʒemænan æceras oððe ʒærs, ʒan ða ðonne þe *þæt* ʒeat aʒon 7 ʒebeten ðæm oðrum ðe heora dæl ʒetynedne hæbben ðone æfwyrdlan, ðe ʒær ʒedon sy, abiddon heom æt ðam ceape swylc

42, 1. riht swylce hit cyn sy. Gyf ðonne hryðera hwylc sy ðe beʒas brece 7 ʒa in ʒehwær 7 se hit nolde ʒehealdan se hit aʒe oððe ne mæʒe, nime se ðe hit on his æcere ʒemete 7 ofslea 7 nime se aʒenfriʒa his flæsc 7 ðolie ðæs oðres.

43. Ðonne mon beam on wuda forbærne 7 wyrðe yppe on ðone ðe hit dyde, ʒylde he fulwite, ʒesylle syxtig

43, 1. scill., forðam ðe fyr bið ðeof. Gyf mon afylle on wuda *well* maneʒa treowe 7 wurð *þæt* eft undyrne, forʒylde ðreo treowa ælc mid ðrittiʒ scill; ne ðearf he heora ma ʒyldan, wære heora swa feola swa heora wære, forðan seo eax bið melda, nalæs ðeof.

44. Gyf mon ðonne aceorfe an treow *þæt* mæʒe ðrittiʒ swina understandan 7 wurð undyrne, ʒesylle syxtiʒ

44, 1. scill. Gafolhwitel æt hiwisce sceal beon syx peneʒa wurð.

45. Burhbryce man sceal betan hundtwelftiʒ scill. Cyninʒes 7 bisceopes, ðær his rice bið. Ealdormannes hundeahtatiʒ scill. Cyninʒes ðeʒnas syxti scill. Gesiðcundes mannes landhæbbendes fif 7 .XXX. scill. 7 bið ofsacan.

---

41. Second diff. in chapters from EH (cf. XXXV) | orʒes, *B* new above, B, Borʒes H | man | — deð End of p. 34 in B — ‖ **42.** ciorlas | ʒærstûn habban | al. ʒedal land above to tyn-nanne | nabben | ʒân | ðam | heora, o above | betyned- | habben | ðonne, first n above | ʒedôn | aft. sy new 7 ab. B | abidden | heom, o ab. | swylc cynn sy, vac. hit ‖ **42,1.** hriðera, e ab. | ʒehwilc | ðæt for ðe | ʒa ʒehwær in | ʒehealden, ʒe ab. | se þe hit, þe ab. | flæcs | ðoliʒe‖ **43.** man | wurðe | ʒilde | fulwite, second l new and small B, fullwite, second l ab. H | .LX.‖ **43, 1.** well new over eras. B, welmaniʒe H | treowa wyrð eft, vac. þæt | forʒilde | .XXX. | he nan mâ ʒildan | heora, feola, heora,

9*

124

XC.

46. Ðonne mon monnan betybð *þæt* he ceap forstele
oððe forstolenne ʒefeormie, *þonne* sceal he be .LX. bida

46, 1. onsacan þære þiefðe, ʒif he aðwyrðe bið; ʒif ðonne
enʒlisc onstal ʒa forð, onsace *þonne* be twyfealdum;
ʒif hit ðon*ne* bið wilisc onstal, ne bið se að na ðy

46, 2. mara; ælc mon mot onsacan frymþe 7 werfæhðe,
ʒif he mæʒ oððe dear.

.XCI.

47. Gif mon forstolenne ceap befehð, ne mot hine mon
tieman to ðeowum men.

.XCII.

48. Gif hwelc mon bið witeðeow niwan ʒeðeowad 7
hine mon betybð *þæt* he hæbbe ǽr ʒeðiefed ǽr hine
mon ʒeðeowode, þon*ne* ah se teond ane swinʒellan
æt him; bedrife hine to swinʒum be his ceape.

.XCIII.

49. Gif mon on his mæstenne unaliefed swin ʒemete,

49, 1. ʒenime þonne .VI. scill. weorð wed; ʒif hie *þonne*
þær næren oftor *þonne* æne, ʒeselle scill. se aʒenfriʒea
7 ʒecyðe *þæt* hie þær oftor ne comen be þæs ceapes

49, 2. weorðe; ʒif hi ðær tuwa wæren, ʒeselle tweʒen .scill.;

49, 3. ʒif mon nime æfesne on swynum, æt þryfinʒru*m*
þæt ðridde, æt twyfinʒrum *þæt* feorðe, æt þymelum
þæt fifte.

.XCIIII.

50. Gif ʒesiðcund mon þinʒað wið cyninʒ oððe wið
kyninʒes ealdormonnan for his inhiwan oððe wið his
hlaford for ðeowe oððe for friʒe, nab he þær nane
witerædenne, se ʒesið, forðon he hi*m* nolde ǽr yfles
ʒestieran æt ham.

XCV.

51. Gif ʒesiðcund mon landaʒende forsitte fierd, ʒeselle
.CXX. scill. 7 ðolie his landes, unlandaʒende .LX. scill.,
cierlisc .XXX. scill. to fierdwite.

---

46. oððe for End of p. 99 in E |

Continuation of Variants from p. 125.

first e in yfeles ab. || **51.** mann, second n ab. | .CXX. | þoliʒe | Landaʒende .LX.
scillinʒa | Ceorlisc, o ab. | .XXX., vac. scill. | wite, ferd new ab. B, fyrdwite H ||

46.   Ðonne mon mon betyhð *þæt* he ceap forstæle oððe
forstolene ʒefeormie, ðonne sceal he be syxti hida

46, 1. ætsacan ðære ðeofðe, ʒyf he andwyrde bið. Gyf ðonne
enʒlisc mon stalað, ʒa forð ætsace be twyfealdu*m*; ʒyf
hit ðonne *biþ wylisc* onstal, ne bið se að na ðe mare;

46, 2.   ælc man mot ætsacan fyrmðe 7 werfæhðe, ʒyf he
mæʒe oððe dêar.

47.   Gyf mon forstolene ceap befehð, ne mot hine mon
tymon to ðeowan men.

48.   Gyf hwylc mon bið witeðeow niwan ʒeþeowad
7 hine mon betyh *þæt* he hæbbe ær ʒeðeofad ær hine
mon ʒeðeowade, ðonne ah se teond ane swinʒelan æt
him; bedrife hine to swinʒlum be his ceape.

49.   Gyf mon on his mæstene unalufed swin ʒemete,

49, 1. ʒenime ðonne syx scill. wurð wed. Gyf hi ðonne
ðær næron oftor ðonne æne, ʒesylle scillinʒ se aʒenfriʒa 7 ʒecyðe *þæt* hi ðær oftor ne comon be ðæs

49, 2. ceapes wyrðe. Gyf hi ðær tuwa wæron, ʒesylle tweʒen

49, 3. scill; ʒyf mon nime æbesne on swinum, æt ðryfinʒrum
þæt ðridde, æt twyfinʒru*m* *þæt* feorðe, æt ðumelu*m*
þæt fifte.

50.   Gyf ʒesiðcund mon ðinʒað wið cynʒ oððe wið
cynʒes ealdormannu*m* for his inhiwan, oððe wið his
hlaford for ðeowe oððe for friʒe, nah he ðar nane
witerædene, se ʒesiþ, forðon he nolde him ær yfeles
ʒestyran æt ham.

51.   Gyf se siðcunde man landaʒende fyrde forsitte,
ʒesylle hundtwelftiʒ scill 7 ðolie his landes, unlandaʒende syxti scill., ceorlisc ðrittiʒ scill. to wite.

---

46. man | mon, ann above new, B, mon- H | forstolenne | ʒefeormiʒe |
sceal, a above | .LX. | ðyfðe | aðwyrðe ‖ **46, 1.** enʒlisc onstal ʒa forð,
onsace ðonne | biþ wylisc new above B, biþ wilisc H | onstâl | að mare,
vac. na ðe ‖ **46, 2.** onsacan | mæʒʒ, second ʒ above | dear, new r added
B, dearr H ‖ **47.** man | forstolenne | tyman | menn ‖ **48.** hwylc above
man | man | betyhð | swinʒlum, l above BH ‖ **49.** man | unalyfed | .VI. | weorð |
wedd ‖ **49, 1.** ænne new ab. scillinʒ B | — friʒa 7 ʒe End of p. 36 in B — | hy |
næron for ne comon ‖ **49, 2.** twiʒa | .II. ‖ **49, 3.** man | ab. ðryfinʒrum new
spic B | ðridde, ð uncrossed B | ðumelum, new y stroke B, ðymelum
H ‖ **50.** man | cyninʒ | wiþ his ealderman | innhiwum | friʒe, ʒe ab. |
þær | nan | witerædene | forþon ðe he him nolde ær yfeles ʒestyran æt ham,

.XCVI.

52.   Se ðe diernum ʒeðinʒum betyʒen sie, ʒeswicne hine be .CXX. hida þara ʒeðinʒea, oððe .CXX. scill. ʒeselle.

.XCVII.

53.   Gif mon forstolenne man befo æt oþrum 7 sie sio hand oðcwolen sio hine sealde þam men þe hine mon ætbefenʒ, tieme þonne þone mon to þæs deadan byrʒelse swa oðer fioh swa hit sie, 7 cyðe on þam aðe be .LX. hida þæt sio deade hond hine him sealde; þonne hæfð he þæt wite afylled mid þy aðe, aʒife

53, 1.   þam aʒendfrio þone monnan; ʒif he þonne wite hwa ðæs deadan ierfe hæbbe, tieme þonne to þam ierfe 7 bidde ða hond þe þæt ierfe hafað þæt he him ʒedô þone ceap unbeceasne oþþe ʒecyðe þæt se deada næfre þæt ierfe ahte.

.XCVIII.

54.   Se þe bið werfæhðe betoʒen 7 he onsacan wille þæs sleʒes mid aðe þonne sceal bion on þære hyndenne an kyninʒæde be .XXX. hida, swa be ʒesiðcundum

54, 1.   men swa be cierliscum, swa hwæþer swa hit sie; ʒif hine mon ʒilt, þonne mot he ʒesellan on þara hyndenna ʒehwelcere monnan 7 byrnan 7 sweord on þæt werʒild,

54, 2.   ʒif he ðyrfe; witeðeowne monnan wyliscne mon sceal bedrifan be .XII. hidum swa ðeowne to swinʒum, enʒliscne be feower 7 .XXX. hida.

.XCVIIII.

55.   Ewo bið mid hire ʒiunʒe sceape scill. weorð oþ þæt .XII. niht ofer eastran.

.C.

56.   Gif mon hwelcne ceap ʒebyʒð 7 he ðonne onfinde him hwelc unhælo on binnan .XXX. nihta, þonne weorpe

---

52. hine be .CXX. End of p. 100 in E ‖ **53, 1.** unbeceasne, un dim ‖ **54.** æde, first part of æ dim ‖ **54, 1.** sweord dim ‖ **55.** Ewo, E dim ‖ **56.** Ends with p. 101 in E, dim on lower left hand corner ‖

Continuation of Variants from p. 127.

hwylce unhælo | .XXX. | he ðone ceap to handa, ceap ab. | þam syllend new above to handa B | swerize | facen ‖

52.   Se ðe dyrnum ʒeðinʒðum betoʒen sy, ʒeclænsie he hine be hundtwelftiʒum bida ðara ðinʒa oððe hundtwelftiʒ scill. ʒesylle.

53.   Gyf man forstolenne man befo æt oðrum, 7 sy seo hand acwolon ðe hine sealde ðam men ðe hine mon ætbefenʒ, tyme ðonne ðone man to ðæs deadan byrʒenne, swa oðer feoh swa hweðer swa hit sy, 7 cyðe on ðem aðe be feortiʒ hida þæt seo deade hand hine him sealde; ðonne hæfð he þæt wite afylled mid

53, 1. ðu aðe, aʒyfe ðam aʒendfrêo ðone man. Gyf he ðonne wite hwâ ðæs deadan yrfe hæbbe, tyme ðonne to ðam yrfe 7 bidde ða hônd þe þæt yrfe hafað þæt he him ʒedô ðone ceap unbesacene, oððe ʒecyðe þæt se deade næfre þæt yrfe ahte.

54.   Se ðe bið werfæhðe betoʒen 7 he ætsacan wylle ðæs slæʒes mid aðe, ðonne sceal beon on ðære hyndene an cyninʒæðe be ðrittiʒ hida, swa be ʒesiþcundum

54, 1. men swa be ceorliscum, swa hweðer swa hit su. Gyf hine mon ʒylt, ðonne mot he ʒesyllan on ðæra hyndenna ʒehwylcre monnan 7 byrnan 7 sweord on þæt werʒyld,

54, 2. ʒyf he ðurfe. Witeðeowne monnan wyliscne man sceal bedrifan be twelf hyndum swa ðeowne to swincum, enʒliscne be seo wær 7 ðrittiʒ hida.

55.   Eowu bið *mid* hire ʒeonʒe sceape scill. weorð oð þæt feowertyne niht ofer easton.

56.   Gyf mon hwelcne ceap ʒebyʒeð 7 he ðonne afinde him hwylcne unhæle on binnon ðrittiʒ nihta ðonne

---

52. ʒeðinʒum | ʒeladie hine, vac. he |.CXX.|ʒeþinʒa|.CXX. | **58.** befð | opcwolen | hine æt befenʒ, vac. mon | þone man above | to þære byrʒenne ðæs deadan mannes | þæm | .LX. | wite | ðu, last stroke erased B, ðy H | 7 above aʒife | aʒen-friʒe | aʒendfrêo End of p. 37 in B | **53, 1.**þanne|hand| hafeþ | ʒedô | deada | **54.** wer, new r put in marg. B | onsacan | wille | sleʒes | .XXX. | cierliscum | hwæðer | su, new y stroke B, sy H | **54, 1.** man above ʒylt | ân for on | hyndenna, first n above | ʒehwylcere, first e ab. | monna | werʒild | **54, 2.** man | wiliscne | .XII. hidum | swincum, l above c new B, swinʒ-um H | be .XXXIIII. hida H, (seo wær st. feower B) | **55.** Eowu, new e ab. u B | mid new ab. hire B | ʒeonʒan | .XIIII. nyht | easton, new r ab. B, eastran H | **56.** man | hwylcne | him on

þone ceap to honda oððe swerie þæt he him nan facn on nyste þa he hine him sealde.

.CI.

57.   Gif ceorl ceap forstilð ꝸ bireð in to his ærne ꝸ befehð þærinne mon, þonne bið se his dæl synniᵹ butan þam wife anum, forðon hio sceal hire ealdore hieran; ᵹif hio dear mid aðe ᵹecyðan þæt hio þæs forstolenan ne onbite, nime hire ðriddan sceat.

.CII.

58.   Oxan horn bið .X. pæninᵹa weorð.

.CIII.

59.   Cuu horn bið tweᵹea pæninᵹa, oxan tæᵹl bið .scill. weorð, cus bið fifa; oxan eaᵹe bið .V. pæninᵹa weorð,

59, 1. cus bið scill. weorþ; mon sceal simle to bereᵹafole aᵹifan æt anum wyrhtan .VI. wæᵹa.

.CIII.

60.   Se ceorl se ðe hæfð oðres ᵹeoht ahyrod, ᵹif he hæbbe ealle on foðre to aᵹifanne, ᵹesceawiᵹe mon, aᵹife ealle; ᵹif he næbbe, aᵹife healf on fodre, healf on oþrum ceape.

.CV.

61.   Ciricsceat mon sceal aᵹifan to þam healme ꝸ to þam heorðe þe se mon on bið to middum wintra.

.CVI.

62.   Þonne mon bið tyhtlan betyᵹen ꝸ hine mon bedrifeð to ceape, nah þonne self nane wiht to ᵹesellanne beforan ceape, þonne ᵹæð oðer mon seleð his ceap fore, swa he þonne ᵹeþinᵹian mæᵹe on ða rædenne þe he him ᵹa to honda oð ðæt he his ceap him ᵹeinnian mæᵹe; þonne betyhð hine mon eft oþre siðe ꝸ bedrifð

---

59. first bið above line, but old ‖

Continuation of Variants from p. 129.
mon | midde‖ 62. man | nah þonne . . . . . . beforan ceace on margin in H | nane | ᵹesyllanne | seleð, second e ab. | ræde-ne | vac. him before ᵹeinni-an | — ᵹeinnian End of p. 39 in B — | mon ab. eft | bedrife þ, last e above | forh new before nylle, old forh erased B, forð nele forstandan se þe, þe ab. H | ceap ær | hine | þonne ab. | þoliᵹe | þonne above | vac. se | he above him ‖

weorpe ðone ceap to handa oððe swerie þæt he him
nan facn on nyste ða he hine him sealde.

57.   Gyf ceorl ceap forstylð 7 bereð into his ærne 7
befehþ ðær inne, ðonne *biþ* his dæl synniʒ butan ðam
wife anum, forðan heo sceol hire ealdre byran; ʒyf heo
dear mid aðe ʒecyðan þæt *heo* ðæs forstolenan ne onbite,
nime hire ðæne ðriddan dæl ðære æhta.

58.   Oxan horn bið feowertyne peniʒa wurð.

59.   Cu horn tweʒea peniʒa wurð. Oxan tæʒl bið *.IIII.*
peoneʒa wurð. Cu tæʒl bið fif peneʒa wurð. Oxan
59, 1. eaʒe bið fif peoneʒa wurð. Cu bið scill. weorð; mon
sceal symble to bereʒafole aʒyfan æt anum wyrhtan
syx weʒa.

60.   Se ceorl se ðe hæfð oðres oxan ahyred, ʒyf he
hæbbe ealle on foðre to aʒyfanne, ʒesceawiʒe mon,
aʒyfe ealle; ʒyf he næbbe, aʒyfe healf on foðre, healf
on oðrum ceape.

61.   Cyricsceat man *sceal* aʒyfan to þam ba*l*me 7 to
ðam heorðe ðe se man on bið to middan wintra.

62.   Ðonne mon bið tyhtlan betoʒen 7 hine mon bedrifeð to ceace, nah ðonne sylf nan wiht *to* syllanne
beforan ceace, ðonne ʒæð oðer man sylað his ceap
fore, swa he ðonne ʒeðinʒian mæʒe on ða ræddene ðe
he him ʒa to handa oð þæt he his ceap him ʒeinnian
mæʒe; ðonne betyhð hine mon eft oðre siðe 7 bedrifþ

---

57. ciorl | forsteleþ | byrð | huse, above it al. ærne | mann bef. befehþ,
hitt after, new B, hit man ðær inne befehð H | — ðær in End of p. 38
in B — | biþ bef. his dæl, scyldiʒ above synniʒ new B, bið his dæl
scyldiʒ H | ðon | sceal | hlaforde for ealdre | new h above eo B, heo H | hire
ðriddan ʒescead‖ 58. teon | peniʒa, prob. orig. so, now penn, last stroke new
B, peninʒa H | weorð ‖ 59. Each capital begins a line in B, making
appar. five chapters, not so H | Cû | bið .V. | peninʒa | weorð | before
peoneʒa *.IIII.* over erasure new B, scill. H | weorð | Cû bið .V. peninʒa |
.V. | peninʒa | weorð | Cû | eaʒe above cu new B ‖ 59, 1. mon, large M
new B | simle | aʒyfen | .VI. pund wæʒa ‖ 60. ciorl | vac. se | hæfð, ð old
over h B, hæbbe H | ʒeoht, e ab, for oxan | vac. aʒyfe ealle | aʒife ‖ 61.
sceal new above aʒyfan B, sceal H | balme, l over eras. B, healme H |

to ceape: ʒif hine forð nele forstandan se ðe him ær
ceap foresealde 7 he hine þonne forfehð, poliʒe þonne
his ceapes se ðe he him ær foresealde.

.CVII.

63.   Gif ʒesiðcund mon fare, þonne mot he habban
his ʒerefan mid him 7 his smið 7 his cildfestran.

.CVIII.

64.   Se ðe hæfð .XX. hida, se sceal tæcnan .XII. hida
ʒesettes landes þonne he faran wille.

.CVIIII.

65.   Se ðe hæfð .X. hida, se sceal tæcnan .VI. hida
ʒesettes landes.

.CX.

66.   Se ðe hæbbe þreora hida, tæcne oþres healfes.

.CXI.

67.   Gif mon ʒeþinʒað ʒyrde landes oþþe mare to ræde-
ʒafole 7 ʒeereð, ʒif se hlaford him wile þæt land
aræran to weorce 7 to ʒafole, ne þearf he him onfôn,
ʒif he him nan botl ne selð, 7 þolie þara æcra.

.CXII.

68.   Ʒif mon ʒesiðcundne monnan adrife, fordrife þy
botle, næs þære setene.

.CXIII.

69.   Sceap sceal ʒonʒan mid his fliese oð midne sumor
oððe ʒilde þæt flies mid twam pæninʒum.

.CXIIII.

70.   Æt twyhyndum were mon sceal sellan to monbote
.XXX. scill., æt .VI. hyndum .LXXX. scill., æt .XII.-

70, 1. hyndum .CXX. scill.; æt .X. hidum to fostre .X. fata
hunies, .CCC. hlafa, .XII. ambra wilisc ealað, .XXX.
hluttres, tu eald hriðeru oððe .X. weðeras, .X. ʒees,
.XX. henna, .X. cesas, amber fulne buteran, .V. leaxas,
.XX. pundwæʒa foðres 7 hundteontiʒ æla.

---

64. Ends with p. 102 in E ‖ 66. begins third Ot. fragm. (cf. App. A),
from which foll. variants: 67. Ʒif, i above y | londes ‖ 69. þæt flys ‖
70. syx hyndum ‖ 70, 1. wilisces ‖

to ceace: Gyf he hine nylle forstandan forh se ðe him
ær ceap foresealde 7 he him ðonne forfehð, ðolie
ðonne his ceapes se ðe he him ær foresealde.

63. Gyf zesiðcund man fare, ðonne mot he habban
his zerefan mid him 7 his smið 7 his cildfestran.

64. Se ðe hæfð twentiz hida, se sceal tæcan twelf
hida zesettes landes, ðonne he faran wylle.

65. Se ðe hæfð tyn hida, se sceal tæcan syx hida
zesettes landes.

66. Se ðe hæbbe ðreo hida, tæce oðres healfes.

67. Gyf mon zeðinzað zyrde landes oððe mare to
rædezafole 7 zeerað, zyf se hlaford him wyle þæt
land aræran to weorce 7 to zafole, ne ðearf he him
onfon, zyf he him nan botl ne sylþ, 7 ðolie ðara acera.

68. Gyf mon zesiðcundne monnan adrife, fordrife ðy
botle, næs ðære setene.

69. Sceap sceal zonzan mid his flyse oð midne sumor
oððe zylde þæt fleos mid twam penezum.

70. Æt twyhundum were man sceal syllan to monbote
.XXX. scill., 7 æt syxhyndum hundeahtatiz scill., æt
70, 1. twelfhyndum hundtwelftiz. Æt tyn hidum to fostre
tyn fata hunies, ðreo hund hlâfa, twelf ambra wylisces
ealoð, ðrittiz hlutres, twa ealda ryðeru oððe tyn weðeras,
7 tyn zees 7 twenti henna 7 tyn cysas, amber fulne
buteran, fif leaxas, twentiz pund weza fodres 7 hund-
teontiz æla.

---

64. .XX. | tæcnan, first n ab. | .XII. | wille ‖ 65. .X. hida landes |
tæcnan, first n ab. | .VI. ‖ 66. .III. hida landes | tæcne, n ab. | oðres
healfes hides zesettes | 67. man zyrde landes zeþinzeð | zeereð | wile |
slihð for sylþ | 7 þolize his æcera ‖ 68. mann | 69. zilde | flys | .II. ‖
70. hundum, y stroke new B, hyndum H | manbote | .LXXX. | .XII. | — twelf
hyn End of p. 40 in B — | .CXX. ‖ 70, 1. .X. | .X. fata hunizes | .CCC. hlafa,
fa ab. | .XII. ambres, s ab. | wilisces, es ab. | .XXX. hluttres, first t ab. |
.II. ealde, last e ab. | hryþeru | .X. weþeras | Insertion new on marg. B |
.X. zês 7 .XX. | .X. | buteran, e ab. | .V. | .XX. | pund ab. wæza | .C. ‖

.CXV.

71.   Ʒif mon sie wertyhtlan betoʒen 7 he hit þonne
ʒeondette beforan aðe 7 onsace ǽr, bide mon mid þære
witerædenne oð ðæt se wer ʒeʒolden sie.

.CXVI.

72.   Gif mon werʒild ðeof ʒefehð 7 he losiʒe ðy dæʒe
þam monnum ðe hine ʒefoð, þeah hine mon ʒefð ymb
niht, nah him mon mare æt ðonne fulwite.

.CXVII.

73.   Gif hit bið nihteald þiefð, ʒebeten þa þone ʒylt
þe hine ʒefenʒon swa hie ʒeþinʒian mæʒen wið cyninʒ
7 his ʒerefan.

.CXVIII.

74.   Gif ðeowwealh engliscne monnan ofslihð, þonne
sceal se ðe hine ah weorpan hine to honda hlaforde

74, 1. 7 mæʒum oððe .LX. scill. ʒesellan wið his feore; ʒif
he þonne þone ceap nelle foreʒesellan, þonne mot hine
se hlaford ʒefreoʒean, ʒielden siððan his mæʒas þone
wer, ʒif he mæʒburʒ hæbbe freo, ʒif he næbbe, heden

74, 2. his þa ʒefan; ne þearf se friʒe mid þam þeowan
mæʒʒieldan, buton he him wille fæhðe ôfaceapian, ne
se þeowa mid þy friʒean.

.CXVIIII.

75.   Gif mon ceap befehþ forstolenne 7 sio hond tiemð
þonne, sio hine mon ætbefehþ, to oþrum men, ʒif se
mon hine þonne onfon ne wille 7 sæʒþ þæt he him
næfre þæt ne sealde ac sealde oþer, þonne mot se
ʒecyðan, se ðe hit tiemþ to þære honda, þæt he him
nan oðer ne sealde buton þæt ilce.

.CXX.

76.   Gif hwa oðres ʒodsunu slea oððe his ʒodfæder,
sie sio mæʒbot 7 sio manbot ʒelîc; weaxe sio bot be
ðam were swa ilce swa sio manbot deð þe þam hlaforde

---

74. mæʒum End of p. 103 in E || 75. forstollenne | hond tymð ||

Continuation of Variants from p. 133.

ab. se, eras. after ʒe and cyþan on marg. B, þonne mot se ʒecyðan H |
tymð, t made out of c B | þære || 76. weaxe, W new out of w B ||

71.   Gyf mon sy wertyhlan betoʒen 7 he hit ðonne
ʒeandette beforan aðe 7 onsace ær, abide mon mid
ðære witerædenne oð þæt se wer ʒeʒolden sy.

72.   Gyf mon werʒyld ðeof ʒefehð 7 he losie ðu dæʒe
ðam mannum ðe hine ʒefoð, ðeah hine man ʒefð ymbe
niht, nah him mon mare æt ðonon fulwite.

73.   Gyf hit bið nihteald ðyfð, ʒebeten ða ðone ʒylt
ðe hine ʒefenʒon swa hiʒ ʒeðinʒian maʒon wið cyninʒe
7 his ʒerefan.

74.   Gyf ðeowwealh enʒliscne man ofslihð, ðonne sceal
se ðe hine ah weorpan hine to handa hlaforde 7 maʒum

74, 1. oððe syxtiʒ scill. ʒesyllan wið his feore.   Gyf he
ðonne ceap nelle foresyllan, þonne mot hine se hlaford
ʒefreoʒan, ʒyldan syððan his maʒas ðone wer.   Gyf
he mæʒborh hæbbe freo, ʒyf he næbbe, heden his ða

74, 2. ʒefan; ne ðearf se friʒêa mid ðam ðeowan men
ʒyldan, buton he him sylle fæhðe ofaceapian, ne se
ðeowa mid ðam friʒean.

75.   Gyf mon ceap befehþ forstolene 7 seo hand tymð,
ðonne seo hine mon ætbefehð ðe to oðrum men, ʒyf se
mon hine onfon nylle 7 sæʒð þæt he him næfre þæt
ne sealde, ac sealde oðer, ðonne *mot* se ʒecyþan, se
ðe hit tymð to ðara handa, þæt he him nan oðer ne
sealde buton þæt ilce.

76.   Gyf hwa oðres ʒodsunu slêa oððe his ʒodfæder,
sy seo mæʒbot 7 sêo manbot ʒelic; weaxe seo bot be
ðam were swa ilce swa seo manbot deð þe ðam

---

71. abide man | ræde-ne ‖   72. werʒildþeof | losi-e | ðu, new y stroke
B, ðy H | monnum | ʒefð | ymb | nyht | man | ðonne for ðonon ‖   73. nyht |
hy ʒeþinʒian | cyninʒ ‖   74. man, second new n above B, man H | þe above
hine | hine ab. after weorpan | .LX. ‖   74, 1. þone ceap | nylle | foreʒesyllan |
þonne, onne new at end of line B, þonne H | ʒildon | sioðan | mæʒburh | nis
ðonne ða ʒefan ‖   74, 2. — mid ðam End of p. 41 in B —| þeowan mæʒʒyldan
butan | wille for sylle | ofaceapian, first a ab. ‖   75. man | æt befehð to
oðrum men, vac. ðe | man hine þonne | þæs ceapes ab. after nylle | mot

76, 1. sceal; ʒif hit þonne kyninʒes ʒodsunu sie, bete be
76, 2. his were þam cyninʒe swa ilce swa þære mæʒþe.   Ʒif
        he þonne on þone ʒeonbyrde þe hine sloʒ, þonne æt-
        fealle sio bôt þæm ʒodfæder swa ilce swa þæt wite
        þam hlaforde deð; ʒif hit biscep sunu sie, sie be
        healfum þam.

76, 2. ætfealle Ot, æ fealle E | second sie above, but old E ||

76, 1. ʼhlaforde sceal. Gyf hit ðonne kyninʒes ʒodsunu sy, bete be his were ðam cinʒe swa *ilce* swa ðære mæʒðe.

76, 2. Gyf he ðonne on ðone ʒeonbyrde ðe hine sloh, ðonne ætfealle seo bot þam ʒodfædere, swa *ilce* swa *þæt* wite ðam hlaforde deð; ʒyf hit bisceop sunu sy, sy be healfum ðem.

76, 1. Gif hit þonne sy cyninʒes ʒodsunu, þonne above | cyninʒe | *ilce*, prob. orig. so, new same over eras. B, same H ‖ 76, 2. ðæm ʒodfæder | ilce, see note on 76, 1, B, same H | biscop | sunu, down stroke erased below first u B | þam seo bote ‖ In B follows: We cwedon be ðam blaserum etc. In H, as CXXI, the same, after which there is a space of two lines ‖

APPENDICES.

Italics for parts wanting in Ot and supplied from E. Abbrev. forms retained, but with period after word instead of line over last letter as in Ms. Ot. prefers þ to δ, espec. initial. For description of Ms. see pp. 12, 19, 25.

XVII. hiora, hi above the line, but old.

APPENDICES.

hundni3onti3 *scill.* oþres bisceopes 7 ealdorm*onnes*
.LX. scill. twelf*hyndes* monnes .XXX. scill. syx*hyndes*

40, 1. .XV. scill. ceorles edorbryce . *V. scill.* 3if þisses hw*æt*
3elimpe þenden fyrd *ute sie oþþe* in lencten fæst*en*

40, 2. hit sie twybo*te. 3if mon in lenct*enne hali3 *ryht in*
folce butan leafe *alec33e 3ebete mid .CXX. scill.*

41. Se mon se þe boc*land* hæbbe 7 him his .XXXVII.
mæ3as *læfden þonne setton we þæt he hit ne moste*
sellan of his mæ3bur3e 3if þær bið 3ewrit oððe
3ewitnes þæt hit þara manna *forbod* wære þe hit
on fruman 3es*tryndon 7 þara þe hit him* seald*on* þ. he
swa ne mote 7 þ*æt* þonne on cynin3*es* 7 on bisceop*es*
3ewitnesse 3erecce beforan *his mæ3um.*

42. Eac we beoda*ð se mon se þe his 3efan* .XXXVI*II.*
*h*amsittend*ne* wite þæt he ne *f*eohte ær þam he *him*

42, 1. *ryhtes* bidde. 3yf he mæ3*nes* hæbbe þ. he his 3*efan*
beri*de* 7 inne besitte 3eheal*de* hine .VII. niht *inne*
7 *h*ine on ne feohte 3if he inne 3eþoli*an wille* 7 þon
ne ymb .VII. niht 3if he wille on *hand 3an 7 wæpenu*
sel*l*an 3ehealde hine .XXX. nih*ta 3esundne* 7 *hine*

42, 2. his ma3um 3ebodie 7 his *friondum 3if he cirican*
þonne 3eierne sie þonne be *þære cirican are swa we*

42, 3. ær bufan cwædon. 3yf he þonne þæs mæ3enes ne *hæbbe*
þæt he hine inne *besitte ride to þam ealdormen*
bidde hine *fultumes 3if he him fultuman ne*

42, 4. *wille ride to cynin3e ær he feohte. Eac swelce*
3if mon becume on his 3efan 7 *he hine ær ham*

SECOND FRAGMENT. (FOL. 50.)

fæstne ne wite. Ʒif he wille h*is* *wæpen* sellan hine
mon ʒchealde .XXX. nihta 7 hine *his* freondum
ʒecyþe. ʒyf he *ne wille* his wæpenu sellan þonne
mot he feohtan on hine. Ʒif *he wille* on hond ʒan
7 *his wæpenu sellan* 7 *hwa ofer þæt on* him feohte
ʒielde swa wer swa wunde *swa he ʒewyrce* 7 wite

42, 5. 7 *hæbbe his mæʒ* forworh*t*. *Eac we cwæðað* þ. mon
mote mid his hlaforde feohtan orwiʒe ʒif mon *on*
þone hlaforde *fiohte swa mot se hlaford mid þy* men

42, 6. feohtan. *æfter þære* ilcan wisan *mon mot feohtan*
mid his ʒeborene mæʒe. Ʒif hine mon on woh on
feohteð buton wið his hlaforde *þæt we* ne lyfað

42, 7. 7 mon *mot feohtan orwiʒe ʒif he ʒemeteð* o*þ*erne
æt his ænum wife betynedum durum o*þþe un*
der anre reon *oþþe æt* his dehter *æwum borenre*
oþþe æt his sweos*ter* borenre oþþe æt *his medder*
þe wære to æwum wife forʒyfen his *fæder.*

43. *Eallum* frioum monnum þas daʒas sien .*XXXVIIII.*
forʒyfene butan þeowum monnum 7 *esne wyrhtan*
.XII. daʒas on ʒehhol 7 *þone dæʒ þe crist þone*
deofol oferswiþde 7 scs. *ʒreʒorius ʒemynd dæʒ*
7 .*VII.* daʒas to eastro*n* 7 .*VII. ofer* 7 *an dæʒ æt*
sce. pe*tres* tide 7 sce. paul*es* 7 *on hærfeste þa ful*
lan *wican* ær sca. *marian mæssan* 7 *æt eallra*
haliʒra weorþunʒe anne dæʒ 7 .*IIII. wodnes*
daʒas on .*IIII. ymbren wicum þeowum monnum*
eallum sien forʒifen þam þe him leofost sie

42, 7. sweoster borenre, cannot have been æwum bor., no room for
æwum; this clause is found above the line in E, and on the margin of
H, which latter, with Lamb, has æwum ‖ **43.** oferswiþde, d above.

APPENDIX A. MS. OT.

ʒesettes landes. .CX.

66. Se þe hæbbe þreora bida *tæcne oþres healfes.* .CXI.

67. Ʒyf mon *ʒeþinʒað* ʒyrde londes *oþþe mare to ræde*
ʒafole 7 ʒeereð ʒif se hlaford him *wile þæt land aræ*
ran to weorce 7 *to* ʒafole ne þearf *he him onfon ʒif*
he him nan botl ne selð 7 *þolie þara æcra.* .CXII.

68. Ʒif mon *ʒesiðcundne monnan adrife fordrife þy*
botle næs þære *setene.* .CXIII.

69. Sceap sceal ʒonʒan *mid his fliese oð midne sumor*
oþþe ʒilde þæt flys *mid twam pæninʒum.* .CXIIII.

70. Æt twyhyndum were *mon sceal sellan to mon bote*
.XXX. *scill.* æt syx *hyndum .LXXX. scill. æt .XII.*

70, 1. *hyndum .CXX. scill. æt .X. hidum to* fostre .X. *fata*
hunies .CCC. hlafa .XII. ambra wilisces ea*l*að
.XXX. *hluttres tu* eald hriþeru oþþe .X. weðeras
.X. ʒees .XX. henna .X. cesas amber fulne *buteran*
.V. *leaxas* .XX. pundwæʒa fodres 7 hund *teontiʒ*
æla. .CXV.

71. Ʒif mon sie *wertyhtlan betoʒen* 7 *he hit þonne*
ʒeondette beforan aðe 7 *onsace ær bide mon mid*
þære *wite rædenne oð* ðæt se *wer ʒeʒolden sie.*

72. Ʒif mon *werʒild þeof ʒefehþ* 7 *he losiʒe* .CXVI.
ðy *dæʒe þam* monnum *þe hine ʒefoð þeah*
hine mon *ʒefo ymb niht nah him mon mare*
æt *þonne fulwite.* .CXVII.

73. Ʒif hit bið *nihteald þiefð ʒebeten þa þone ʒylt*
þe hine *ʒefenʒon swa hie ʒeþinʒian mæʒen*

---

67. Ʒyf, i above y. ‖ **70, 1.** fodres perhaps foðres ‖ ll of scill,
end of 70, is last of the part reset as fol. 52, fostre and all below is
from 53 ‖ This page most charred and blackened of all: the little that
can be deciphered costs great labour.

THIRD FRAGMENT. (FOL. 52—53.)

wið cyning 7 *his ʒerefan.* .CXVIIƖ.

74.   *Ʒif þeow wealh enʒlisc*ne monnan ofslihð þonne
      sceal se þe hine ab weorpan hine to honda hlaforde

74, 1. 7 *mæʒum oþþe* .LX. scill. ʒesellan *wið* his feore. ʒif he
        þonne þone ceap nelle foreʒesel*l*an þonne mot
        *hine se hlaford ʒefreoʒean ʒield*en siþþan his mæʒ
        as þone wer ʒif he mæʒburʒ hæbbe freo ʒif he

74, 2. *næbbe heden his þa ʒefan ne* þearf se friʒe mid
        *þam þeowan mæʒʒieldan buto*n he him wille fæhþe
        ofaceapian ne se þeowa mid þy friʒean. .CXIX.

75.   Ʒif *mon ceap be*fehþ *forsto*llenne 7 *sio* hond tymþ
      þonne sio hine mon æt befehð to oþrum *men ʒif*
      se mon hine *þon. onfon ne* wille 7 sæʒþ þ. he him *næfre*
      þ. ne sealde *ac* sealde oþer þonne mot *se ʒecyð*an
      se þe hit tiemþ to þære honda þ. he him nan oþer ne
      sealde buton þ. ilce.   .CXX.

76.   Ʒif hwa oþres ʒodsunu slea *oþþe his ʒodfæder sie*
      sio mæʒbot 7 sio manbot *ʒelic weaxe sio bot*
      be þam were swa ilce swa sio *manbot* deð þe þam

76, 1. *h*laforde sceal. *ʒif hit þonne kyninʒes ʒodsunu*
        sie bete be his were þam cyninʒe swa ilce swa þære

76, 2. *mæʒþe.* ʒif he þonne on þone ʒeonbyrde þe hine
        sloʒ þon. ætfealle sio bot þæm ʒodfæder *swa*
        *ilce swa þ. wite þa*m hlaforde deð *ʒif hit biscep*
        sunu sie sie be healfum þam.

What remains of this page is quite legible, the fire having attacked the other side more directly. All in 74, also llenne, ð to oþr, wille 7 sæʒþ, onne mot, belongs to the upper fragment (52); Ʒif, p be, and all below, to the lower (53).

142

æfter *þam wære awendende* þas ure domas.

1. Ærest we *bebeoda*þ þte ʒodes .XLV.
ðeowas hiora ryht reʒol on ryht heal
den. æfter þæ. we bebeodað þte ealles fol
ces æw 7 domas þus sien ʒebealdenne .XLVI.

2. Cild binnan .XXX. nyhtu. sie ʒefullod. ʒif hit
swa ne sie .XXX. scill. ʒebete. Ʒif hit ðon.
sie dead buton fulwihte ʒebete he hit
mid eallu. þæm þe he aʒe. .XLVII.

3. Ʒif þeowmon werce on sunnan dæʒ be his
hlafordes hæse sie he freoh 7 se hlaford

3, 1. *ʒeselle .XXX.* scill. *to wite. ʒif* þon. se þeowa
butan his ʒewitnysse wyrce þolie his

3, 2. hyde. *ʒif* ðon. se friʒea þy dæʒe wyrce
buton hlafordes hæse þolie his freotes .XLVIII.

4. Ciric sceattas sien aʒifene be Sce. mar
tines mæssan. Ʒif hwa þ. ne ʒelæste sie he
scildiʒ .LX. scill. 7 be .XII. fealdu. aʒife
ðone ciric sceat. .XLVIIII.

5. Ʒif hwa sie deaþes scyldiʒ 7 cirican ʒeær
ne habbe his feorh 7 bete swa him

5, 1. ryht wisie. Ʒif hwa his hyde forwer
ce 7 cirican ʒeirne sie hi. sio swinʒel
le forʒifen. .L.

6. Ʒif hwa ʒefeohte on kininʒes huse sie he

Italics for the parts wanting and supplied from E. Abbrev. retained
with period after the abbrev. inst. of mark over last letter, as in Ms. Note
that from upper right-hand corner of second page and from upper left-
hand corner of third most is gone; on the double leaf these are contiguous.
For information concerning Ms. see pp. 13, 20, 26.

FIRST LEAF.

scyldiʒ ealles *his ierfes* 7 *sie on cyninʒes dome*

6, 1. hwæþer he lif habbe *þe næbbe.* ʒif hwa on
mynster ʒefeohte *hund twelftiʒ scill ʒe*

6, 2. bete. ʒif *hwa on ealdormonnes huse oð*
ðe on oðres ʒeþunʒenes witan ʒefeohte .LX.
scll. ʒebete 7 oðer .LX. *scill ʒeselle to wite.*

6, 3. ʒif mon on ʒafolʒildan huse oððe on ʒebu
res ʒefeohte .CXX. scill. *to wite ʒeselle*

6, 4. 7 þam bure .VI. scill. 7 þeah *hit sie on mid*
dan felda ʒefeohtan .CXX. *scill. to wite sie*

6, 5. *aʒifen.* ʒif ðonne bið on ʒebeorscipe ʒeciden
7 oðer *hiora mid* ʒeðylde *hit forbere ʒeselle*
se oðer .*XXX. scill. to wite.* .*LI.*

7. ʒif hwa sta*lie swa his wif nyte* 7 *his bearn ʒe*

7, 1. selle .LX. scill. *to wite.* ʒif he ðonne stalie on ʒe
witnysse eall*æs his hiredes ʒonʒen hie*

7, 2. ealle on ðeowot .X. wintre *cniht mæʒ*
beon þeofðe ʒewitæ. .*LII.*

8. ʒif hwa hine ryhtes bidde *beforan hwelcum*
scirmen oððe oðru. dema*n* 7 *a*biddan *ne*
mæʒe 7 hi. wed sellan nelle ʒebete mid .XXX.
scill. 7 binnan .VII. nyhtu. ʒedo hine ryh
tes weorðe. .*LIII.*

9. ʒif hwa wræce do ær ðon he hi. ryhtes bidde
þ. he hi. onnime aʒife 7 forʒylde 7 ʒebete

7, 2. ʒewitæ or ʒewitte.

144

mid .XXX. scill. .LIIII.

10. ꝟif hwa binnan þam ꝣemæru. ures rices
reaflac ⁊ niednæme do aꝣife he þone
reaflac ⁊ ꝣeselle .LX. scill. to wite. .LV.

11. ꝟif hwa his aꝣenne ꝣeleod bebycꝣe þeow
ne oððe friꝣne þeah he scildiꝣ sie ofer
sæ forꝣielde hine his were. .LVI.

12. ꝟif þeof sie ꝣefonꝣen swelte he deaðe oððe
his lif be his were monna liese .LVII.

13. ꝟif hwa beforan biscope his ꝣewitnesse
⁊ his wed aleoꝣe ꝣebete mid hund twelf
tiꝣum scill. .LVIII.

13, 1. Þeofas we hatað .VII. men. from .VII. hloð

14. oð .XXXV. siððan bið here. se ðe hloðe be
tyꝣen sie ꝣeswicne he hine be .CXX. hida
oððe swa bete. .LVIIII.

15. Se ðe here teame betiꝣen sie he hine
be his wereꝣilde aliese oððe be his

15, 1. were ꝣeswicne. se að sceal byon healf be
huslꝣenꝣum. .LX.

15, 2. Þeof sið þan he bið on kininꝣes bende

16. nah he þa swycne. Se ðe þeof ofslehð
he mot ꝣeceþan mit aþe þ. he hine syn
niꝣne ofsloꝣe nalles þa ꝣeꝣildanum.

17. Se þe forstolen flæsc findeð .LXI.

___

12. liese or læse.

7 ʒederneð ʒif he dear he mot mid aðe ʒecyðan
þæt he hit aʒe, se ðe hit ofspereð he *ah þ. meld*
feoh.   .LXII.

18.   Cirlisc mon ʒif he oft betwyʒen wære *ʒif*
       he æt siþestan sie ʒefonʒen slea mon hon*d*
       oððe fot.   .LXIII.

19.   Cyninʒes ʒeneat ʒif his wer biþ twelf hun*d*
       scill. he mot sweriʒen for sixtiʒ hida *ʒif*
       he bið huslʒenʒa.   .LXIIII.

20.   Ʒif forcund mon oððe fremde buton weʒe
       ʒeond wudu ʒonʒe 7 ne hrime ne horn *blawe*
       for ðeof he bið to profianne oððe to slean
       ne oððe to lesanne.   .LXV.

21.   Ʒif mon ðon. þæs ofslæʒenan weres bidde
       he mot ʒecypan þæt he hine for ðeofðe
       ofsloʒe nalles þæs ofslæʒenan ʒeʒildan

21, 1. ne his hlaford. ʒif he hit dirneð 7 wierðeð
       ymb lonʒ yppe þon. remeð he þæm deadan
       to þæm aðe þ. hine moton his mæʒes unsinʒian.

22.   Ʒif þin ʒeneat stalie 7 losie ðe ʒif .LXVI.
       þu habbe berʒan manna ðone þæs anʒeldes.
       ʒif he næbbe ʒeld ðu þ. anʒelde 7 ne sie him
       no ðy ðinʒodre.   .LXVII.

23.   Ʒif mon elþeodiʒne ofslea se kininʒ ah twæd
       ne dæl weres ðriddan dæl sunu oððe mæʒes.

APPENDIX C. BOTH TEXTS OF

MS. B, p. Ðis is ðæt fri ð ðæt ælfred cyninc 7 ȝyðrum cyninȝ
83, l. 15. 7 ealles anȝelcynnes witan 7 eal seo ðeod ðe on east
ænȝlum beoð ealle ȝeeweden habbað 7 mid aðum ȝe-
feostnod for hy sylfe 7 for heora ȝinȝran, ȝe for
ȝeborene ȝe for unȝeborene, ðe ȝodes miltse recce oððe

1.   ure.   Ærest ymb ure landȝemæra: up on temese, 7
ðonne up on liȝan, 7 andlanȝ liȝan oð hire sæwylm,
ðonne on ȝerihte to bedan forda, ðonne up on usan oð

*P. 84. 2. wætlinȝa stræt.   *Ðæt is ðonne, ȝif man ofslæȝen
weorðe, ealle we lætað efen dyrne enȝliscne 7 deniscne,
to .VIII. healf mearcum asodenes ȝoldes, buton ðam
ceorle ðe on ȝafollande sit 7 heora liesenȝum, ða syndan

3.   eac efen dyre æȝðer to .CC. scill.; 7 ȝif man cyninȝes
ðeȝn beteo manslihtes, ȝif he hine ladian dyrre, do he
þæt mid .XII. cininȝes ðeȝnum; ȝif ma ðone man betyhð ðe bið læssa maȝa ðone se cyninȝes ðeȝn, ladiȝe
he hine mid .XI. his ȝelicena 7 mid anum cyninȝes
ðæȝne; 7 swa æȝehwilcre spræce ðe mare sy ðone
.IIII. mancussas; 7 ȝyf he ne dyrre, ȝylde hit ðryȝylde

4.   swa hit man ȝewyrðe. 7 þæt ælc man wite his ȝetyman
5.   be mannum 7 be horsum 7 be oxum.   7 ealle we
cwædon on ða dæȝe ðe mon ða aðas swor þæt ne
ðeowe ne freo ne moton in ðone here faran butan leafe
ne heora nan ðe ma to us; ȝif ðonne ȝebyriȝe þæt for
neode heora hwylc wið ure biȝe habban wille oððe we
wið heora mid yrfe 7 mid æhtum, ðæt is to ðafianne
on ða wisan þæt man ȝislas sylle friðe to wedde 7
to swutulunȝe þæt man wite ðæt man clæne bæc hæbbe.

Variants of Lamb. from Text 1: fryþe | cyninȝ | eastenȝlum | ȝe-
fæstnod | hi ‖   2. Headed Be ofslæȝenan mannes were | ofslaȝen | butan |
ðæm | lysinȝum | syndon ‖   3. Headed Be ðeȝnum ðe betoȝene synd |
mon | manslihtes beteo | dô | cyninȝes | st. ma ðone man, mon ðonne
ðeȝn | ðeȝne for ðæȝne | æȝhwylcre | ðonne | ȝif | dyrne | ȝyld | ðry-
ȝyld | mon ‖   4. Headed Be ȝetymum | And, vac. þæt ‖   5. ðæm st. ða | nân |
hwylce | hæbban | mon | fryþe | vac. to wedde 7 | swutelunȝe | mon | mon |
clæn | marg. al. flæsc ‖ On both Mss. all the names of the places are
scribbled on the margin.

TREATY BETWEEN ÆLFRED AND GUTHRUM.

P. 6. Ðis is þæt fri𝔬 𝔬æt ælfred cynȝ 7 ȝu𝔬rum cinȝ 7 ealles anȝelcynnes witan 7 eal sêo 𝔬eod 𝔬e on eastenȝlum beo𝔬, 7 ȝesworen habba𝔬 ȝe for hy sylfe ȝe for heora ofsprynȝ.

1. Ærest ymbe heora landȝemæra: andlanȝ temese þonne up on liȝean, andlanȝ liȝean o𝔬 hire æwylm, 𝔬anon on ȝerihta to beda forda, þanon upon on usan

2. o𝔬 wætlinȝa stræt. 7 hi cwædon, ȝyf mon ofslæȝen wur𝔬e, eal we leta𝔬 efen dyrne enȝliscne 7 denisce, þæt is to .VIII. healf marcum asodenes ȝoldes, buton 𝔬am ceorle 𝔬e on ȝafollande sit, 7 hêora lysynȝon. . . . . .

3. 7 ȝyf man cynȝes 𝔬eȝen beteo manslihtas 7 he hine ladian durre, do hê þæt mid .XII. cynȝes þeȝnas 7 ȝyf mon 𝔬one man betyh𝔬 þe bi𝔬 læssa maȝa, ladie hine .XI. his ȝelicena, 7 anum cyninȝes 𝔬eȝene.

5. 7 ealle hiȝ ȝecwædon 𝔬a man þa a𝔬as swor þæt na𝔬or ne we on 𝔬one bêre faran buton leafe, ne heora non 𝔬a ma to us, buton man trywan 7 betwynan ȝyslas sylle, fri𝔬e to wedde 7 to swutelunȝe þæt man mid rihte fare, ȝyf þæt ȝeneodiȝe, þæt ure æniȝ to o𝔬rum fæce mid yrfe and mid æhtum.

Above Text II, red Alfredes Laȝa Cyninȝes. Above swor new cweþ, making ȝecweþen prob., on marg. new 7 mid aþum ȝefæstnod | ofspryn underlined and to ȝ inȝran added new ‖ 2. 7 hi cwædon, on marg. þæt is þonne | lysynȝon, eras. here, on which þa sy ndoneac efendyre new; æȝþer twa hund scyll. follows above and on marg. ‖ 5. 𝔬a ma, e new above a of 𝔬a ‖

See for information p. 16. and Schmid, Einl. XXXVIII — XXXIX. Text I is the original form.

Lightning Source UK Ltd.
Milton Keynes UK
UKHW020846211122
412567UK00007B/1579